The War of the Bavarian Succession 1778-1789

Prussian Military Power in Decline?

Alexander Querengässer

Helion & Company

Helion & Company Limited
Unit 8 Amherst Business Centre
Budbrooke Road
Warwick
CV34 5WE
England
Tel. 01926 499619
Email: info@helion.co.uk
Website: www.helion.co.uk
Twitter: @helionbooks
Visit our blog at http://blog.helion.co.uk/

Published by Helion & Company 2023
Designed and typeset by Mach 3 Solutions (www.mach3solutions.co.uk)
Cover designed by Paul Hewitt, Battlefield Design (www.battlefield-design.co.uk)

Text © Alexander Querengässer 2023
Illustrations © as individually credited
Maps by George Anderson © Helion and Company 2023
Colour plates by Alexandr Chernushkin © Helion and Company 2023

Cover figure: Musketeer, Prussian Freiregiment von Münster Nr.4 (artwork by Alexandr Chernushkin © Helion and Company 2023). Cover background: Saxon troops on the march, 1779 (Anne S.K. Brown Collection).

Every reasonable effort has been made to trace copyright holders and to obtain their permission for the use of copyright material. The author and publisher apologise for any errors or omissions in this work, and would be grateful if notified of any corrections that should be incorporated in future reprints or editions of this book.

ISBN 978-1-804511-87-9

British Library Cataloguing-in-Publication Data.
A catalogue record for this book is available from the British Library.

All rights reserved. No part of this publication may be reproduced, stored in a retrieval system, or transmitted, in any form, or by any means, electronic, mechanical, photocopying, recording or otherwise, without the express written consent of Helion & Company Limited.

For details of other military history titles published by Helion & Company Limited, contact the above address, or visit our website: http://www.helion.co.uk

We always welcome receiving book proposals from prospective authors.

Contents

Introduction		iv
1	The Empire after the Peace of Hubertusburg	9
2	The Road to War	21
3	Opposing Forces	26
4	The War	74
5	The Peace of Teschen	123
6	Further Developments	128
Conclusion		132

Appendices
I	Order of Battle and Deployment of the Imperial and Royal Austrian Army, 1 July 1778	136
II	Order of Battle and Formation of the Allied Prussian-Saxon Army on July 1, 1778	142
III	Composition of the Prussian Armies in 1778	146

Bibliography	150

Introduction

The War of the Bavarian Succession never was and – for I am under no illusion that this book will change matters – probably never will be of special interest to eighteenth-century military historians, as it was a short war without major battles and so lacks the adventurous flair of say the Seven Years War or the parallel War of American Independence. Even contemporaries mocked it a *Kartoffelkrieg* (potato war), as the prime concern of soldiers was not avoiding being killed by the enemy, but instead avoiding starving to death. It can be considered uninteresting because it appears indecisive. The alleged indecisiveness of eighteenth-century warfare plays a vital role in modern scholarship. Personally, I am sceptical about this, because what might appear as an indecisive outcome always turns out to be the ability of one belligerent to deny his opponent to the opportunity to fight the war on his own terms through either invading a country or forcing a battle. If this is the central strategic and operational objective of one party the results of a war might appear inconclusive, but are far from it, as the party that did not want any political, territorial or strategic changes achieved its goals and denied the opponents' wish for change. This is basically what happened in the War of the Bavarian Succession, even if the peace-making process and peace determinations are somewhat more complex. But the fact that the Austrians fought the Prussians to a standstill, and denied Frederick the Great the possibility to add to his laurels, was an important achievement. This is often explained as a growing risk-aversion by an aging king or as a first sign of a military system which had passed its zenith and was showing its first cracks, before being annihilated by the 'new' Napoleonic system of warfare. Apart from the later interpretation being very difficult, even flawed, this interpretation overplays two factors – which, however, have their justification – at the cost of two others: the increasing efficiency of the Austrian army, and the inherent weaknesses of Prussian war making, which had been visible before but had not previously had a decisively negative effect.

These, however, are the factors which I want to analyse more clearly in this book. Prussian war-making in this conflict therefore has to be put in the greater context of Frederick the Great's reign, as the War of the Bavarian Succession can be and, and sometimes is, considered as the 'Fourth Silesian War' (First 1740-1742, Second 1744-1745, Third – or Seven-Years War – 1756-1763), even if Silesia was not the prize to win. But the major opponents

– Austria and Prussia – were the same, while Bohemia was an important theatre of war just as in all the three former conflicts.

At the beginning of this project, it was my intention to do much more archival research. However, COVID cut through this plan, as either archives were closed, traveling aggravated, or budgets frozen. I was therefore unable to consult the archive in Vienna, which is certainly a weakness, I must admit. But as there is nothing like 'the' history of an event, but always just 'a' history, I still consider this to be an important contribution to this conflict, as there is no modern study of this war. Where it lacks in archival documentation, it has been able to draw on published sources. Additionally, I was able to visit the archives at Dresden, where I could draw from plentiful material. A trip to Berlin was all for nothing, thanks to Prussian bureaucracy. However, the archive of the Prussian War Ministry was destroyed in the Second World War by a bomb attack, so most documentation directly related to the army is lost forever and all I was looking for were a few correspondences of officers. Much of the general description of the campaign therefore has to draw on printed sources.

A hint of the cultural change sometimes described as the 'Printing Revolution' is given by the fact that immediately after the war several multi-volume histories appeared on the German market.[1] These are valuable sources for the modern scholar. Johan Seyfahrt was a kind of an early modern war correspondent. He followed the armies during the campaigns and so was an eyewitness of the events he described. His two volumes were written down in winter 1780 from material he had compiled during the campaigns. However, as a hint of how subjective sources are and how difficult or even impossible it is to write objective history, Seyfahrt in his introduction mentions letters he had received from military leaders, accusing him of giving distorted accounts against which the author defended himself by arguing that he sought to compile information, not interpret it. Another short history of the war was written by Friedrich II himself: this has to be read with great care, but still is of great interest, because the king gives his very open assessments about the characters of the protagonists.[2] Nearly a century later, a first – and so far the only – longer academic study of the war was written by Eduard Reimann which is also very detailed with regard to its political background.[3] Kurd von

---

1   Carl von Seidel, *Versuch einer militärischen Geschichte des bayerischen Erbfolge-Kriegs, im Jahre 1778: Im Gesichtspunkte der Wahrheit betrachtet* (Königsberg: unknown publisher, 1781); Johann Seyfarth, *Unpartheyische Geschichte des Bayerischen Erbfolgekriegs in welcher nicht allein aus allen bey Gelegenheit desselben erschienen Staatsschriften Auszüge geliefert und von allen kriegerischen Vorfällen die beyderseitige Berichte angeführt, sondern auch in den beygefügten Anmerkungen alle vorkommende Städte, Dörfer etc. beschrieben und die Lebensumstände der merkwürdigsten Personen aus zuverlässigen Nachrichten beygebracht worden* (Leipzig: Paul Gotthelf Kummer, 1780).
2   Gustav Berthold Volz (ed.), *Die Werke Friedrichs des Großen in deutscher Übersetzung*, (Berlin Reimar Hobbing. 1913), Vol.5, pp.99-133.
3   Eduard Reimann, *Geschichte des Bayerischen Erbfolgekrieges* (Leipzig: Duncker und Humblot, 1869).

Schöning presented another important volume, based on the letters of the Prussian king and his brother.[4]

The best introduction to the Prussian and Austrian armies of this age are still those written by Christopher Duffy.[5] German scholarship is somewhat dated, however, the works of Curt Janyand Hans Bleckwenn about army organisation and uniforms are still valuable.[6] Modern scholars, following the war and society approach, expanded our understanding of the Prussian army, but we still lack a comprehensive modern study for the army as a whole, as is provided by Michael Hochedlinger for the Austrian army.[7] There is also good scholarship about the Saxon army of that time. Beside the standard three volume work of Friedrich August Francke and Oskar Schuster, which focuses on structure and campaigns and whose second volume deals with the time treated in this book, there is the work of Stefan Kroll about the life of ordinary men in the eighteenth century. However, more detailed are the works of Johannes Hoffmann and Rudolf Mielsch. Hoffmann wrote his doctoral thesis about the army organisation on the eve of the war,[8] while Mielsch published a long essay about the operations of the army during the war.[9]

In the following chapters I will give a detailed introduction to the historical background of the Bavarian succession crisis, before presenting the complicated diplomatic negotiations on the eve of the war. Wars cannot be analysed without a close look at the participating armies, so this will be done before a narrative and analysis of the conflict is given. As it is my intention to qualify Prussian military capability in the late eighteenth century, I finally have to give an overview of the conflicts Prussia was involved in after 1779. This is not a mere add on to elongate the book, but is required to explain how difficult it is to qualify military capability. Every army has its limits with regard to what it could achieve, and I will argue that Prussian military capability even during Friedrich II's high time had stronger limitations than many historians admit. On the other hand, every limitation has to be put into the context of the tasks an army had to tackle, and, despite its limitations, the Prussian army was one of the largest and strongest in Europe and operated

---

4   Kurd Wolfgang von Schöning, *Der Bayerische Erbfolgekrieg ... nach der Original-Correspondenz Friedrich des Grossen mit dem Prinzen Heinrich und seinen Generalen aus den Staats-Archiven bearbeitet* (Berlin – Potsdam: Ferdinand Riegel, 1854).

5   Republished by Helion and Company: Christopher Duffy, *The Army of Frederick the Great* (second edition) (Warwick: Helion and Company, 2020); Christopher Duffy, *Instrument of War. Volume 1 of the Austrian Army in the Seven Years War* (Warwick: Helion & Company, 2020).

6   Curt Jany, *Geschichte der Königlich Preußischen Armee bis zum Jahre 1807. Vol 3 1763-1807* (Berlin K. Siegismund 1929); Hans Bleckwenn (ed.), *Das altpreußische Heer. Erscheinungsbild und Wesen 1713-1807* (Osnabrück: Biblio-Verlag, 1970-2007); Hans Bleckwenn, *Unter dem Preußen-Adler. Das brandenburgisch-preußische Heer 1640-1807* (Munich: Bertelsmann, 1978).

7   Michael Hochedlinger: *Austria's Wars of Emergence. War State and Society in the Habsburg Monarchy 1683-1797* (London: Longman, 2003).

8   Johannes Hoffmann, *Die kursächsische Armee 1769 bis zum Beginn des Bayerischen Erbfolgkrieges* (Leipzig: S. Hirzel, 1914).

9   Rudolf Mielsch, 'Die kursächsische Armee im Bayerischen Erbfolgekrieg`, in NASG 53 (1932), pp.73-103 and 54 (1933), pp.46-74.

INTRODUCTION

quite successfully in the late 1780s and in the 1790s. It would therefore be foolish to draw a sagging line from the Seven Years War to the catastrophe of Jena and Auerstädt with the War of the Bavarian Succession as a station on it that gives a first hint for a doomed army. This is a very foolish and teleological interpretation, which has its roots in nineteenth-century history writing, but is still repeated by modern historians.

All dates in this book are given according to the Gregorian calendar, which was in use all over the empire. Most places in Bohemia and Silesia had German names and in fact many Bohemian cities had a huge German population. These are the names that can be found in the sources, too. However, for better identification their respective modern Czech or Polish names will always be given in brackets.

With this book I will not only try to provide a first full English-language narrative of this conflict, but also give a more balanced account of Prussian military capability during the age of Frederick the Great.

THE WAR OF THE BAVARIAN SUCCESSION 1778-1789

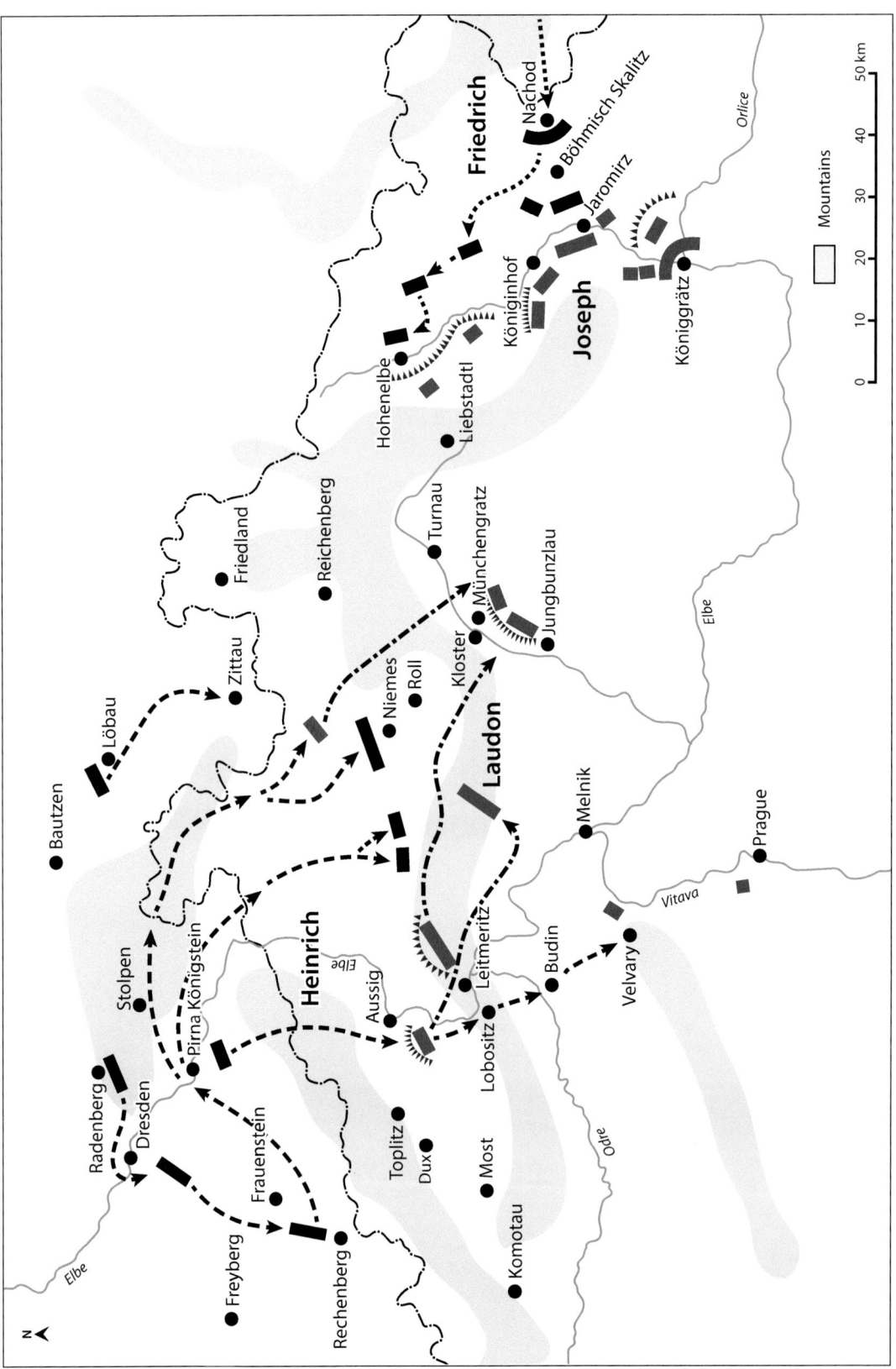

The theatre of war 1778–1779.

1

The Empire after the Peace of Hubertusburg

The Treaty of Hubertusburg, signed on 15 February 1763, ended the Seven Years War within the Holy Roman Empire. It left Austria and especially Prussia exhausted but clearly the major powers within the Empire. Other German states which started the eighteenth century with huge ambitions, especially Saxony and Bavaria, were now clearly second rank powers, both on the Imperial but especially on the European scale. Many historians saw this as a result of the recent war, but in fact both Saxony and Bavaria had lost political weight within Europe as a result of the War of the Austrian Succession. Both states started this conflict with huge ambitions, as both their electors had been married to daughters of the former Emperor Joseph I, nieces of the dead Carl VI and cousins of his successor Maria Theresia. While Bavarian elector Carl Albrecht acted as rival to Maria Theresia's husband Franz von Lothringen for the Imperial crown, Saxony wanted a part of the territorial inheritance of the Habsburg empire to gain a land bridge to Poland, which was united with the electorate in a personal union since the reign of Augustus the Strong (as Friedrich August I, Elector of Saxony 1694-1733 and Augustus II, King of Poland 1697-1733).

While Saxony had made secret plans with Russia in 1738 for a surprise attack on Austria in the case of Carl VI's death (which seemed extremely likely to happen in 1738 due to a serious illness),[1] it was Prussia which triggered the War of the Austrian Succession with an attack on Silesia in 1740. Friedrich II of Prussia was able to benefit from an alliance with France but also with Saxony and Bavaria, both of which hoped to win their share of the cake. While Bavaria was at first successful and Carl Albrecht became Emperor Carl VII with the votes of all electors (meaning that of Saxony and Prussia, too), Saxony's hopes to gain a land bridge to Poland was not only disappointed, but after the Prussian conquest of the province, trade and communication between the two countries was complicated. Saxony switched sides and returned to the Habsburgs for the Second Silesian War

---

1   Rudolf Beyrich, 'Der geheime Plan der kursächsischen Räte zur Österreichischen Erbfolge vom Jahre 1738`, in NASG 37 (1916), pp.56-67.

(1744-1745), but, again, it was a very unsuccessful contest with the country invaded by Prussia in 1745, the army beaten at the Battle of Kesselsdorf and the country forced to sign the humiliating Treaty of Dresden, which forced it to pay a contribution of one million thalers to its northern neighbour.[2] The military situation for Bavaria was not much better, the country being repeatedly invaded and conquered by Austrian forces and after Carl Albrecht's surprising death in January 1745 his successor decided not to run for the Imperial crown but instead signed a treaty with Austria and gave his vote to Maria Theresia's husband.

High debts troubled both electorates which led to a cut in expanses for the military, a situation similar to that seen in Saxony after the end of the Great Northern War in 1717 and in Bavaria after the end of the War of the Spanish Succession in 1714. Saxony still appeared to be a stronger power compared to Bavaria, due to the Polish Crown on the head of elector Friedrich August II (or Augustus III of Poland, reigned 1733-1763), but there was no form of political or administrative union between the two countries. Poland even stayed neutral in the War of the Austrian Succession and except for a few squadrons of Polish Uhlans serving with the Saxon army there was no union of the respective forces notwithstanding that this would have added considerable military potential to the Saxon army, which during 1745 reached a peak of approximately 50,000 men. It would also have put Prussia under serious pressure, due to the geopolitical nature between these states. Poland not only surrounded the province of Eastern Prussia, but it also had a long frontier with Silesia and would have opened this province to attack from the east.

But while Augustus III made some attempts at reform within Poland after 1745, there was no attempt for a real union with his electorate and the resulting weakness of both states was felt on the diplomatic theatre of Europe. Augustus' prime minister Heinrich Graf von Brühl immediately after the Peace of Dresden developed plans for a '*renversement des Alliances*', or reversal of alliances, trying to draw France into an anti-Prussian coalition. But this did not become a serious option until the Austrian chancellor Wenzel of Kaunitz took up the idea,[3] and it only became a reality due to the Convention of Westminister between Prussia and Britain in early 1756 which in itself was an answer to the French occupation of British-held Minorca. The resulting Seven Years War only cemented the situation that Saxony found itself in after 1745 and with the death of Friedrich August II and his sickly son Friedrich Christian on whom the hopes of reformers had been pinned, any idea of holding up the union with Poland was given up.

Early Modern Warfare in Europe is characterized by large, wide-ranging, succession crisis, like the War of the Palatine Succession (in the English-speaking world known as Nine Years War 1688-1697), War of the Spanish Succession (1701-1713/14), War of the Polish Succession (1733-1735) and

---

2   Alexander Querengässer, *Kesselsdorf 1745. Eine Entscheidungsschlacht in der Frühen* (Berlin: Zeughaus Verlag, 2020).

3   René Hanke, *Brühl und das Renversement des alliances. Die antipreußische Außenpolitik des Dresdner Hofes 1744 – 1756* (Münster e.o.: LIT Verlag, 2006).

War of the Austrian Succession (1740-1748). These continental consequences were again fought over in the Seven Years War (1756-1763). The later conflict left the central-European powers Prussia and Austria exhausted. However, in the early 1770s the next contested succession crisis was already in the air. The Bavarian elector Maximilian III Joseph was without a male heir. To strengthen the relations between the Wittelsbach and Habsburg dynasty – which had been in jeopardy since his father ran successfully for Holy Roman Emperor – Max Joseph in 1765 arranged a marriage between his sister Maria Josepha and Emperor Joseph II. Unfortunately, his sister died two years afterwards, but the short-lived marriage created new claims to the Bavarian inheritance on the part of Austria. However, the strongest claim definitely lay with the other major branch of the Wittelsbach dynasty, which ruled the Palatinate. The claims of both houses were by '*Erbvereinigungsverträgen*' (union in inheritance pacts). Such treaties had been signed between lines of a dynasty or even between different dynasties in Germany since the Late Middle Ages. For example, Prussia had built up claims to Pomerania with such a contract signed in 1529. Bavaria and the Palatinate signed four during the eighteenth century: in 1746, 1766, 1771 and 1774. The quick succession of contracts in the decade before the outbreak of the war clearly demonstrates that the Wittelsbachs wanted to keep Bavaria.

Another strong pretender was the dynasty of the Wettins, the electors of Saxony. In a double marriage, Max Joseph had married the Saxon princess Maria Anna Sophia in 1747, while his sister Maria Antonia married her brother Friedrich Christian, prince elector. The promising enlightened prince died a few months after his father, so that his son became new elector of Saxony as Friedrich August III. However, as, he was yet underage, a regency was established under his mother and his uncle Prince Xaver, who during the Seven Years War successfully commanded the reformed Saxon troops within the French army. In 1768 Friedrich August took over the government. There was no real desire in Saxony to take over Bavaria and Maria Anna's rights confined themselves to the typical *Weiberlehen* (women's fiefs), which, however, included smaller territories or the possibility of substantial financial compensation which Saxony did not want to eschew after the dowager-electress conveyed her claims to her son in 1776.[4]

Max Joseph finally made preparations for the succession of the senior branch of the Wittelsbach dynasty, which held the electorate of the Palatinate. This was the line, which descended from the unlucky 'Winter King' Friedrich IV, who became King of Bohemia in 1620 only for his army to be decisively beaten at the White Mountain. Following his defeat, he lost his title as elector to the Bavarian branch of the dynasty. This transfer of a title, while not unseen in the history of the Empire – after the War of the Schmalkaldic League, the title of the elector of Saxony was also transferred from the Ernestine to the Albertine Branch of the Wettins – created much tension and resistance within the protestant territories. To settle the problem, it was decided in the Treaty of Westphalia (1648) to create a new electorate for the Palatinate. The

---

4   Emil Reiman, 'Friedrich August III. und Carl Theodor', in NASG 4 (1883), pp.316-339.

treaty also resolved that if one branch of the Wittelsbachs died out, the other could only take over for a son or by abdicating one title in favour of a son, so that two secular electorates were not held by one dynasty.

Interestingly Carl IV Theodor, Elector of the Palatinate, was not really interested in Bavaria even though it was the larger and richer principality. While he was popular with his population and was seen as an enlightened prince who promoted art and science, on the other hand he was influenced by many mistresses and an increasing horde of illegitimate children, who had to be provided for. On top of this, his enlightened patronage ran counter to his childish wish to recreate the old Burgundian kingdom, a European power along the Rhine.

On 30 November 1777 Maximilian III Joseph died in Munich of smallpox. Immediately after his death the Bavarian chancellor called for a secret council, inviting the Palatine ambassador Ludwig Heinrich von Hammer and presented him with a patent, a declaration by the late elector in which he announced to his people that Bavaria should fall to his cousin from the Palatine. This patent was published the same day and a courier sent to Mannheim.

Joseph II in the meantime was not even willing to wait for negotiations with Carl Theodor. As soon as Max III Joseph was dead, two Austrian corps entered Bavaria. One commanded by *Feldmarschalleutnant* Peter von Langlois consisted of seven regiments of infantry, two of cuirassiers, one of dragoons and 60 guns and marched for Schärding; the second, commanded by *Generalmajor* Franz Josef Kinsky with six regiments of infantry, one of dragoons and 10 guns headed for Waldmünchen. In every town and village they reached they destroyed the Bavarian seals on public buildings and exchanged them for the Imperial eagle, clearly demonstrating Joseph's claim. The Bavarian troops were ordered to retreat without offering any resistance. Joseph officially took possession of the Imperial fiefdoms, the landgraviate of Leuchtenberg, the counties of Wolfstein, Haag, Halse and Schwabeck, the baronies of Hohenwaldeck and Hohenschwangau or a couple of smaller territories or (in most case judicial) rights. At the same time the Emperor declared that everybody who was able to present legal claims would be heard by him. While Joseph enforced his rights as Holy Roman Emperor, his mother forwarded claims on behalf of the house of Austria, namely the barony of Mindelheim in Swabia, the Bohemian fiefdoms in the Upper Palatinate, and Straubing. In all three cases century old conditions were presented, the oldest concerned Straubing which had been presented to Albrecht of Austria in 1426 by King Sigismund.

All these negotiations demonstrated the complicated nature of the early modern state, especially within the Empire. While even contemporaries spoke of 'Bavaria' as they spoke of 'Prussia' and 'Austria', these were no nation or territorial states in the sense of the nineteenth century. Instead, these constructs had grown out of Medieval feudal systems that had not lost any of their judicial legitimacy. Over time small territories, or certain rights over territories, had been obtained by dynasties. Some of them could be integrated into bigger territories, some of them kept their own constitutional rights. The link between the different parts was the ruler and if any idea of a superior

THE EMPIRE AFTER THE PEACE OF HUBERTUSBURG

Elector Maximilian III Joseph of Bavaria. (Public Domain)

THE WAR OF THE BAVARIAN SUCCESSION 1778-1789

Elector Charles Theodor of Bavaria. (Public Domain)

level existed, it was the dynasty so that we can speak of a dynastic state. In the case of the Empire this was further complicated by the fact that the Emperor was in theory the suzerain of all imperial estates and able to seize fiefdoms, especially after the death of a vassal. In practice the heritability of dynastic territories was long established, but this did not free their rulers to formally receive them as fiefdoms after their succession, a practice which offered income and/or influence for Vienna.

While Carl Theodor was still en route to Munich, the Palatine envoy at Vienna, Heinrich Joseph baron von Ritter, was presented on 3 January 1778 with a treaty in which the new elector would cede any claims to the territories claimed by Austria. In return Joseph and his mother accepted him as elector in the remaining territories and undertook to pay substantial equalisation payments. Friedrich II later gave a black comment about this incident:

> The elector Palatine, who was in Munich, turned pale at this news [of the Austrian invasion]; a panic fright clouds what little of his mind he has; his cowardice was the deciding factor, and to his shame he signed an agreement by which he ceded two-thirds of Bavaria to Austrian territorial greed.[5]

The first to raise his voice against this arrangement was the Count Palatine of the Rhine Carl August Christian. Because Carl Theodor had not yet produced a legitimate heir and the claims of his many illegitimate sons were not accepted even by his own estates, the Count Palatine was the next successor in case of his death. He argued that an agreement between Austria and a Bavaria which might become his inheritance could not be made without him. Accordingly, he sent his secretary Philip Jacob Poschinger to the Imperial diet and demanded that Austria should return all the territories. The basis for this were old Imperial privileges, the Golden Bull of 1359, the 1648 Treaty of Westphalia, and other rights guaranteeing the indivisibility of Bavaria. The emerging succession crisis threatened to become an international one as Carl August Christian turned to France and Sweden as the guarantee powers of the Treaty of Westphalia and additionally to Prussia and Denmark. However, he had to fight his fight more or less alone and did not turn to war. Instead, he repeatedly presented his case at the Imperial diet and tried to influence public opinion by printing his memorials. However, he stubbornly insisted that, according to historical treaties of which the oldest – and so highest ranking – was the family treaty of Pavia from 1329, Bavaria could not be divided. Amazingly, while he lacked any allies willing to back him in his case, he even refused the dowager-electress of Saxony her share in the inheritance instead of searching for an alliance. The only real backing Carl August Christian received came from the Bavarian estates, which also rejected the fragmentation of the country and forwarded memorials against it to Carl Theodor and Joseph II.[6] In this complicated situation Friedrich II, who was unwilling for Austria to make any territorial gains, also sent count Eustachius Görtz to Munich. In secret negotiations the count made clear that

---

5   Volz (ed.), *Die Werke Friedrichs des Großen*, Vol.5, p.100.
6   Seyfarth, *Unpartheyische Geschichte*, pp.54-62.

Carl August Christian should not ratify the treaty signed by his uncle and the Emperor and that Prussia would probably back him.

Friedrich II was well aware that an Austrian occupation of Bavaria would be unpopular not only within the Empire and with the other bruised heirs, but also with the other major European powers, France and Russia. His envoys in Paris and St Petersburg were ordered to figure out the attitude of Louis XVI and Catherine II. In general, while none of the continental powers was favourable to the idea of an increase of Austrian power, neither Russia nor France had a major interest to fight a war about it. For Russia, Austrian gains offered the possibility to argue for compensation in Eastern Europe or at least for a favourable reception for Russian expansion at the cost of Turkey or Poland. Louis XVI in turn was Joseph's brother-in-law and Austria and France had been allies since the *renversement des alliances* in 1757. Such alliances never have been signed for eternity, but at the turn of 1778 France was at the brink of another war with Britain, joining the American rebels. While this would not involve significant numbers of French troops, the past conflicts, especially the Nine Years War, the War of Spanish Succession and the Seven Years War, had clearly demonstrated that even a major power like France was unable to simultaneously maintain a fleet fighting the leading sea power and an army to face the major land powers. Paris had learned its lesson and decided to put the focus on the navy for the coming conflict with Britain. However, as Friedrich II made clear in his own history of the war, this decision was not initially clear to him:

> In this great conflict of interests the King felt more hampered by the uncertainty of the position of the Great Powers than by the attitude of Austria. France was allied with Austria by the Treaty of Versailles: had she come to an understanding with the Emperor or not? Had this one promised the French cessions in Flanders if they agreed to his usurpation of Bavaria? Did they prefer the Treaty of Versailles to the guarantee of the Peace of Westphalia? In short, would they remain neutral in the coming turmoil, or would they stand by Austria? It was of the utmost importance to be fully aware of all these points, in order not to rush into an undertaking whose consequences could not be foreseen.[7]

But Friedrich quickly found out that even while Austria's line of action was unpopular with the court of Versailles, France was going to stay neutral in part in allowance for the queen but especially because of its high levels of debt, a fact the king later on clearly recognized:

> For the fitting out of so many ships work was being done in all shipyards; England, by a secret article of the last peace of 1763, had limited the French fleet to twelve ships of the line. Now sixty new ones were under construction. All the money that could be mustered with difficulty went to the fleet, and nothing was left for other purposes.[8]

---

7   Volz (ed.), *Die Werke Friedrichs des Großen*, Vol.5, pp.101-102.
8   Volz (ed.), *Die Werke Friedrichs des Großen*, Vol.5, p.102.

France had indeed put a focus on naval expansion since 1774, raising its funds from 20 million livres that year to 200 million in 1778.[9] On the other hand, the occupation of Bavaria also strengthened Austria's position in southwestern Germany, close to the border to France, so Louis XVI and his ministers were not unfavourable to Prussia challenging the Austrian claim.

While Paris officially was linked to Vienna, but stayed neutral, St Petersburg was allied to Berlin, but also hesitated to act. While the tsardom had had an interest in the Empire since the troops of Peter the Great marched through northern Germany during the Great Northern War, the immediate concern of Russia were relations with Turkey. These were strained since the Peace of Küçük Kaynarca (1774), because Russia tried to strengthen its grip on the Crimea. Friedrich expected that Austrian diplomats would try to fuel the situation in Constantinople. The king asked France for help, because the Bourbon kingdom at this time had the biggest influence at the Porte, as it was its major trading partner and regularly sent military advisers. A plague epidemy which struck the eastern Mediterranean in 1778 and forced the sultan to flee Constantinople further helped to cool down the mood of the Ottomans.

In the meantime, on 7 January the Saxon Privy Councillor Adolf Alexander Baron von Zehmen also arrived in Munich. He had orders to seal the electoral archive and present the Saxon claims for Maria Anna's heritage. However, Zehmen found the archive and all territories taken over by the new elector. His demand to seal the archive was rejected and Zehmen left Munich in protest two days later.

Although a legal exchange, the treaty between Carl Theodor and Joseph II was witnessed by many German powers with distrust. In Saxony dowager-electress Maria Antonia was unwilling to leave the succession crisis with empty hands. She was a very ambitious woman and broke with her brother-in-law Prince Xaver in 1765, after he officially and in the name of her son Friedrich August III abdicated any claim for the Polish succession. Her husband Friedrich Christian had been willing to continue the Saxon-Polish union. In fact, Xaver's declaration was meaningless, as the Polish nobility already in 1764 had elected Stanislaw Poniatowski as new king, who was also the favourite of Russia and there was no chance of any candidate winning an election without Russian backing. But after this serious setback, which reduced the Wettins from royal status to that of ordinary imperial princes, Maria Antonia was at least willing to enlarge the electorate.

On 20 January the Austrian chancellor Graf Kaunitz invited all foreign ambassadors, among them Johann Hermann count Riedesel, the Prussian ambassador, to give them an official declaration of the occupation of Bavaria and present the legal claims, mentioned above. Riedesel sent a communiqué to Berlin and Prussia soon formulated a note of protest, publishing it on 6 February 1778. According to the Prussian view, the Bohemian fiefdoms in the Upper Palatinate could not fall back to the crown, because the Treaty of

---

9   See Jeremy Black, *From Louis XIV to Napoleon. The Fate of a Great Power* (London: Routledge, 2003), p.218. Black in general gives a very good account of the diplomatic problems and political choices of France in this time.

Westphalia had stipulated that they fall to the Palatinate. Mingolfsheim could not be taken over without the consent of the Empire – not the Emperor. The Elector of the Palatinate could not legally split his territories because of entail treaties. Friedrich II threatened that he as Imperial elector could not stand idle by while the Emperor was threatening the Imperial constitution but must react, if the Austrian troops were not withdrawn from Imperial estates. With this declaration Friedrich fixed the roles of good and bad in this dispute, probably not as he saw it, but as he wanted to have it seen by the public and by all Imperial estates. The Emperor was going to violate the Imperial constitution, ruling as a despot, and so forcing Prussia to defend it.

Interestingly, a few years earlier Prussia itself had suggested a takeover of Bavaria by Austria, when a first partition of Poland was under discussion. Friedrich suggested this to the Austrian envoy in May 1770, who promptly rejected the idea and said to the Prussian king, that Austria never usurped anyone's territory. In the first partition of Poland in 1772, Austria gained Galicia with a population of more than two and a half million people. This partition aroused fear within the other two major powers of Europe: France, and especially Britain, which once more feared for the safety of Hannover.[10]

To Friedrich II's declaration Kaunitz answered 10 days later, declaring the treaty with the Palatinate legal, as it was agreed to by both parties and its contents were of no concern to third parties. The occupation of Bavarian territory happened afterwards and was not done by Austrian troops, but by troops of the respective Imperial circles. This, however, was a judicial dodge, as Austria provided most of the troops in the respective circles: furthermore, such a move needed the consent of a circle assembly, which never took place. Kaunitz also underlined that the parts of the Upper Palatinate in question still were Bohemian fiefdoms. He also declared that Bavaria never was a real electorate or inseparable duchy, which was also not true, as the electorate which was given to Maximilian I, Duke of Bavaria, during the Thirty Years War was confirmed in the Treaty of Westphalia.

Prussia, too, saw the augmentation of Habsburg power in this region with reluctance. Josephs ambitions were clear: Bavaria should be a compensation for the loss of Silesia, and it would be more than that for it gave the Habsburg dynasty an important electoral vote. That Joseph secured his new possessions by having Austrian troops march into Bavaria further complicated the geopolitical situation, as the Upper Palatinate bordered the Franconian margravates of Ansbach and Bayreuth, ruled by junior branches of the Hohenzollern, which themselves were threatened with extinction. In this case, Berlin wanted to take over both territories. Already in spring 1777 the Prussians received information about the Austrians preparing magazines on the border from Bohemia to Bavaria,[11] a clear sign that the Austrians were preparing for war.

---

10 Jeremy Black, *The Rise of the European Powers 1679-1793* (London: Edward Arnold, 1990), pp.125-126.
11 Prussian Academy of Sciences (eds), *Politische Korrspondenz Friedrichs des Großen* (Berlin: Reimar Hobbing, 1925-1929), Vol.39, Nr. 25412, p.142.

THE EMPIRE AFTER THE PEACE OF HUBERTUSBURG

Bavarian grenadiers, c.1780. (Anne S.K. Brown Collection)

An Austrian military presence close to both margravates threatened Prussia's claims. Already during the winter, Friedrich II prepared for war, writing to the governor of Königsberg, *Generalleutnant* von Sutterheim on 26 January: 'I cannot write you something positive at the moment, but apparently it will come to war.'[12] In his history of the war Friedrich described his mobilisation as a defensive act, a reaction to the Austrian army concentrating regiments from Flanders, Italy, and Hungary in Bohemia:

> As soon as such a considerable force of troops gathers on the frontier of a province, the welfare of the state dictates that one also arm oneself if one does not wish to have one's neighbour dictate laws. For this reason, the king mobilized his troops to raise two armies of 80,000 men each. One, under Prince Heinrich, was to assemble near Berlin in order to be able to unite quickly with the Saxons, if the Emperor attempted an incursion into Saxony. The other, which the king wanted to lead himself, had its assembly point in Silesia.[13]

Joseph's rashness played into Friedrich's hands, who at the time and later on presented himself as protector of the Imperial constitution against a despotic Emperor:

> At this critical moment it was important to take sides. Either a strong dam had to be built against the torrent, which threatened to flood everything if nothing stopped it, or every imperial prince had to renounce his privilege of freedom. For if the imperial estates remained inactive, they seemed to be tacitly giving the Emperor the right, which he wanted to presume, to dispose despotically of the defunct imperial fiefdoms. This, however, was bound to lead to the general overthrow of the imperial laws, treaties, hereditary fraternities, and privileges that secured the imperial princes' property.[14]

---

12   Prussian Academy of Sciences (eds), *Politische Korrspondenz*, Vol.40, Nr. 25898, p.59.
13   Volz (ed.), *Die Werke Friedrichs des Großen*, Vol.5, p.104.
14   Volz (ed.), *Die Werke Friedrichs des Großen*, Vol.5, p.100.

2

The Road to War

Prussia was able to take the role as defender of the minor states, as Saxony, Zweibrücken and Mecklenburg all appealed to Berlin for help. Because of that a self-confident Riedesel was able to present another declaration to Kaunitz on 9 March which once more rejected all Austrian claims and their evidences. He now demanded that the Maria Theresia – interestingly there was no talk of Joseph II – should withdraw her troops and restore the old order. To this Austria gave no answer for nearly four weeks.

Austria astonishingly alienated the friendly elector by demanding that Saxony reduce her army to 4,000 men, rendering it absolutely meaningless, hand over the fortress of Königstein which guards the Elbe River between Dresden and the Bohemian border, and allow free passage for Austrian ships on that same river and for Austrian troops through the whole country. These demands seriously threatened the reputation of the elector, who – also less powerful than the Emperor and the Prussian king – was still one of the leading princes of the empire. The insistence on a reduction of the army proves that the electoral troops, even if too small for an independent foreign policy, were still a factor in the bigger game.

However, the relations between Saxony and Austria had already soured, as Austria had previously blocked a Saxon occupation of the baronies of Schönburg, Bohemian fiefdoms within southwestern Saxony, which had rejected Saxon suzerainty for centuries. In 1776 the quarrels escalated and Saxon troops occupied the town of Glauchau. Both the elector and Maria Theresia as Queen of Bohemia struggled over traditional rights, with the Austrians also sending troops. Prussia offered its mediation and so was able to improve relations with Saxony on the eve of the Bavarian crisis. The smaller affair about the Schönburg baronies was not settled until 1779.[1]

Interestingly, the Prussian minister von Hertzberg made an offer to the Saxon envoy in Berlin, Graf Zinzendorf. Saxony should assign all land eastwards of the Black Elster River to Prussia in exchange for Prussia's prospective entitlement of the Frankish margravates; Bayreuth and Ansbach. As long as the ruling dynasties survived, Prussia would pay 300,000 thalers

---

1 Jacek Kordel, *Sachsen, Preußen und der Emperorhof im Streit um die Schönburgischen Herrschaften (1774-1779)* (Leipzig: Leipziger Universitätsverlag, 2021).

per annum. The same offer was made by the Prussian envoy in Dresden, but, after discussing the matter with his ministers, the elector turned it down.[2]

This snubbing of Friedrich August directly led to a treaty between Prussia and Saxony signed on 18 March 1778 in which Berlin guaranteed Saxon claims to the Bavarian inheritance. A secret convention of 2 April also stipulated military cooperation. In the event of war, the Saxon army should be directly subordinated to the Prussian king. To avoid quarrels between the two officer corps, however, the army should be used as a cohesive body and not mixed with Prussian troops. If a mixing of troops could not be avoided, the most senior officer should take command in every case. As commander of a combined army of Saxon and Prussian troops the elector agreed to Prince Heinrich (1726-1802), a very experienced and highly regarded general, who won the last battle of the Seven Years War in Europe on Saxon soil at Freiberg.

According to the secret treaty, Dresden kept a Saxon garrison and became a huge depot, while Prussian troops marched into the small Saxon fortress of Torgau, farther north on the Elbe River, which also became an important forward magazine. Prussian hospitals also were established in Torgau and at Wittenberg, another Saxon fortress on the Elbe, while the main Saxon hospitals were concentrated in Dommitzsch and Schmiedeberg between both of those cities.

The treaty further forbade officers to change service between both armies, and stipulated that deserters were to be handed over. Friedrich also had to guarantee the good behaviour of his troops. Saxony was now an ally and not, as in the Seven Years War, 'the flour bag, that could be raped always'[3].

In the meantime, Saxony protested at the Imperial diet against the actions of the new Bavarian elector. The Saxon representative von Loeben demanded the inheritance of the dowager-electress and rejected any claim of Carl Theodor for the Bavarian inheritance. This protest definitely had its weight as a new elector has to be accepted by the electoral college and if Saxony was able to win over the other electors this could destabilize Carl Theodor's position. The representative of the Palatinate in turn rejected the Saxon protests and declared that the territorial and financial properties of Bavaria still had to be inventoried and that no claims for inheritance could be fulfilled before this was properly done.[4] However, contrary to this assertion Austria's claims – especially those of Maria Theresia – had already been fulfilled. The negative stance of the Palatinate demonstrated to the Saxons that if they did not wish to be excluded from any inheritance, they too had to resort to force. In the face of Austrian military superiority, the acceptance of the Prussian offer was now the only political solution.

To this oral response Saxony answered with another declaration printed on 1 April in which it prompted the Palatinate to present documentation of

---

2 Mielsch, 'Die kursächsische Armee im Bayerischen Erbfolgekrieg`, p.76; Reiman, 'Friedrich August III. und Carl Theodor`, pp.321-328.
3 Quoted from: Alexander Querengässer, '"Ich bin Meister vom Lande, und es muß geschehen, was ich befehle". Saxony`s Significance for Prussia`s War Efforts in the Seven Years War', in Alexander Querengässer, *The Battle of Rossbach 1757. New Perspectives on the Battle and Campaign* (Warwick: Helion, 2022), pp.120-141, here p.121.
4 Seyfarth, *Unpartheyische Geschichte*, pp.28-29.

fiefdom for all Bavarian territories claimed to be male fiefs. The declaration also stated that Saxony forwarded its protests to the Empress-queen in January and had not yet received an answer, because Maria Theresia herself acted as new allodial ruler in Bavaria, denying Saxony its share. Because of that, Saxony felt forced to accept the Prussian offer for military assistance and join forces with Friedrich II. This was further justified by accusations that Austria already had started hostilities in Lusatia.

On 1 April Kaunitz finally gave an answer to the Prussian ultimatum of 9 March, declaring that the Empress would not resign any of her legal claims and snubbing Prussia by asserting that no third Imperial estate had the right to act as judge or guardian of the other. The Empress had the power and the will to make war against everybody who acted otherwise.[5]

Friedrich was well aware of this rebuke, but gave a conciliatory answer on 22 April, rejecting the charges and demanded to know how Vienna was going to settle that conflict. Once more he declared that the Emperor, who was acting to the benefit of his own dynasty, was not the unrestricted ruler of the empire, but more like a *primus inter pares*. This in turn was rejected in a very discursive note by Kaunitz of 7 May in which he once more declared that it was not Joseph the Emperor who has acted, but Maria Theresia as Archduchess of Austria and that the Emperor could not – and here he tried to turn Friedrich's arguments against him – involve himself in their bilateral treaties. Kaunitz also once again declared that the troops occupying Bavaria were troops of the circle, not of Austria. Additionally, he claimed that the Empress was willing to settle all open points with Saxony and Mecklenburg while the appeal of the Duke of Zweibrücken should be discussed by the Emperor and the Imperial diet.[6]

While this exchange of declarations and notes was going on, a conference was held at Berlin between the Austrian envoy Johann Ludwig Joseph Graf Cobenzl and the Prussian ministers. Cobenzl tried to put the pressure on Prussia, declaring that if Prussia rejected the takeover of Bavaria by Austria, the house of Habsburg in a similar fashion would reject the reversion of the Franconian margravates of Ansbach and Bayreuth to Prussia. To avoid war Friedrich should put himself into the Empress' position and accept the treaties signed with Carl Theodor. In this case Austria would guarantee Berlin's claim on the two margravates.

What was thought to be a clever comparison and cheap swap of interests by Cobenzl only served to provoke Prussia. Instead of preventing an enlargement of Austria, Friedrich's own territorial interests suddenly had been threatened. The Prussian ministers declared that both cases could not be compared, but offered a compromise. Austria should gain two districts between the Danube and Inn but had to hand back all the rest of Bavaria, while Saxony had to be properly compensated. This was unacceptable to Vienna. The two districts were nothing more than an obvious handout to save one's face, while it was clear to everybody that it would be lost. Accordingly, the court in Vienna rejected the offer. On 7 June – after the mobilisation in Prussia, Austria and

---

5   Seyfarth, *Unpartheyische Geschichte*, p.82.
6   Seyfarth, *Unpartheyische Geschichte*, pp.83-85.

Saxony had already started – Cobenzl presented another compromise, which in fact just repeated the first offer with regard to Bavaria and Ansbach and Bayreuth. Prussia and Austria would guarantee their respective claims and mediate a solution for the Saxon claims. There was no more talk of those of Mecklenburg and Zweibrücken. This was probably due to the fact that only Saxony could raise substantial forces and so underlines the importance of the smaller armies within the empire.

Friedrich himself had left Berlin on 6 April for Silesia, where he took his quarters at Frankenstein (Ząbkowice Śląskie). His army here consisted of 30,000 troops, but reinforcements from the garrisons in Pomerania and East Prussia were en route. The king established a fortified camp at the heights of Pieschkowitz (Pieskowicze), close to the border to Bohemia. His left was protected by the fortress of Glatz and in his front the Prussians dammed a small rivulet to add further protection to their camp.

While the Prussians were preparing for war, a courier from the Emperor reached Friedrich's camp. In a letter to the king, Joseph II tried to convince him of his peaceful intention, which only provoked the reply that in this case Joseph should abandon his claims to Bavaria. In a second letter Joseph tried to justify his claims. Shortly thereafter the Emperor sent a third courier suggesting negotiations through the Austrian envoy in Berlin, Cobenzl. Friedrich suspected Joseph was just trying to buy time to finish his own mobilisation. However, as the Prussian army itself was not yet prepared and because it was essential to his policy to demonstrate his own peacefulness, he accepted the offer without building up false hopes.

> The Austrians presented all their bad evidence, which was victoriously refuted by the Prussian ministers. Nevertheless, the Viennese court did not want to give up their plans of conquest in the least. Finally, in order to put an end to this fruitless war of words, the Austrians were hired. Ultimatum: if they did not agree to return most of Bavaria to the Elector Palatine, this refusal should be taken as a declaration of war.[7]

Friedrich later on accused Joseph of provoking a war to obtain the independence of his mother and this assessment appears correct.

---

7 Volz (ed.), *Die Werke Friedrichs des Großen*, Vol.5, p.105.

THE ROAD TO WAR

Emperor Joseph II in front of his troops. (Anne S.K. Brown Collection)

3

Opposing Forces

Prussia

Friedrich II's success in the first two Silesian Wars certainly came as a surprise to his contemporaries, but it was not out of the blue. In 1740, his father, Friedrich Wilhelm I, had left him a numerically strong and well-trained army, a full state treasury and – in comparison with other European countries – an efficiently organized state.

Especially with regard to the officer corps, primarily made up of noblemen, certain of the military's social disciplinary functions cannot be denied. Since primogeniture (right of the first-born) was in force in Prussia and in the Protestant country a church career was not an attractive alternative for noble families' subsequent children, the military was an important outlet for the local nobility. Friedrich Wilhelm I recognized the danger that young Prussian nobles could also seek their fortune in other countries, either in the military or in a government career. He put a stop to this and forbade the nobility from serving in foreign armies. The war entrepreneur of the seventeenth century who enjoyed far-reaching autonomous rights, gradually became a service nobility.[1] Therefore, many Prussian families sent sons to the military, who were to be trained accordingly in the various cadet institutions established in the country. However, these measures were inconsistent across the country. The officer corps was mainly dominated by nobles from the Kurmark and Pomerania. In the richer provinces, such as Kleve, the comparatively poorly

---

[1] In any case, in 1702, Friedrich I had already prohibited his own nobles from performing military service abroad, Friedrich Wilhelm I only renewed these instructions. See Carmen Winkel, '"Getreue wie goldt" oder "malicieus wie der deuffel"? Der brandenburg-preußische Adel und der Dienst als Offizier' in Lorenz Friedrich Beck and Frank Göse (ed.), *Brandenburg und seine Landschaften. Zentrum und Region vom Spätmittelalter bis 1800* (Berlin: Lukas Verlag, 2009), pp.202-203, see more generally pp.199-219; Carmen Winkel, 'Eine Frage der Ehre – Das preußische Offizierskorps als ständische und militärische Elite', in Eberhard Birk, Thorsten Loch and Peter Andreas Popp, *Wie Friedrich 'der Große' wurde. Eine kleine Geschichte des Siebenjährigen Krieges* (Freiburg i. Br. – Berlin – Vienna: Rombach, 2012), pp.85-89., Rolf Straubel, *'Er möchte nur wissen, daß die Armée mir gehöret'. Friedrich II. und seine Offiziere. Ausgewählte Aspekte der königlichen Personalpolitik* (Berlin Brandenburgische Landeshauptarchiv, 2012), pp.22-26, 41-44.

paid military service was much less attractive to the nobility.² Although it was possible in principle for non-commissioned officers to rise to the officer ranks or for non-nobles to hold this rank (especially with technical troops such as artillery and engineers), these cases remained extremely rare and after the Seven Years War Friedrich tried to get bourgeoise elements out of the officer corps. Service in the military was not an engine for social advancement.³

The chances of promotion in the officer corps were also far from good. Fifty-four percent of officers who left service between 1713 and 1786 had not even obtained the position of company commander.⁴ Military service had a high standing in the Prussian society, visually expressed by the fact that the king – Friedrich Wilhelm I and Friedrich II – wore uniforms. On the flip side, however, Friedrich II demanded of his officers that they sacrifice themselves for their service. While the king usually encouraged ordinary soldiers to marry and have children, he was reluctant to see an officer enter into marriage.⁵ Even a request for leave could quickly arouse the king's displeasure, especially when it was made in times of war. In reply to *Major von Sparr* of the Dragoon Regiment Bayreuth, who asked for a few days' leave in 1744, the king answered gruffly 'A young, healthy man who requests an absence during a campaign should be ashamed to death.'⁶

The Prussian army's recruitment system changed drastically under the Soldier King (*Soldatenkönig*), Friedrich Wilhelm I. Until the time of Friedrich I, the officers responsible for recruitment mainly resorted to recruiting 'volunteers' domestically and abroad. However, military service was poorly paid and therefore unattractive to large parts of the population working in agriculture and urban commerce. As a result, many recruits had been pressed into military service using force. But those same soldiers who had made better money in their previous professions and had been recruited against their will quickly tended to desert. Friedrich Wilhelm I recognized this evil and immediately after taking power forbade forced recruiting – at least domestically.⁷ Abroad, the Prussian recruiters remained dreaded and

---

2   See Winkel, '"Getreue wie goldt" oder "malicieus wie der deuffel"?', p.203; Winkel, 'Eine Frage der Ehre', pp.85-86.
3   See Winkel, *Im Netz des Königs. Netzwerke und Patronage in der preußischen Armee 1713-1786*, pp.39-61; Martin Meier, 'Rekrutierung, Ausbildung und Drill im friderizianischen Heer' in Eberhard Birk, Thorsten Loch and Peter Andreas Popp, *Wie Friedrich 'der Große' wurde. Eine kleine Geschichte des Siebenjährigen Krieges* (Freiburg i. Br. – Berlin – Vienna: Rombach, 2012), pp.96-101.
4   See Georg Hebelmann, *Das preußische 'Offizierskorps' im 18. Jahrhundert. Analyse der Sozialstruktur einer Funktionselite* (Münster: Uni Press, 1998), p.276.
5   See Straubel, *Friedrich II. und seine Offizier*, p.431.
6   Quoted from Grosser Generalstab (eds), *Die Kriege Friedrichs des Großen. Teil 2*, Vol.2 Hohenfriedberg, p.124. The example here is only representative of the monarch's general, negative attitude toward officers taking leave or being absent – see Carmen Winkel, 'Ziele und Grenzen der königlichen Personalpolitik im Militär' in Frank Göse (ed.), *Friedrich der Große und die Mark Brandenburg. Herrschaftspraxis in der Provinz* (Berlin: Lukas Verlag, 2012), pp157-158, pp.144-162; Straubel, *Friedrich II. und seine Offiziere*, pp.466-473, 486-491.
7   See Ralf Pröve, 'Zum Verhältnis von Militär und Gesellschaft im Spiegel gewaltsamer Rekrutierungen (1648-1789)', *Zeitschrift für Historische Forschung* 22 (1995), pp.191-223; Michael Sikora, 'Massenhaft Soldaten' in Bernd Sösemann and Gregor Vogt-Spira (eds),

unwelcome visitors. In 1724, the Elector of Saxony even had 858 muskets handed out to border villages in Lower Lusatia, so that the inhabitants could protect themselves from unauthorised forced recruitment from the neighbouring country![8] Recruitment by force seriously strained Prussia's relations to her neighbours, notably Saxony, Hannover, but most of all Mecklenburg.

A remnant of the former war enterprise system was manifested in the recruiting system, which, incidentally, was retained up to the Prussian reforms in the nineteenth century, because it was based on a certain arbitrary selection of recruits on the part of the recruiting officers. On the other hand, the cantonal system established by Friedrich Wilhelm in 1733 was a model of state order. Prussia, apart from the Rhine provinces of Kleve, Moers and Geldern, was evenly divided into conscription districts (cantons – *Kantone*) which would comprise about 5,000 to 6,000 households. The military-capable male population was included in lists which made available the expendable – that is to say, the socially or economically incompletely-integrated – parts of the population for service in the army. To do so, the army's administration used church records, which at that time were the most accurate statistical record of the population. Excluded from military service were, in addition to the two economic urban centres of Berlin and Magdeburg, precisely those population sectors which were indispensable for the smooth functioning of the economy (and thus for the raising of taxes): above all, urban craftsmen, free farmers and also the educated classes. As a result, primarily unemployed day labourers and part-time workers were conscripted. However, they did not serve continuously in the regiments, but were only assembled for a few weeks in order to be trained.[9] Thus, for most of the year, their labour power remained available to the economy (for example during the harvest months). More recent research has now deduced from the time discrepancies between the short service times and the cantonists' long leave periods or the recruits'

Friedrich der Große in Europa. Geschichte einer wechselvollen Beziehung (Stuttgart: Franz Steiner, 2012), Vol.II, pp.217-220, see more generally pp.216- 232.

8   See Matthias Hoffeins, 'Alltagsleben mit einer Grenze. Brandenburgs südliche Grenzregion in der Frühen Neuzeit' in Lorenz Friedrich Beck and Frank Göse (ed.), *Brandenburg und seine Landschaften. Zentrum und Region vom Spätmittelalter bis 1800* (Berlin: Lukas Verlag, 2009), pp.72-77; see more generally pp.69-107. As an older investigation with a focus on the relationship with Mecklenburg see Wilhelm von Schultz, *Die preußischen Werbungen unter Friedrich Wilhelm I. und Friedrich dem Großen bis zum Beginn des Siebenjährigen Krieges mit besonderer Berücksichtigung Mecklenburg-Schwerins* (Schwerin: Schulze, 1887).

9   See Curt Jany, 'Die Kantonverfassung Friedrich Wilhelms I.', FBPG 38 (1926), pp.225-272; Hartmut Harnisch, 'Preußisches Kantonsystem und ländliche Gesellschaft. Das Beispiel der mittleren Kammerdepartements' in Bernhard R. Kroener and Ralf Pröve (ed.), *Krieg und Frieden. Militär und Gesellschaft in der Frühen Neuzeit* (Paderborn and Munich: Ferdinand Schöningh, 1996), pp.137-165, for the origin of the cantonal system especially see pp.140-144; Hans Bleckwenn, 'Bauernfreiheit durch Wehrpflicht. Ein neues Bild der altpreußischen Armee?,' in Wehrgeschichtliches Museum Rastatt (ed.), *Die Bewaffnung und Ausrüstung der Armee Friedrichs des Großen. Eine Dokumentation aus Anlass seines 200. Todesjahres* (Rastatt: Wehrgeschichtliches Museum Rastatt, 1986), pp.1-14; Meier: 'Rekrutierung, Ausbildung und Drill im friderizianischen Heer', pp.97- 98; Thomas Wollschläger, *Die Military Revolution und der deutsche Territorialstaat. Determinanten der Staatskonsolidierung im europäischen Kontext 1670-1740* (Norderstedt: BOD, 2004), pp.154-157.

off-duty time (*Freiwächter Zeit*) that a predominantly military-dominated socialisation of the Prussian cantonal soldiers could not have taken place.[10]

However, this argument, justified only by the brevity of active service, falls short. Two simple measures challenge this argument. On the one hand, the soldier continued to be subject to military jurisdiction. This protected him, for example, from beatings by his landlords, free peasants or master craftsmen, with whom he earned his wages during his off-duty time, which clearly distinguished him from civilian unskilled workers. The landlord and company commander were only rarely the same person.[11] The soldier's well-defined legal status was symbolically emphasized by 'the King's coat' (*des Königs Rock*), which he continued to wear, especially during Sunday church services, and which reminded both himself and those around him of his rights and duties.[12] That, too, made him little different from British, French, Austrian or Saxon soldiers, who were also on leave for long periods of time, who were able to gain civilian employment and wore uniforms. Thus, perhaps it is not possible to speak of a Prussian special path. However, the attempt to socially discipline the soldier outside of his active service can by no means be dismissed. Perhaps it had a slightly stronger effect in Prussia because the army's share of the total population was comparatively high and in the garrison locations – the cities – in some cases up to 40 percent. The fact that representatives of the estates from various provinces asked the king to limit the military jurisdiction only to the cantonists actually conscripted into regiments also suggests that there was an attempt to inculcate the cantonists militarily. Friedrich gave in and placed the enrolled men – that is to say, the cantonists who were not actively on duty – back to civilian jurisdiction before the beginning of the Seven Years War.[13] If the company commander in the regiment had been the lord of the manor, as older scholarship has claimed, such demands would have ceased. The extent to which the authoritarian state's inculcation and disciplining of the soldier actually succeeded still needs further research.[14]

The composition of the Prussian army of cantonists and foreigners fluctuated greatly in the eighteenth century. In peacetime Friedrich II preferred recruiting foreigners, because the local cantonists were required

---

10   See Harnisch: 'Preußisches Kantonsystem', pp.147-148.
11   See Frank Göse, 'Zwischen Garnison und Rittergut. Aspekte der Verknüpfung von Adelsforschung und Militärgeschichte am Beispiel Brandenburg-Preußens', in Ralf Pröve, *Klio in Uniform? Probleme und Perspektiven einer modernen Militärgeschichte der frühen Neuzeit* (Cologne – Weimar – Vienna: Böhlau, 1997), p.121, and more generally pp.109-142. Similarly, Hans Bleckwenn, 'Altpreußischer Militär- und Landadel. Zur Frage ihrer angeblichen Interessengemeinschaft im Kantonwesen', Zeitschrift für Heereskunde 49 (1985), pp.93-95.
12   See Jany, 'Die Kantonverfassung', pp.231-242.
13   See Frank Göse, '"… die Racce davon so guht ist, das sie auf alle art meritiret, conserviret zu werden". Das Verhältnis Friedrichs des Großen zum brandenburgischen Adel' in Frank Göse (ed.), *Friedrich der Große und die Mark Brandenburg. Herrschaftspraxis in der Provinz* (Berlin Lukas Verlag, 2012), pp.104-132, here p.114.
14   Wolfgang Neugebauer, 'Staatsverfassung und Heeresverfassung in Preußen während des 18. Jahrhunderts', in Peter Baumgart, Bernhard R. Kroener and Heinz Stübing (ed.), *Die preußische Armee zwischen Ancien Régime und Reichsgründung* (Paderborn: Ferdinand Schöningh, 2009), pp.27-44.

THE WAR OF THE BAVARIAN SUCCESSION 1778-1789

Two Prussian officers and two troopers of the Gendarmes, c.1775. The officer far-left is in gala dress. (Anne S.K. Brown Collection)

for the economy. As a result, only seven percent of the enrolled cantonists were drafted in.[15] Losses caused by death, wounding and desertion were largely replaced by cantonal troops, who were to become the backbone of the army during the Seven Years War. In 1763, the Prussian army consisted of more than two-thirds citizens (68.4 percent) and just under a third foreigners (31.6 percent).[16] Friedrich himself therefore stated after the war: 'The cantons make the regiment immortal, because they continue to replace their losses.'[17]

In peacetime, the soldiers were mainly quartered in the Prussian cities. The barracking of the regiments was slow, not least due to a lack of money. For the cities, the quartering of a regiment was both a curse and a blessing. On the one hand, it increased the number of consumers by about 1,800 persons. The soldier spent his two-thalers pay, which he received on six dates each month, mainly in the municipal taverns and in the markets. Professions such as innkeepers, bakers and butchers benefited greatly from the resulting increase in demand. The soldier's basic care was thus ensured, which is why, if he did not have any duties, he could provide his labour below the usual wage

---

15 See Bernhard R. Kroener, 'Die materiellen Grundlagen österreichischer und preußischer Kriegsanstrengungen 1756 – 1763`, in Bernhard R. Kroener (ed.), *Europa im Zeitalter Friedrichs des Großen. Wirtschaft, Gesellschaft, Kriege* (Munich: Oldenbourg Verlag, 1989), pp.47-78, p.50.
16 See Kroener, 'Die materiellen Grundlagen', p.51.
17 Harnisch, 'Preußisches Kantonsystem', p.137.

level, much to the annoyance of the guilds and especially of the journeymen, for whom it created dangerous competition.[18]

Moreover, the system of quartering was not due only to a lack of funds for the construction of the barracks. Although Friedrich's 1752 political testament recommended an increase in the construction of military residences for married soldiers and their wives, it at the same time noted: 'By the way, the regiments lose [men] if they place the unmarried soldiers in barracks.'[19] The quartering of troops was supposed to prevent desertions. The 'host' thus took on a civilian control function. Conversely, however, the soldier also monitored the host.[20]

All these deep ranging measures did not bring about a general militarisation of Prussian society as a whole, as older scholarship once asserted.[21] In order to better understand the possibilities of the state's inculcation of individual soldiers, it will be necessary in future, in addition to using the statistics – which are only marginally interpretable – to find and comparatively evaluate the testimonies of simple soldiers. Prussia was already perceived by contemporaries as a particularly militaristic state. One French diplomat even said, 'Every Prussian is born a soldier.'[22] Similarly, the Danish Minister Johann Hartwig Graf Bernstorff, who made the same judgement and claimed that Friedrich 'had turned his states into an *army camp* and his *people* into an army.'[23] In the light of the canton system's complete encompassing of the population capable of military service, these statements have their own significance. However, many contemporaries received only an incomplete insight into the Prussian military system, since their views were mainly based on what they saw in Potsdam and Berlin, cities that were not representative of the conditions throughout Prussia. On the other hand, their observations that the Prussian military system was clearly different from that in their homeland should not be rejected too quickly, for in the end the nimbus of the Frederician army was more marked by external perception, than by its actual efficiency. For example, Bernhard R. Kroener limited and qualified the value of the statements of contemporary eyewitnesses, writing:

---

18   See Holger Th. Gräf, 'Militarisierung der Stadt oder Urbanisierung des Militärs? Ein Beitrag zur Militärgeschichte der frühen Neuzeit aus stadtgeschichtlicher Perspektive' in Ralf Pröve (ed.), *Klio in Uniform?* (Cologne– Weimar – Vienna: Böhlau Verlag, 1997), pp.89-108.
19   Volz (ed.), *Die Werke Friedrichs des Großen*, Vol.7, p.183.
20   See Pröve, Der Soldat in der 'guten Bürgerstube', pp.201-202.
21   See Otto Büsch, *Militärsystem und Sozialleben im alten Preußen 1713 – 1807. Die Anfänge der sozialen Militarisierung der preußisch – deutschen Gesellschaft* (Berlin: De Gruyter, 1962), pp.71-74; Gerhard Oestreich, 'Strukturprobleme des europäischen Absolutismus', Vierteljahreshefte für Sozial- und Wirtschaftsgeschichte 55 (1969), pp.329- 347.
22   In the original, '*Tout Preussien est né soldat*', quoted from Bernhard R.Kroener, '"Eine Armee, die sich ihren Staat geschaffen hat"? Militärmonarchie und Militarismus', in Bernd Sösemann and Gregor Voigt-Spira (ed.), *Friedrich der Große in Europa. Geschichte einer wechselvollen Beziehung* (Stuttgart: Franz Steiner 2012), Vol.II, pp.233-249, here p.241.
23   Quoted from Johannes Kunisch, 'Friedrich der Große als Feldherr', in Johannes Kunisch, 'Friedrich der Große als Feldherr', in Johannes Kunisch (ed.), *Fürst – Gesellschaft – Krieg. Studien zur bellizistischen Disposition des absolutistischen Fürstenstaates* (Cologne – Weimar – Wien: Böhlau 1992), pp.83-106, here pp.88-89.

> The flaws of the system hidden behind the shiny facade, the limited governmental penetration of the region, the assertions of standing reserve rights in the various provinces and the negotiation compromises that accompany it, on the other hand, only allowed external observers to perceive things imperfectly.[24]

So even if Berlin might not be representative for Prussia as a whole, its martial description by Wraxall differs obviously from that he gave of Vienna, 'a picture of tranquillity', or Dresden. Of Berlin he wrote:

> An air of silence and dejection reigns in the streets, where at noon-day scarcely any passengers are seen, except soldiers [...] The splendid fronts of the finest houses, frequently conceal poverty and wretchedness. A colonnade, hardly inferior to the Louvre, proves, when inspected, to be only a casern, or a barrack.[25]

'The soldier must fear his officers more than the enemy.'[26] These famous words of Friedrich II have become firmly anchored in the collective memory to this day and determine our perception of service in the Prussian army. It would be wrong to completely accept the picture of the corporal who used the cane, which always hung from a button on his uniform, to beat a slow recruit. At the time of the Enlightenment, this trope was overused in order to denounce avoidable grievances. It was by no means the case that the Prussian recruit should have his drill exercises beaten into him. On the contrary, the drill manuals made it extremely clear that new recruits should not be sent on guard duty in the first two weeks and that the new and understandably unfamiliar musket drills should be explained to them with calm and understanding.[27] The study by Sascha Möbius, who for the first time deals with the question of what motivated the Prussian soldier in battle, is also fundamental. He concludes that primarily religious motives and identification with his own regiment were the reasons.[28]

However, drill manuals merely laid down rules which set a standard and did not establish compliance with it. Not every sergeant who mastered the corresponding exercises from the textbook had the appropriate skills to pass on his knowledge in a didactic manner. Some recruits' poor performance would all too often have been neither the result of lack of motivation nor of

---

24   Kroener: 'Eine Armee, die sich ihren Staat geschaffen hat?', p.241.
25   Nathaniel Wraxall, *Memoirs of the Courts of Berlin, Dresden, Warsaw and Vienna* (Dublin: T. Cadell and W. Davies, 1799) Vol.1, pp.101-102.
26   Quoted from Volz (ed.), *Die Werke Friedrichs des Großen*, Vol.6, p.314 (Aus der Instruction für die Kommandeurs der Kavallerie Regimenter (11. Mai 1763) = from the instructions for Cavalry Regiment Commanders dated 11 May 1763.
27   See Meier, 'Rekrutierung, Ausbildung und Drill', pp.92, 100; Sikora, 'Massenhaft Soldaten', pp.225-226.
28   See Sascha Möbius, *Mehr Angst vor dem Offizier als vor dem Feind?. Eine mentalitätsgeschichtliche Studie zur preußischen Taktik im Siebenjährigen Krieg* (Saarbrücken: VDM Verlag Dr. Müller e. K., 2007), pp.16-30, 99-134. Predominantly relying on Möbius' study is also Ilya Berkovich, *Motivation in War. The Experience of Common Soldiers in Old-Regime Europe* (New York: Cambridge University Press 2017), pp.31-32. Additionally, as an introduction see Martin Guddat, *Grenadiere, Musketiere, Füsiliere. Die Infanterie Friedrichs des Großen* (Hamburg: Nikol Verlag. 1986), pp.38-43.

understanding, but probably the NCOs' inadequate instruction and teaching capabilities. Beating was therefore not an instructional principle, but rather an unconscious expression of the instructor's own failure – which was surely irrelevant to the recruit in the end. The fact that instruction by caning was commonplace quickly became established in the collective memory and was expressed not least in the lyrics of a contemporary soldier's song: 'Gentlemen, do not be surprised, when one deserts / We are burdened with beatings like the dogs.'[29] Nevertheless, Georg Heinrich von Berenhorst,[30] actually a strict critic of the Frederician army, wrote in 1798 in the first volume of his 'Reflections on the Art of War': 'The beatings became fewer; but I believe, not based on orders, but because of increasing humanity.'[31] However, such a trend is only noticeable after the War of the Bavarian Succession, starting around the 1780s.[32]

In the Prussian economy, the military was of increased significance in comparison with other countries. A major problem for the production of weapons and ammunition was the country's paucity of natural resources. There were only a few mining locations for inferior iron ore, and a copper mine in Rothenburg an der Saale. Tin for the production of gun bronze, lead for casting musket balls, and high-quality iron for steel production had to be imported, with the British Isles and Sweden being important trading partners.[33]

Friedrich Wilhelm I had made intensive efforts to establish and expand a Prussian armaments industry. When he came to power, there were only a few pre-industrial production plants, such as the Berlin Cannon Foundry (*Berliner Kanonengießerei*, founded in 1645), the *Eberswalder Kupferhammer*, the brass works in Finow and the ironworks (*Eisenhütte*) in Zehdenick. The lack of suitable places of employment was tantamount to a shortage of skilled workers. Although the king created sizeable financial incentives to recruit skilled craftsmen from established European weapons production sites, such as the Suhl and Liège musket manufactures or the Solingen sword-makers (*Solinger Schwertfegerstätten*), few workers responded to this call. Subsequently the country's respective craftsmen themselves had to be

---

29 '*Ihr Herren, nehmt's nicht Wunder, Wann einer desertiert/ Wir werden wie die Hunde mit Schlägen strapeziert.*' Quoted from Sikora, 'Massenhaft Soldaten', p.226.
30 For his role as a critic of the Frederican military system see Heinz Stübig, 'Berenhorst, Bülow und Scharnhorst als Kritiker des preußischen Heeres der nachfriderizianischen Epoche' in Peter Baumgart et al. (eds), *Die Preußische Armee zwischen Ancien Regime und Staatsgründung* (Paderborn etc.: Schöningh, 2009), pp.108-111, and more generally pp.107-120.
31 Quoted from Georg Heinrich von Berenhorst, *Betrachtungen über die Kriegskunst, über ihre Fortschritte, ihre Widersprüche und ihre Zuverläßigkeit, Erste Abtheilung* (Leipzig: Fleischer Verlag 1798), p.156.
32 For this, see Johannes Kunisch, 'Friedensidee und Kriegsidee im Zeitalter der Aufklärung' in Johannes Kunisch, *Fürst – Gesellschaft – Krieg. Studien zur bellizistischen Disposition des absolutistischen Fürstenstaates* (Cologne – Weimar – Vienna: Böhlau, 1992), pp.131-159.
33 See Dieter H. Kollmer, 'Die Versorgung der preussischen Armee mit kriegswichtigen Ressourcen im Zeitalter Friedrichs des Großen' in Eberhard Birk, Thorsten Loch and Peter Andreas Popp, *Wie Friedrich 'der Große' wurde. Eine kleine Geschichte des Siebenjährigen Krieges* (Freiburg i. Br. – Berlin – Vienna: Rombach, 2012), pp.77-84, here p.78. More dated, but still providing an interesting insight is Paul Rehfeld, 'Die preußische Rüstungsindustrie unter Friedrich dem Großen' in FBPG 55 (1944), pp.1-31.

THE WAR OF THE BAVARIAN SUCCESSION 1778-1789

Prussian uniform schema, c.1761. (Anne S.K. Brown Collection)

trained. However, this required a lengthy development process, because the corresponding technical expertise was not passed on from a master to a journeyman, nor through books or educational institutions, but still just orally. It took several generations and Prussia's own development before its arms manufacturers could keep up with established manufacturing facilities in this sector. In the Seven Years War, Prussian weapons were therefore still of a comparatively poor quality.[34]

Initially the army remained heavily dependent on imports. During Friedrich Wilhelm I's first improvements to the army in the 1710s and 1720s, large quantities of muskets were purchased in Liège. In 1722, the Berlin businessmen David Splittgerber (1683-1764) and Gottfried Adolph Daum (1679-1743) founded the 'Royal Prussian Gun Factory' (*Königlich Preußische Gewehrfabrique*). Contrary to what is often portrayed, this was a private venture, not a state factory, but one generously supported by the king with privileges and capital. In this way, the founders finally succeeded in finding 170 masters and journeymen in Liège. In its first year, the factory was already able to produce 10,000 weapons of all kinds – muskets, pistols, edged weapons, cuirasses. By 1726, its capacity had already risen to 15,000 weapons. The 1723 Prussian musket model, based on the French M 1717 musket, was replaced by an improved version in 1740. The soldiers later referred to the 143.4 cm long and 5.5-kilogram (12 lbs.) weapon as a 'cow's foot' (*Kuhfuss*) due to the shape of its butt and the strong recoil when fired.[35]

In addition to the manufacture of weapons, the production of uniforms was of enormous importance to the army. In a regulation of 1714, Friedrich Wilhelm I stipulated that the Prussian army should receive new uniforms every two years. In 1725, the duration of wear for coats was reduced to one year. In 1713, the Royal Warehouse (*Königliche Lagerhaus*) in Berlin was founded for their production, which was responsible for the central supply of uniform pieces to the regiments. The warehouse awarded corresponding orders to local craftsmen or had uniforms made in people's homes. In order to protect the textile industry, the export of local wool was criminalized by a 1718/19 edict, and in 1720 the import of wool was also prohibited. Although this led to a drastic fall in wool's price by up to 50 percent, it nevertheless had a positive effect on the development of domestic wool production.[36] In order to keep up with the army's increasing demand, the amount of cloth required to produce an infantry coat was already drastically reduced under Friedrich Wilhelm I's government. While a tailor needed five ells of cloth per coat in 1714, in 1725 it required only 2 ¾ ells, a saving of 55 percent. The export ban

---

34 See Kollmer, *Versorgung*, pp.78-79; Heinrich Müller, *Das Heerwesen in Brandenburg und Preußen von 1640 bis 1806. Die Bewaffnung* (Berlin: Brandenburgisches Verlagshaus, 2001), pp.56-64.
35 See Eugen A. Lisewski and Peter Andreas Popp, 'Die Waffen der friderizianischen Infanterie' in Eberhard Birk, Thorsten Loch and Peter Andreas Popp, *Wie Friedrich 'der Große' wurde. Eine kleine Geschichte des Siebenjährigen Krieges* (Freiburg i. Br. – Berlin – Vienna: Rombach, 2012), pp.108-114; Müller, *Die Bewaffnung*, pp.86-89.
36 See Kollmer, *Versorgung*, pp.79-80; Klaus-Peter Merta, *Das Heerwesen in Brandenburg und Preußen von 1640 bis 1806. Die Uniformierung* (Berlin: Brandenburgisches Verlagshaus, 2001), pp.44-46.

also reduced the wool price from 14 to 11 Groschen per ell. As a result, the Soldier King was able to uniform 48,000 soldiers in 1725 even more cheaply than only 33,000 in 1714.[37]

The acquisition of Silesia also significantly increased Prussia's economic power. The new province had significant deposits of coal and iron. In Breslau (Wroclaw) a cannon foundry existed, which was further expanded by Friedrich II and until 1745 alone produced 444 new guns.[38] However, it was precisely in this sector that the Prussian arms industry had significant deficits because of a lack of qualified craftsmen to cast artillery pieces. In 1756, 30 cannon that had been made in Berlin had to be melted down because they had significant defects. But an angry Friedrich could not even afford to punish the craftsmen, because he had no available replacements for them. However, the master was sentenced to having to recast the cannons at his own expense. Things were not going any better in the Breslau Foundry, which eventually in 1759 led to the king arresting the foundryman there. In 1757, for this, he still managed to recruit a new master from the Netherlands for the Berlin plant, who mastered the new solid casting process. Until then, the Prussian cannon had been cast with the help of a core spindle. If it was not placed exactly in the centre, the gun's barrel ended up with walls of variable thickness, which caused it to become unusable more quickly. In the solid casting process, the bore was subsequently drilled out, which also led to a more standard calibre.[39]

However, more than half of the money available for the 'armament requirements' in Prussia was used for the procurement of food. The royal domains had a key position for grain production. Centrally controlled by the Royal War- and Domain Chamber (*Königliche Kriegs- und Domänenkammer*), they supplied much of the grain needed for the army. Friedrich kept the crops in warehouses and did not sell them freely on the market, which allowed prices to be regulated by the state. However, the king wanted to hold back the reserves created with it for as long as possible and instead preferred to supply his army in the enemy's country, as was shown by the ruthless plundering of the occupied Bohemian territories in 1742, 1744, 1757, 1758 and 1778-1779.[40]

---

37 See Joachim Niemeyer, 'Die Dessauer Spezifikationen von 1729 und 1737' in *Fürst Leopold I. von Anhalt Dessau (1676-1747) 'Der Alte Dessauer'. Ausstellung zum 250. Todestag* (Dessau: Museum für Naturkunde und Vorgeschichte Dessau, Museum für Stadtgeschichte Dessau, Museum Schoß Mosigkau Dessau, 1997), p.46, see more generally pp.45-49; J.L.P. von Scheffler Knox, 'Die preußische Sparsamkeit im Spiegel der Bekleidungsordnung', *Zeitschrift für Heeres- und Uniformkunde* 7 (1959), pp.7-12.

38 See Kollmer, *Versorgung*, p.81.

39 See Volker Schmidtchen, 'Der Einfluß der Technik auf die Kriegführung zur Zeit Friedrichs des Großen', in Bernhard R. Kroener (ed.), *Europa im Zeitalter Friedrichs des Großen. Wirtschaft, Gesellschaft, Kriege* (Munich: Oldenbourg Verlag, 1989), pp.121-142, pp.129, 136; Martin Guddat, *Kanoniere, Bombardiere, Pontoniere. Die Artillerie Friedrichs des Großen* (Hamburg: Nikol Verlag 1992), pp.27-28.

40 See Kollmer, *Versorgung*, pp.82-83.

Since the reign of Friedrich Wilhelm I, dark blue had been the dominant colour of Prussian uniform coats.[41] The regiments differed by different coloured turnbacks of the coattails and sleeves and the coats' lace trim, as well as the colour of the breeches and waistcoats, with buff dominating. The musketeers wore black hats with white or yellow trim around the edges, the grenadiers had tall mitre hats with a tin plate, the fusiliers a smaller variant of it. Ammunition was carried in a large leather cartridge box supported by a wide white leather bandolier worn across the chest, while swords and bayonets were on a waist belt worn over the waistcoat. In 1741, the king increased the number of cartridges carried from 30 to 60 rounds. In 1740, the infantry regiments wore knee-high white linen gaiters. Black gaiters made their first appearance the following year and in 1744 Friedrich introduced them as winter clothing for all regiments. Additionally, the field equipment included a calfskin pack carried on a single strap over the right shoulder, as well as a tin canteen. In the pack, the soldier carried the items he needed daily: spare shirts and trousers, gaiter buttons, stockings, gloves, cutlery, brush and comb, possibly a mirror, shoe polish, gaiter hook (this was needed to close the buttons), tools for the musket, cleaning cloths and oil. Additionally, three wooden tent pegs were tied to the pack. The soldier carried his food in a separate white linen bag, which was also carried over the right shoulder. In the first two Silesian Wars, the men sharing a tent took turns carrying the field cooking pot. Only starting in 1748 was this carried by an extra pack horse.[42]

All the kit put enormous strain on the infantryman and limited him above all in his mobility. During the Second Silesian War, the soldiers were positioned also particularly close together. The 1743 Regulations decreed in this regard: 'There must be equal and not too great a distance between all the squad members, that is arm to arm, and that people can touch one another. Therefore, the soldiers should not stand as far apart as before.'[43] This worked on the training ground, where the soldiers drilled without field equipment (pack, bread bag, canteen), but not on the battlefield.

---

41 As before, the significant works on the history of Prussian uniforms include: Hans Bleckwenn, *Die friderizianischen Uniformen 1753 bis 1786* (Dortmund: Harenberg Verlag, 1984), four volumes including available actual artifacts, and Daniel Hohrath, *Friedrich der Große und die Uniformierung der preußischen Armee von 1740 bis 1786* (Vienna: Militaria Verlag, 2011). See also more generally Merta, *Die Uniformierung*, which, however, summarizes the time after 1740 only in a cursory manner. An older description in at Carl Kling, *Geschichte der Bekleidung, Bewaffnung und Ausrüstung des Königlich Preußischen Heeres* (Weimar: Königl. Kriegsministerium 1902/1906/1912). Furthermore see the exhibition catalogue: *Die Bewaffnung und Ausrüstung der Armee Friedrichs des Großen. Eine Dokumentation aus Anlaß seines 200. Todestages* (Rastatt, 1986).

42 See Hohrath, *Friedrich der Große und die Uniformierung*, pp.63-129; Duffy, *Frederick the Great*, p.116.

43 '*Zwischen allen Rotten muß egale und nicht zu weite Distance sein, als daß Arm an Arm ist, und das die Leute sich rühren können; Daher die Rotten nicht so weit voneinander stehen sollen wie bishero.*' Quoted from *Reglement für die Königl. Preussische Infanterie, worinn enthalten: Die Evolutions, das Manual und die Chargirung, und wie der Dienst im Felde und in der Garnison geschehen soll, Auch wornach die sämtlichen Officiers sich sonst zu verhalten haben. Desgleichen wie viel an Tractament bezahlet und darvon abgezogen wird, auch wie die Mundirung gemachet werden soll* (Unknown Publisher, 1743), p.33.

THE WAR OF THE BAVARIAN SUCCESSION 1778-1789

Prussian troops, c.1775. From left to right an engineer, a cadet, a jäger and a soldier of a freibataillon. (Anne S.K. Brown Collection)

The Prussian infantry's strength in the field was based on both its firepower and cold steel. According to the Regulations of 1743, the musket was loaded in 11 steps with a total of 16 movements. After firing it, the soldier brought the musket to his right side and the placed the hammer with the flint into the resting position. Then he took a cartridge from the cartridge box, bit it with his teeth (hence, men with bad teeth could not serve in the military), poured some powder onto the pan and closed the pan lid. The musket was then swung around and held on the left side of the body so that the muzzle pointed upwards. The soldier put the rest of the powder and the ball into the barrel, pulled out the ramrod, turned it and rammed the load down the barrel with its help, then pulled the ramrod out again, put it in the shaft and then shouldered the musket.[44] There are many myths about the Prussian troops' methods of loading and the rate of fire. With the method described, it was in no way possible to fire more than four shots per minute, because in addition to the loading steps described, there were still cocking the hammer, aiming the musket, and firing it. The latter alone took at least one or two seconds, because just by pulling the trigger the musket ball was not fired immediately. First, the hammer hit the pan lid with the screwed-in flint, opening it and simultaneously releasing glowing sparks. They ignited the powder on the pan, so that a jet of fire passed through the touchhole igniting the propellant charge inside the musket, which in turn sent the ball on its way. It could take up to two seconds after firing before the soldier was able to recover his musket. With four shots per minute, that would be eight seconds, leaving only 52 seconds, or 13 seconds per charge, for the remaining steps. The loading became more difficult with each shot, because the powder left thick residues in the barrel, so that the ball had to be rammed down with more force each subsequent time. Descriptions that the soldiers simply rolled the bullet down the barrel like marbles, tamped them gently or even spitting into the barrel to hold them in place, belong to the realm of (film) myths. For at the same moment that the powder and bullet were in the muzzle, the weapon was ready to fire. A soldier, who was still putting the muzzle up to his mouth, risked blowing off his own head. The risk of injury was similarly high when the weapon was rammed. The construction of the muskets was still very primitive at the time and the Prussian muskets were among the worst in Europe. The fine powder smoke residue penetrated into every crack and settled on all the components of the lock. It could therefore very possibly happen that the bolt holding back the cocked hammer was so badly coated with powder that the hammer released due to the shock of the ramming and the weapon fired. The drill regulations of their time also served as 'safety instructions' and were designed so each man in a closed formation could load his musket without endangering himself or his comrades. Spitting bullets into the barrel or ramming the weapon while charging contradicted this logic. How difficult inserting the musket ball could be is also shown by an important technical innovation that gave the Prussian regiments a significant advantage over their Austrian opponents in the first two Silesian

---

44 See *Reglement 1743*, pp.58-59.

Wars: the iron ramrod. As early as 1698, Leopold of Anhalt Dessau is said to have introduced the iron ramrod to his own regiment and, starting in 1730, successively in the entire Prussian army. While the wooden ramrods still being used in all the other armies could break as soon as bullets had to be rammed into thickly encrusted barrels, the Prussian infantrymen were now immune from this problem: however, the iron ramrods could bend depending on the quality of production.[45]

Leopold also introduced firing by division or platoon in the Prussian infantry. During the War of the Spanish Succession, he became convinced of the effectiveness of this method used by the English and Dutch troops. Administratively a Prussian battalion consisted of six companies, though the sixth, the grenadier company, was formed with other units in separate grenadier battalions. In battle, the musketeer companies were divided into four divisions of two platoons each, and the officers were distributed among them based on their seniority. Up until 1740 the Prussian infantry stood four ranks deep, then Friedrich ordered them to form in three ranks, which became mandatory for the entire army per an instruction issued on 20 June 1742. The divisions and platoons were numbered from right to left as one to four, and five to eight respectively. When conducting division or platoon firing, it always began first on the extreme right, then the outer leftmost formation, then the firing continued alternating unit by unit to the centre. In this way, the entire battalion kept up a steady fire.[46] According to the Regulations of 1743, volley fire of the whole battalion should be avoided, instead officers should ensure that there were always several platoons with 'their muskets on their shoulders',[47] ready to fire. In battle, increased emphasis was placed on absolute discipline, the soldiers 'also must be sharply ingrained so that they should neither chat nor make noise, and perform their actions so "it is like they're on the training ground."'[48] This should be used to ensure smooth and fast firing, but at the same time to impress the enemy with the uniformity of their movements. The 'silence' was especially necessary so that between the salvos the soldiers could still understand their officers' commands.

The accuracy of the muskets of that time was extremely poor. A test ordered by Friedrich in October 1755, in which the grenadiers of his bodyguard company (*Leibkompanie*) fired at a wooden wall, 10 paces wide by 10 feet-high (about twice as high as an average soldier), showed meagre results. Kneeling at 300 paces, no more than 13.3 percent, at 200 paces 16.6 percent and at 150 paces only 46.6 percent of the projectiles hit the target. When standing, the results were even more modest, 3.3 percent at 200 and

---

45 See Georg Ortenburg, *Waffen der Kabinettskriege 1650 – 1792* (Bonn: Bernhard & Graefe, 1986), pp.64-65; Rohrschneider, *Leopold I. von Anhalt-Dessau*, pp.62-63.
46 See Marcus Junkelmann, 'Der Militärstaat in Aktion. Kriegskunst des Ancien Regime', in Bernd Sösemann and Gregor Voigt-Spira (ed.), *Friedrich der Große in Europa. Geschichte einer wechselvollen Beziehung* (Stuttgart: Franz Steiner 2012), Vol.II, pp.166-191, here pp.177-179; Guddat, *Grenadiere*, pp.84-85.
47 Quoted from *Reglement 1743*, p.272: '*das Gewehr auf der Schulter haben*'.
48 Quoted from *Reglement 1743*, p.271.

300 paces, and 6.6 percent at 150 paces.[49] The fires of widely spaced battalion lines therefore had primarily a psychological effect.

The right wing was considered the most honoured position, both within the battalion and for the entire order of battle. This is where the elite units were usually positioned. This honour goes back to ancient models. The Greek hoplites already placed their most experienced warriors on the right. The ancient military writers enjoyed a small renaissance in the middle of the eighteenth century. They had already experienced renewed appeal in the late sixteenth century, during the House of Orange's army reforms, when linear formations had been reintroduced. Eighteenth century military writers, such as Maurice de Saxe or the Frenchman Hubert de Folard, suddenly again preferred the use of slashing and stabbing weapons over the musket fire, and de Saxe even advocated the reintroduction of the pike. Friedrich II did not go that far, but in April 1741, he ordered that the infantrymen keep their bayonets fixed. The Regulation of 1743 finally recommended:

> And since the strength of the men and the good order that makes Prussian infantry invincible, the men must be so ingrained, that if the enemy should stand still against all suspicions, their safest and most certain advantage is to advance with levelled bayonets into the enemy, as if the King was standing before them, so that no one could resist them.[50]

Thus, at that time, Friedrich also relied more on the psychological effect of a formation that advanced with a levelled bayonet against the enemy than on the efficiency of platoon firing.[51]

In contrast to the infantry company, the squadron formed the cavalry's basic tactical unit in battle. Cuirassiers and dragoons formed in three ranks. Although Friedrich Wilhelm I had already decreed in 1734 that his dragoons should only attack with drawn swords in battle and not engage in exchanging fire, the Prussian cavalry at the beginning of the First Silesian War relied more on firepower than on impact, which was to prove fatal in the Battle of Mollwitz.[52] The attitude of the Austrians towards the enemy cavalry was correspondingly disdainful. One officer praised the Prussian squadrons' exact manoeuvres, but reprimanded them, 'they sit badly on horseback, as a result of the long stirrups, so that they are not able to use the sabre well. It has been observed that the dragons only have swords, and that they use the tip more than the cutting edge. They are fighting on the spot, which is why they are always thrown.'[53] In retrospect, an anonymous Austrian officer described

---

49 See Jürgen Luh, *Kriegskunst in Europa* (Cologne, Weimar, Vienna: Böhlau, 2004), p.135.
50 Quoted from *Reglement 1743*, pp.275-276.
51 See Möbius, *Mehr Angst vor dem Offizier als vor dem Feind?*, pp.16-27.
52 See Martin Guddat, *Kürassiere, Dragoner, Husaren. Die Kavallerie Friedrichs des Großen* (Hamburg: Nikol Verlag, 1989), pp.76-77.
53 Quoted from Johann Christoph Allmayr-Beck, 'Von Hubertusburg nach Jena. Die preußische Armee am Ende des 18. Jahrhunderts von außen gesehen`, in Peter Baumgart, Bernhard R. Kroener and Heinz Stübing (ed.), *Die preußische Armee zwischen Ancien Régime und Reichsgründung* (Paderborn: Ferdinand Schöningh, 2009), pp.121-132, here p.36.

the equestrian qualities of the Prussian cuirassiers and dragoons as deficient in 1756 and painted an almost grotesque picture:

> ...at the time, the Prussians could neither ride nor defend themselves; their ignorance in the matter made them despondent; yes, they fell under their horses along with the saddles, because they had not even girdled it properly; I take all those who have been there as witnesses, as to whether they had ever seen this many ridiculous riders.[54]

In addition, the Prussian horses were considered too large and heavy.

Therefore, in the following years, Friedrich dealt extensively with reform of the shock cavalry and issued a number of new instructions to increase the horsemen's aggressiveness and shock effect. In a 3 June 1741 letter to Leopold von Anhalt-Dessau, he had already commanded that his cavalrymen should 'get engaged with nothing but the sword.'[55] In instructions issued on 25 July 1744, it stated 'The King thereby forbids all officers from the cavalry, under penalty of dishonourable reduction in rank, to allow in their days an attack by the enemy, but the Prussians must always be attacking the enemy.'[56] By attacking first, the Prussian cavalry should gain a decisive psychological advantage, because often the opposing cavalry regiments did not meet one another at all, but one side gave way before the decisive clash. To put fear into the opponent even before the first drop of blood was spilled, was the goal of any vigorously initiated attack. The July 1745 instructions for the cavalry then set out exactly how such an attack should happen: 'If the general orders is to attack, then the line deploys at a walk, goes to a trot, and, when it is 200 paces from the enemy, it should completely abandon the horses' reins and charge into [the enemy]. The impact must take place with all possible violence and shouting…There is no doubt that the enemy will not endure such attacks.'[57]

The hussars had a special place in Friedrich's army. He had taken over nine squadrons from his father in 1740. Within a short time, Friedrich raised completely new regiments, so that by 1745 there were a total of nine. After the Seven Years War another two were raised, one of them 'Bosniaken' – originally a Balkan people – armed with lances.[58] These each had more than ten squadrons and had a strength of 1,100 to 1,500 men. Initially the hussars were primarily recruited in Hungary, but also in Poland. This cavalry branch had originally evolved in the Hungarian-Turkish border region in the course of the sixteenth century. The Austrian army, and also that of the

---

54 Quoted from Allmeyr-Beck, *Die friderizianische Armee*, p.36.
55 Volz (ed.), *Die Werke Friedrichs des Großen*, Vol.30, p.59.
56 Volz (ed.), *Die Werke Friedrichs des Großen*, Vol.6, p.303.
57 Volz (ed.), *Die Werke Friedrichs des Großen*, Vol.6, p.30. Also see Möbius, *Mehr Angst vor dem Offizier als vor dem Feind?*, pp.30-32. For cavalry reforms see Ullrich Marwitz, 'Friedrich der Große als Heeresorganisator' in Oswald Hauser (ed.), *Friedrich der Große in seiner Zeit* (Cologne, Vienna: Böhlau, 1987), pp.232-233, and more generally pp.213-235.
58 For the development of light troops during this period, see Johannes Kunisch, *Der kleine Krieg. Studien zum Heerwesen des Absolutismus* (Wiesbaden: Steiner, 1973) and Martin Rink, *Vom 'Parheygänger' zum Partisanen. Die Konzeption des kleinen Krieges in Preußen 1740-1813* (Frankfurt a. M.: Peter Lang, 1999).

Elector of Saxony, had already successfully employed hussars in the War of Spanish Succession and the Great Northern War. In the first half of the eighteenth century, the European military appears to have assumed that East Europeans, by their nature, were better suited for irregular warfare, therefor it was preferred to man the early hussar formations from these ethnicities. Friedrich also said that 'a German lad does not make such a good hussar as a Hungarian or a Pole.'[59] The hussars brought their grand, colourful uniforms, jackets decorated with cording, the pelisse that hung from the shoulder, pointed boots and fur caps from their native countries.[60]

The Prussians did not have effective light troops. Their Feldjägerkorps was not used as such, its men rather acting as dispatch riders. During the Seven Years War eight Freikorps were created. Made up of foreigners – especially Saxons – they were used for raiding parties and were notorious for their bad discipline and behaviour. Friedrich despised them as *Geschmeiß* (rabble). In theory they could be used in battle, where Fredrick expected them to protect the flank of an army, but they should not fight in open order but give volleys like ordinary line infantry. After the war all the corps were disbanded, but at the beginning of the War of the Bavarian Succession four new corps were created under the command of *Generalleutnant* Johann Ludwig von Hordt (1719-1789), former Polish colonel Andreas Alexander von Schlichten (1728-1792), *Oberst* Carl Philipp Joseph von Münster (1747-1809) and *Oberstleutnant* Carl Philipp von Pollitz (1733-1805). However, the Prussian light forces were insufficient compared not only to the mass of skilled raiders the Austrians were able to recruit from their Balkan territories. Britain had started to build up light companies within its regiments following its experiences in the Seven Years War, Russia used light infantry with good effect in its wars against the Ottomans and the French too formed some units, while their theorists wrote extensively about them. Friedrich was not willing to develop a light infantry concept and that takes some wonder, as he had bad experiences with the Austrian pandurs and hussars during all his former three wars against the Habsburgs when they repeatedly wrecked his already inefficient supply system. In his instructions to all his general officers of cavalry in 1748 he just advised them to use strong 'detachments' to guard his line of communications against the Austrian irregulars, but it seems that he was not able to grasp the idea that in order to be useful such troops had to be mobile and effective themselves and that purely being mounted was not in itself sufficient to ensure this. The Prussians would pay dearly for this negligence in this war once more. Other German armies, many of them following the Prussian model, were more receptive to this development. Hesse-Cassel, Brunswick-Wolffenbüttel and Ansbach-Bayreuth had sent Jäger formations to America for subsidies, fighting for the British. Carl von Seidel recognized this lack as a major weakness of Prussian war-making in his history of the war, writing that the Austrians' 'knowledge of the country, their certainty not to be betrayed, their good light infantry and our lack of it comes in handy to them in small warfare.'[61]

---

59 Quoted from Duffy, *Frederick the Great*, p.168.
60 See Hohrath, *Friedrich der Große und die Uniformierung*, pp.44-45.
61 Seidel, *Versuch einer militärischen Geschichte*, Vol.I, p.230.

THE WAR OF THE BAVARIAN SUCCESSION 1778-1789

Johann Ludwig von Hordt. (Nationalmuseum (Stockholm))

The artillery was also considerably strengthened by Friedrich after his accession. In 1739, the Prussian Army had only one single artillery field battalion with six companies. One year later Friedrich had a second field battalion raised and in 1745 combined the two into a field artillery regiment. In 1731, *Generalmajor* von Linger had reduced the variety of Prussian artillery pieces and made them much more standardized. From then on only 3-, 6-, 12- and 24-pounders were produced, of which the latter were used as fortress artillery. The field artillery, which was supposed to be limited to these short models, was divided into battalion and battery artillery pieces. The battalion, or regimental, guns were to serve as direct artillery support in battle, comparable to the infantry's heavy weapons in the early twentieth century. After the first two Silesian Wars, Friedrich considered further standardizing his artillery. As early as 1747 he sent artillery officers to France to investigate the French unitary system. Even before the reports were available, the king decided that in the future to that as well as the standardised calibres for cannon there would only be 7-, 10-, 25- and 30-pounder howitzers, as well as 7-, 10, 25- and 50-pounder mortars. At the same time, the elevating screw was introduced. It had been developed in 1732 in Sweden and enabled a considerably faster and more precise positioning of the gun barrel than the old aiming wedges.[62]

In the first two years of the Seven Years War, the light regimental cannon still played a significant role, which was not in the least a result of production numbers. For example, 41 were cast in Prussia in 1756, and in 1757 twenty-three 3-pounders; however, their production was discontinued after that. In contrast, the production of 12-pounders rose from 20 pieces in 1756 to 40 in 1757 and reached a peak of 87 tubes in 1760.[63] The increasing importance of heavy field artillery first became apparent in the Battles of Rossbach and Leuthen, but it first appreciably dominated battle events starting in 1758, which brought significant changes to tactics. The Prussians used more and heavier guns. While 12-pounders were not used as field artillery at the beginning of the war, Friedrich used ever more. At Lobositz in 1756 the Prussians had 28,300 men and 98 cannon (3.4 guns per 1,000 men), at Prague the following year 64,000 men and 192 cannon (3 per 1,000 men). At Torgau in 1760 Friedrich had 50,000 men and 309 cannon (6.1 per 1,000 men).

Historians tend to describe Prussia as the emerging power of the eighteenth century. This might be true at its core, but ignores the fact that of the five major powers of the European system it was by far the weakest in financial and economic terms. The Seven Years War had exhausted the country economically and militarily. Friedrich II himself painted the situation in dark colours in his *Denkwürdigkeiten vom Hubertusburger Frieden bis zum Ende der Polnischen Teilung*:

> Through seven years of war with seventeen field battles and nearly as many, not less bloody, encounters, three sieges which the Prussians has conducted, and five which they endured, not to speak of the operations against the enemy's winter quarters and other very similar operations, the army was very much melted

---

62 See Schmidtchen, *Einfluß der Technik*, pp.136-138; Müller, *Die Bewaffnung*, pp.193-202.
63 Numbers according to Kroener, 'Die materiellen Grundlagen', pp.66-67.

down. A huge part of the best officers and old soldiers were fallen. To connect the dots, one only has to remember, that the victory at Prague alone cost 20,000 men. To this add 40,000 Austrian prisoners and nearly as many Prussians, among them 300 officers, the overcrowding of hospitals with wounded and the fact, that within the infantry regiments were not more than 100 men, which in the year 1756, at the beginning of the war, belonged to them.

Through the loss of more than 1,500 officers, who had fallen in the various encounters, the nobility was robbed of its best forces. In the country there were only old men and juvenile boys. Because of the lack of nobles, numerous officer positions had to be filled with commoners. In some battalions there have not been more than eight serving officers; the other were fallen or wounded or captured. From these sad conditions it easily results, that even the old troops were without order, discipline and accuracy; consequently, they lacked spirit.

This was the condition of the army, when it marched to its old quarters after the Treaty of Hubertusburg. The regiments at that time counted more natives than foreigners; the companies were 162 men strong; 40 of them were disbanded and helped the agriculture to recover. The Volunteer Battalions were used for the completion of the garrison regiments, and they too furloughed the surplus of natives. In the cavalry each regiment released 150 men, the hussars 400. Through these disbandments the countryside got 30,780 peasants back, which it lacked.[64]

In general, the Prussian army is often described as the paradigm of its time, superseding the French as the leading model for Europe. This view – even if it was taken up by contemporaries – has many flaws based on the fact that people – public and historians alike – for a long time tended to reduce the discussion about military effectiveness to an analysis of battlefield appearance. This approach was also dominant within the German historical scholarship of much of the nineteenth and early twentieth centuries, reflecting its failed overestimation of the importance of battles in war. The later popular 'War and Society' approach or the Cultural turn are also not very helpful, as they are analysing armies either before or after a war. Important aspects of war-making, especially logistics and siege warfare, for a long time were not covered when looking at the Prussian army, which revealed a serious lack of capability in both. The territory the Prussians were fighting over was not dominated by fortresses, as for example the southern Netherlands or the Rhineland that were the main area of operations for the French. If the Prussians had to start a siege they often did badly, for example at Prague (1757), Olmütz (1758) or Dresden (1760), all of which were unsuccessful. It can be argued with reason that the Prussians would have done very badly if they had been obliged to operate in the same areas as the French, who, especially under Maurice de Saxe, did very well at siege warfare in the War of the Austrian Succession. This is a reminder of the fact, that there is no one-size-fits-all model of military effectiveness, but that armies had to adopt to the geographical environments that they operate in.

---

64   Volz (ed.), *Die Werke Friedrichs des Großen*, Vol.5, p.69.

Prussian limitations in logistics always came to light when the army operated in Bohemia, especially during the campaigns of 1742, 1744, and 1758, all of which had to be abandoned, because the Austrians were able to cut the Prussian supply lines and the inability of Friedrich's forces to support themselves from within the very hostile countryside.

With these major limitations in the Prussian war making capability, it seems absurd to talk of this army as the best of its time, which is still done in public and academic reading alike. This assumption is flawed not only within the possible European theatres of war, but especially when taking a global perspective. Non-European armies, like the Persians under Nadir Shah or the Chinese under the Qianlong Emperor demonstrated a much higher ability for war-making in various geographical and climatic environments, as well as superb logistics. It is an oversimplified comparison to value Prussian soldiers higher compared to those non-European contemporaries, just because the battlefield performance based on the effective use of firepower and cold steel was more effective. This means nothing, if an enemy was able to bring more of his men to the battlefield thanks to better logistics.

However, despite these flaws, Prussia was very effective when mobilising resources for war, which also is a serious aspect when analysing war making capabilities. The French military theorist Guibert after the Seven Years War calculated the costs of European armies and total war costs of the major powers. The result showed that on the one hand the Prussians had the lowest per capita costs for their army, spending only an annual of 52 million livres for 180,000 men, while the Austrians had to pay 62 million and the French as much as 106 million for just 140,000 men. The Seven Years War cost the French and astonishing 573 million guilders, the Austrians 392 million and the Prussians only 180 million. These differences are in part explained by the fact that France beside a large army also had to maintain the second largest fleet in the world and that global war-making was much more expansive than regional war-making in Europe. The French also paid huge sums as subsidies to their major allies: Russia, Sweden and even Austria and also to small German princes whose troops the French were hiring, for example the re-formed Saxon infantry corps under Prince Xaver. On the other hand, the Prussian total, which was the equivalent of 125 million thalers, already included subsidies received from Britain. A major part of the total was provided by the occupied Electorate of Saxony which paid contributions totalling 48 million thalers or about 38.4 percent of the total costs for of the war.[65]

---

65   See Kroener, 'Die materiellen Grundlagen`, p.76; Carl Görler, 'Studien zur Bedeutung des Siebenjährigen Krieges für Sachsen`, *Neues Archiv für Sächsische Geschichte* 29 (1908), pp.118-149; Jürgen Luh, 'Sachsens Bedeutung für Preußens Kriegführung`, in *Sachsen und Dresden im Siebenjährigen Krieg* (=Dresdner Hefte 68), pp.28-34; Katrin Keller, 'Der Siebenjährige Krieg und die Wirtschaft Kursachsens`, in *Sachsen und Dresden im Siebenjährigen Krieg* (=Dresdner Hefte 68), pp.74-80; Alexander Querengässer: '"Ich bin Meister vom Lande, und es muß geschehen, was ich befehle" – Die Bedeutung Sachsens für die preußischen Kriegsbemühungen im Siebenjährigen Krieg`, in Alexander Querengässer (ed.) *Die Schlacht bei Roßbach* (=Beiträge zur Geschichte des Militärs in Sachsen 2) (Berlin: Zeughaus Verlag, 2017), pp.149-170

So, two of the major reasons that the Prussian was able to sustain the war were the low per capita costs for its military and the ability to outsource a tremendous part of the total war costs to occupied provinces or to cover them with the help of subsidies. If one of these fragile pillars broke away, for example if Friedrich II had been unable to hold on in Saxony for a longer period of time due to a lack of battlefield successes, Prussian victory would have been questionable.

Because of these circumstances Prussia too is described as one of the early modern fiscal military states. This however seems to be a perversion of the concept originally put forward by John Brewer for early modern England which was able to conduct long wars thanks to a wealthy and developing economy, a free banking system and a state that was able to raise low return credits.[66] Prussia in turn had to wage short wars, before its war chest emptied, and nobody knew that better than Friedrich himself. The coffers were filled up in the interwar years thanks to a thrifty policy in part based on huge halfway profitable royal estates. So, while Britain was able to conduct war out of its own strength for a considerable time, Prussia was not, unless it was able to outsource costs, which it did successfully between 1756 and 1763. This, however, is diametrically the opposite of Brewer's original concept of a fiscal military state.

In 1778-1779 Prussia was not able to outsource war cost. This was on the one hand due to the fact that Saxony, which took the lion's share of these costs between 1756 and 1763, was now an ally. However favourable this was in a political sense, in that Prussia could present itself as protector of legitimate Saxon claims, it hit the country hard in economic terms. On the other hand, Prussia was also unable to gain foreign subsidies, because the continental conflict was not mixed with the parallel global encounter of France and Britain in the American War of Independence. Prussia's economic weakness was the same in the 1770s as in the 1740s and 1750s, but circumstances had changed. Friedrich was also unable to extricate any appreciable amount of money from conquered Austrian territory, because he was neither able to campaign successfully in Bohemia, thanks to logistical problems similar to those that the Prussians had faced before, and his inability to force a battle to the Austrians on terms favourable to him.

This situation was also far from new. Public and also academic narratives of the Silesian Wars tend to focus on the string of battlefield successes won by Friedrich, like Hohenfriedberg (1745), Lobositz (1756), Prague, Roßbach, and Leuthen (all 1757) and Zorndorf (1758). However, most Prussian victories in the Seven Years War were won within the first years. Later on Friedrich also suffered a string of serious defeats, like Hochkirch (1758), Kunersdorf and Maxen (1759), and Landeshut (1760). Apart from Kunersdorf, which was mainly fought by Russian troops, these victories were won by the Austrians, who demonstrated increased effectiveness and a certain learning curve. *Feldmarschall* Leopold von Daun (1705-1766), while generally in favour of Fabian tactics, definitely

---

66 John Brewer, *The Sinews of Power. War, Money and the English State, 1688-1783* (London: Unwin Hyman, 1989).

showed a willingness to use an opportunity if it was offered to him, as at Hochkirch and Maxen where Prussian troops were posted in unfavourable terrain. Daun was also very innovative in using columns attacking from various directions.

On the other hand, Friedrich was probably too obsessed with his concept of the oblique attack for which he was praised after the Battle of Leuthen. The king had tried to force this concept on his enemies since Mollwitz (1741), but he was nearly always unsuccessful. At Leuthen he benefited from his good knowledge of the terrain, because the Prussian army had carried out manoeuvres there before the war in 1748. But even at Leuthen, Prussian victory was more due to a successful flanking march than to the application of the concept of the oblique attack. Two years later, when he tried to repeat his success at Kunersdorf, he suffered a crushing defeat because he lacked the necessary knowledge of the terrain and did not undertake sufficient reconnaissance.

Still, the Prussian army went through a significant tactical development during the Seven Years War, which was, however, partly reversed afterwards. Far from being fixed to linear tactics, the infantry operated in flexible columns during the last years of the war. These were first used by Prince Ferdinand of Brunswick in the western theatre, during the Battle of Krefeld (1758) and later also by Friedrich at the Battle of Burkersdorf (1762) and by Prince Heinrich at Freiberg (1762). The role of artillery also increased during the war.

Friedrich's enemies recognized his obsession with the oblique battle order, but also his flexible handling of troops later in the war. Daun was careful of offering battle to Friedrich and instead preferred to employ his troops on a ridgeline, a tactic favoured by the nature of terrain in southern Saxony, Silesia, and Bohemia. From 1758 onwards Friedrich was growing frustrated about his inability to force a battle on his Austrian antagonist on even terms, while he was also unwilling to accept one on Austrian terms. This was the same situation the Prussians were confronted with in 1778-1779. The lack of Prussian success in the War of the Bavarian Succession – which is a basic thesis of this book – was, however, not due to any decline in its war making ability, but due to the limitations always inherent with it during the eighteenth century. These were successfully overshadowed in the Seven Years War thanks to the final Prussian victory, which was due to the death of Empress Elisabeth which led to Russia signing a peace, Austria's exhaustion after France also dropped out of the continental war, and the fact that Friedrich was still able to win a few victories in the later part of the war, when he was able to face the Austrians in more favourable terrain, as at Torgau where he nevertheless took horrible causalities.

It should be clear, then, that the Prussian military capability had serious limitations. This should not be taken to mean that Prussia was weak, but it was definitely the weakest of the five European great powers and its limitations as a military power had roots in both economic factors and the capabilities of its army. These factors, however, cannot be revealed if scholarship focuses on peacetime organisation and battlefield outcomes alone.

Austria

While Austria was unable to win the Seven Years War, it also was not defeated. Instead, the forces which had been reformed after the War of the Austrian Succession gave proof of their new effectiveness and fighting power, inflicting a series of crushing defeats on Frederick the Great. However, army reform is an ongoing and never-ending process.[67] After Joseph II became co-ruler following the death of his father Emperor Franz I in 1765, he ordered a further reform. Joseph was an admirer of Frederick the Great. Apart from organisational and structural reforms, the social standing of the army and officers was further increased. Like Friedrich, Joseph preferred to wear uniform at court, something the Habsburg Emperors before him had never done. Under his reign, the officer in uniform became acceptable at court.

Feldmarschall Franz Moritz Graf von Lacy (1725-1801) was charged with the reform. Lacy was an experienced soldier and military theorist. During the Seven Years War he initially served as a kind of chief of staff to *Feldmarschall* Daun. He was the initiator of the innovative plans for attacks in multiple columns which let to victories at Hochkirch (1758) and Maxen (1759). Being promoted to *Feldzeugmeister* in 1760 he took Berlin for a short time in the same year in collaboration with Russian troops. As an autonomous field commander he was probably inferior to his great rival Gideon Ernst Baron von Laudon, but Lacy was a favourite at court, which was decisive. In 1763 he became a member of the *Hofkriegsrat* and in 1766 its president.

Lacy further professionalised, centralised and institutionalised the army. New regulations were published, standardising drill. The rights of regimental commanders were cut further, the practice of buying commissions limited – but not completely abolished. Regiments were numbered and not named after the commanding officer or *Inhaber*. The 59 infantry regiments were numbered 1 to 59, while the 17 Grenzer regiments, recruited from the Balkan frontier, became 60 to 76. Colonels were introduced to give promotions for company command on the basis of rank and merit, not money. Huge drill camps were held to drill the troops in the new manuals. The organisation of the formations changed too. The cavalry squadron, which so far consisted of two companies, was made the smallest tactical and administrative unit in 1769. Two squadrons formed a division and three divisions a regiment, which made for about 900 men. Regiments of hussars could have four or even five divisions, making for a total of 2,000 men per regiment.

The Austrian artillery was probably the best in Europe after the reforms of Fürst Joseph Wenzel von Liechtenstein in the late 1740s and early 1750s, who paid for new gun material and a better education of the gun crews from his own pocket. The French Gribeauval system was influenced by Liechtenstein's

---

67 Claudia Reichl-Ham, 'Die Armee Maria Theresias (1740-80) und Josephs II. (1780-90), in Peter Fichtenbauer and M. Christian Ortner (eds), *Die Geschichte der österreichischen Armee von Maria Theresia bis zur Gegenwart in Essays und bildlichen Darstellungen* (Vienna: Militaria Verlag, 2015), pp.12-41; Johann Christoph Allmayr-Beck, 'Die Armee Maria Theresias und Josephs II.', in Erich Zöllner (ed.), *Österreich im Zeitalter des aufgeklärten Absolutismus* (=Schriftenreihe des Instituts für Österreichkunde 42) (Vienna: Bundesverlag, 1983), pp.71-83.

OPPOSING FORCES

Austrian *Feldmarschall* Moritz Graf Lacy. (Anne S.K. Brown Collection)

pieces and, while the Russian army also had a very fine artillery, the casting of the Austrian pieces was of a high quality and certainly superior to Prussian guns.[68] The organisation was put on a permanent footing and, instead of an assembly of individually trained gunners, Austria now had 24 companies of 90 men each even in peacetime. Attached to each of these was a company of fusiliers as infantry protection and additional hands. In 1757 the artillery received its first printed manual.[69] Following the death of Liechtenstein in 1772, Franz de Paula, Prince Kinsky (1726-1792) became the new director general of artillery. He further unified the artillery organisation and reformed the 'brigades' into regiments. Heavy guns became more and more important. While in 1753 the field artillery had 200 pieces, four-fifths of them light 3-pounder battalion guns, the total had risen to 648 in 1768 of which just slightly over a half (332 pieces) were 3-pounders.

Kinsky also detached the miners, formed into four companies, from the artillery. Additionally, there existed a sapper company of 186 men, an engineer corps of 98 engineers, and a pontonier battalion: so-called pioneer companies were only created during war time.

Conscription was gradually introduced from 1771. The Habsburg hereditary lands (except the Tyrol) and Galicia were divided in recruiting districts with roughly equal population. Each district had to provide recruits for a 'German' infantry regiment. For this, the male inhabitants had to be gathered in lists and their houses numbered. Recruits were drawn by lot. These conscripts were given a quick training in drill, before they were dismissed, forming a reserve which in the case of war could be quickly mobilised. For this each regiment in war left one small battalion in garrison to train new men. Three-eighths of the recruits were also allowed to be hired from within the Empire. All in all, this organisation was similar to the Prussian canton system.[70]

However, the structure and so the recruiting systems of the Habsburg army varied. While the 'German' regiments recruited in the hereditary lands (which also included non-German territories, like Bohemia), Hungary and Italy provided their own regiments. About 23,000 men during the War of the Bavarian Succession were raised in the Austrian Netherlands alone.[71] The frontier zone on the border to the Ottoman Empire also had its own organisation, providing 17 Grenzer regiments which, at the eve of the war, amounted to an impressive 72,200 infantry and 3,600 cavalry[72] Additional troops could be hired from foreign countries, in most cases small principalities from within the Empire.

The Grenzer regiments and the Hungarian hussars had always given Austria an advantage in small warfare, and it was the conduct of these troops

---

68 Ken McLennan, 'Liechtenstein and Gribeuaval "Artillery Revolution" in Political and Cultural Context', *War and History* 10/3 (2003), pp.249-264.
69 Duffy, *Instrument of War*, pp.299-301.
70 Reichl-Ham, 'Die Armee Maria Theresias', p.13.
71 Hochedlinger, *Austria's Wars of Emergence*, p.317.
72 The best English works with regard to this topic remain Gunther E. Rothenberg, *The Austrian Military Border in Croatia, 1522–1747* (Urbana: University of Illinois Press, 1960) and Gunther E. Rothenberg, *The Austrian Military Border in Croatia, 1740–1881. A Study of an Imperial Institution* (Chicago: University of Chicago Press, 1966).

OPPOSING FORCES

Austrian *Feldmarschall* Prince Franz de Paula Ulrich Kinsky von Wchinitz und Tettau. (Public Domain)

THE WAR OF THE BAVARIAN SUCCESSION 1778-1789

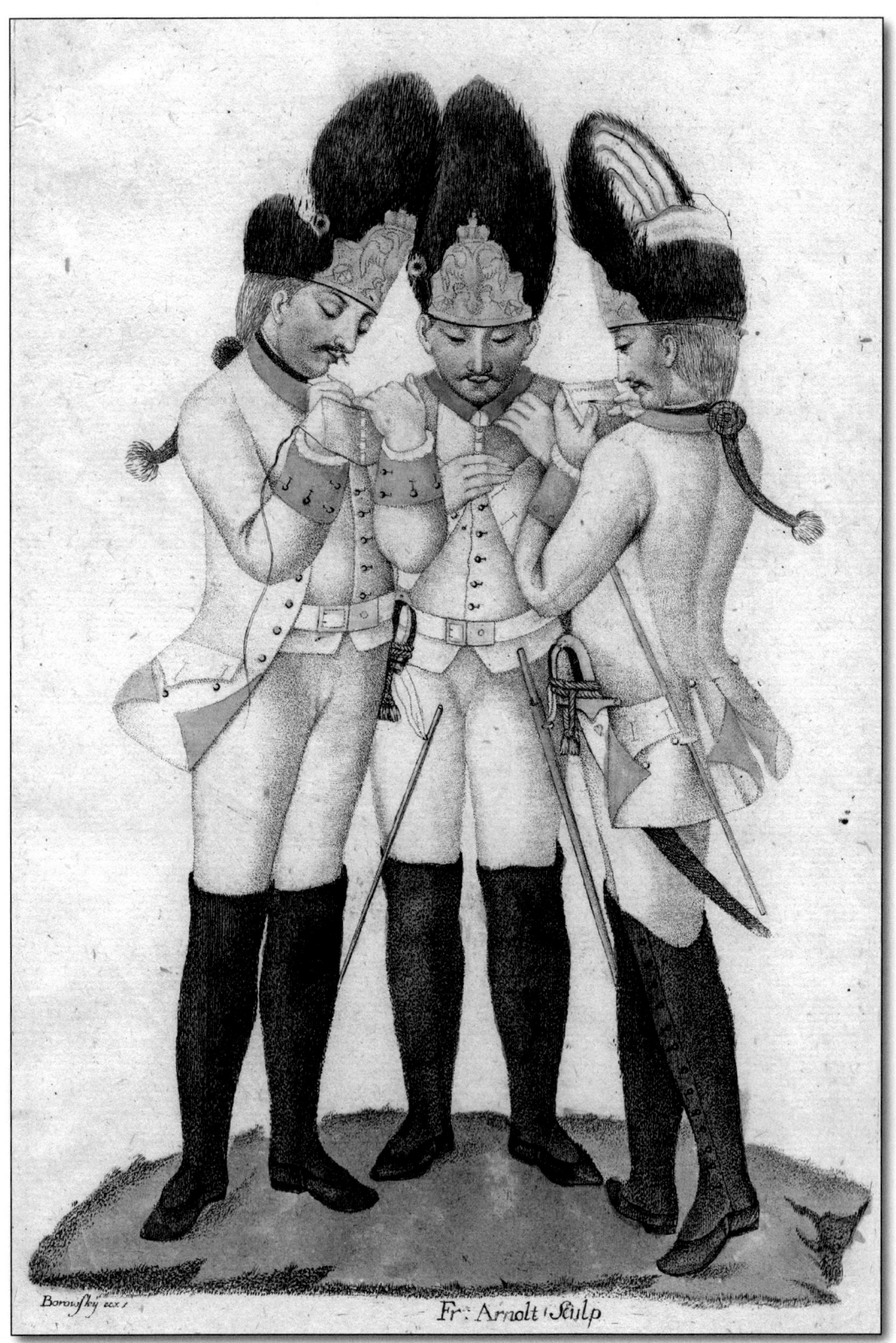

Three Austrian grenadiers. They are NCOs, recognizable by the canes and notebooks. (Anne S.K. Brown Collection)

which wrecked the Prussian supply system in the Bohemian campaigns of 1742, 1744 and especially 1758. Despite the improvements the Prussian army underwent, especially with regard to its hussars, the British traveller Wraxall considered the men from the Balkans as superior:

> It is in the irregular forces which Maria Theresia can bring into the field, that she possesses a great superiority over her adversary. The Croats and Hungarians, fierce, undisciplined, and subject to scarcely any military laws, are attached to the house of Austria by prejudices and predilections of religion, manners, and education, peculiar to themselves. Frederick has no troops of a similar description to oppose them, equally faithful and loyal. The Croat rarely or never deserts: he is even incapacitated by his ignorance of German, from mixing intimately with the soldiers of that nation. A degree of primeval rudeness and simplicity characterizes them, totally unlike the spirit which animates the mercenary stipendiary of modern armies. Fathers of families, followed by their sons, at the command of their Sovereign, cheerfully quit their habitations on the banks of the Drave, the Teiss, and the lower Danube, to spill their blood in her cause. Hithero the Croats have never been considered as regular troops, but, it is now intended to clothe and discipline them like other regiments in the Austrian service. It is a sight equally novel and pleasing to see these corps arrive, dressed in the rude garb of their respective province, and presenting in their whole appearance, a contrast to the soldier of every other European service. From the great magazines in the neighbourhood of this city, they are furnished with arms, accoutrements and all other requisites, before they prosecute their march towards the frontiers.[73]

However, the tendency of eighteenth century military organisation to regularize auxiliary formations by subjugating them to the same strict discipline as regular units – as described by Wraxall – and giving them the same standard drill books robbed them a part of their special qualities, a process also witnessed with the Prussian hussars. However, during the mobilisation additional light troops were raised: a Tyrolian Jägercorps, another Jägercorps, and four Freikorps.[74] So Austria raised the same number of light troops as did Prussia, in addition to the great number it already had. Amazingly, Maria Theresia on the eve of the war wrote to her son that she feared a superiority of the Prussians in light troops: this on the one hand underlines the value given to them by the Austrians, but on the other reveals poor knowledge of the Prussian force structure and of Friedrich's attitude towards these troops.[75]

The reform found its visual expression in the new uniforms. As uniforms during the eighteenth century became tighter – in part out of fashion and in part to spare fabric – they also became less practical. The number of military theorists who criticized this increased. Maurice de Saxe in his *Reveries on the Art of War*, the German version of which was published posthumously in 1757, wrote: 'Our dress is not only expensive, but most inconvenient, the

---

73 Wraxall, *Memoirs of the Courts of Berlin, Dresden, Warsaw and* Vienna, Vol.I, pp.349-351.
74 Seyfarth, *Unpartheyische Geschichte*, pp.104-105.
75 Reimann, *Geschichte des Bayerischen Erbfolgekrieges*, pp.60-61.

THE WAR OF THE BAVARIAN SUCCESSION 1778-1789

Austrian sharpshooter. He seems to be wearing civilian clothes. (Anne S.K. Brown Collection)

soldier is neither shod nor clad. The love of appearance prevails over the regard due to health, which is one of the grand points demanding our attentions.'[76] Saxe suggested coats in the Turkish style with a hood, which also could be used as greatcoats: 'It will be also very warm, prevent colds and fluxes, and give quite a good air.'[77] He also advised soldiers to cut their hair and use a wig of Spanish lambskin. Saxe is probably one of the most prominent, but far from the only critic of eighteenth century Rococo uniforms, even if others did not follow his rather fanciful suggestion of a hooded Turkish-style coat.

However, in Austria the need for more practical uniforms was also appreciated. In her instructions for the introduction of the new uniforms the Empress Maria Theresia in 1767 wrote that it was her intention to make the duties of the common soldier easier for him to perform, for which reason the new manner of dress was to offer better protection against the elements while being no heavier to wear than the old. In the same year the *Monturökonomiekommission* was founded which was ordered to further rationalize and standardize military uniforms. In 1773 the six-volume *Militär-Oekonomikum* was published, which gave a detailed description of the fabric and cut of the uniforms and gave a sketch of everyone.

The new infantry uniform coat introduced in 1769, the '*Röckl*' was completely closed at the front up to the placket and could be buttoned together with 12 buttons. The tails of the skirts were shorter and only reached over the buttocks and no longer down to the hollows of the knees. In quarters, for daily routine or also for hot summer drill, the '*Leibel*', a sleeved waistcoat replaced the older sleeveless pattern. As protection from cold, wind and ice, grey greatcoats, the *roquelors*, were introduced. They reached down to the knees and had a cape as additional protection from the rain. These pieces were very popular, but also expansive and to spare costs they were initially only given out during a campaign, drill camps, or for a march, but in 1775 the *Hofkriegsrat* demanded that they were to stay with the men permanently.[78]

The new uniforms of the Austrian army are ample proof that an eighteenth century military was able and willing to react to criticism and shape uniforms to the need of their soldiers. However, the criticized Rococo-fashion was still dominant in nearly all the major armies, including the Prussian and Saxon, until Russia introduced the Potemkin-uniform in 1786 which shows some similarities with the '*Röckl*'.

For the War of the Bavarian Succession Austria benefited from already having prepared a part of its army for the Bavarian invasion in late 1777. During the spring of 1778 regiments from all over the Empire were marched to Bohemia. Several hundred guns from the arsenals in Vienna were moved to the armies and in Lombardy the army was buying several hundred mules which would be indispensable for logistics in the difficult terrain of the Silesian-Bohemian and Saxon-Bohemian borders.

---

76 Maurice de Saxe, *Reveries or Memoirs concerning the Art of War* (Edinburgh: Sands, Donaldson, Murray and Cochran 1759), p.6.
77 Saxe, *Reveries*, p.7.
78 Hans Edelmair, 'Der Caputrock und seine Aufschläge, Umschläge und Überschläge`, *Pallasch* 31 (2009), pp.31-46.

THE WAR OF THE BAVARIAN SUCCESSION 1778-1789

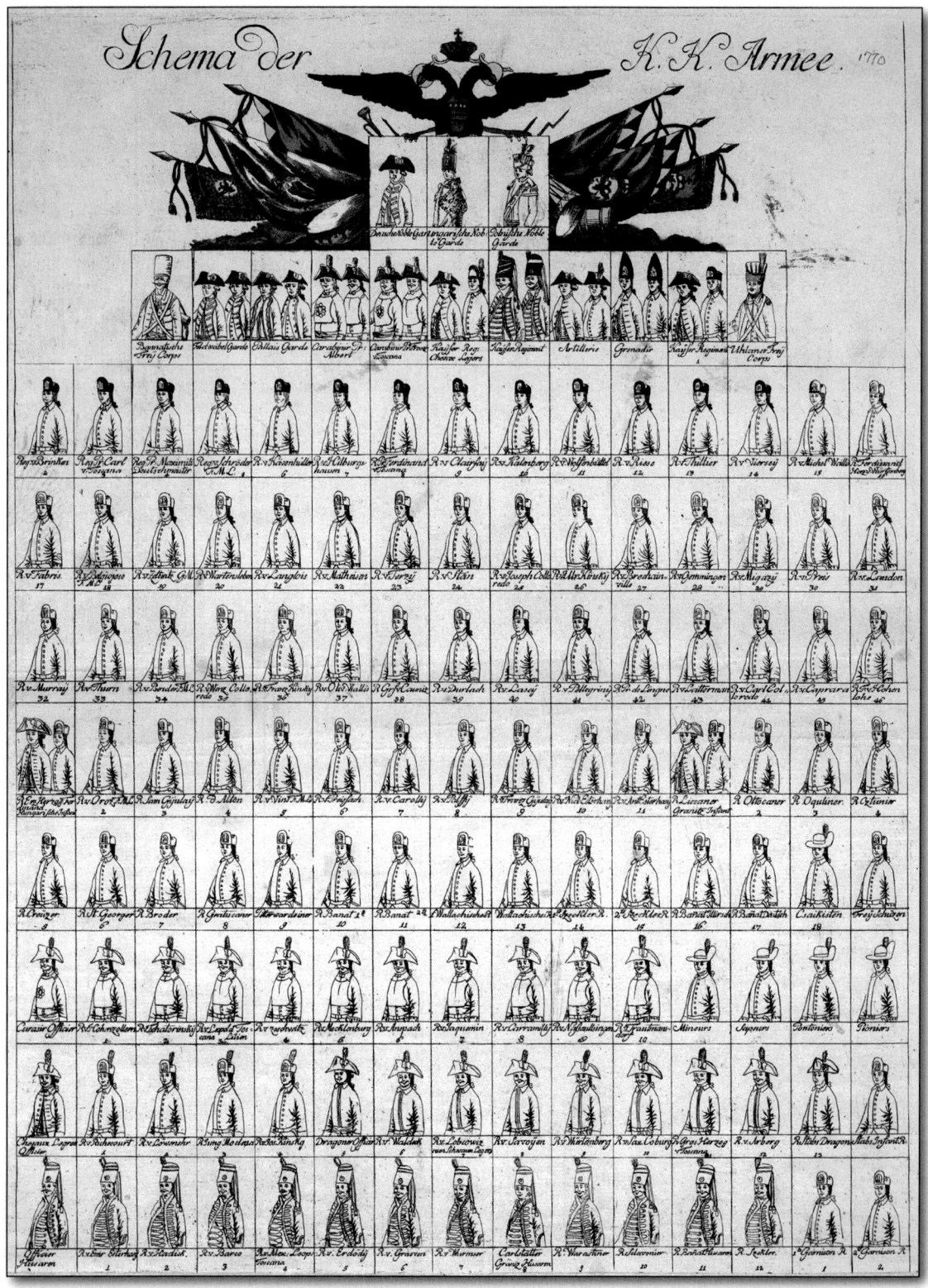

Austrian uniform schema, c.1770. (Anne S.K. Brown Collection)

OPPOSING FORCES

Austrian Military, c.1780. From left to right: officer, German grenadier, German fusilier, Hungarian fusilier, Croat, Czaikist (boatman). (Anne S.K. Brown Collection)

THE WAR OF THE BAVARIAN SUCCESSION 1778-1789

Austrian cavalry, c.1780. From left to right: Hussar, Croat, Chevauxleger, Dragon, Cuirassier. (Anne S.K. Brown Collection)

For the better coordination of the troops, larger formations than regiments had to be formed. Brigades, divisions, and corps were not unknown to eighteenth century armies but they were not permanent formations, and always improvised for certain campaigns. However, these formations needed experienced staff officers and so the regiments were ordered to compile lists of officers who spoke fluent French and were able to draw maps who could be transferred to these new staffs.[79]

The strength of the army rose considerably before and during the war. While it reached a low point in the late Seven Years War with 153,000 men, it rose to 308,000 regulars in 1779 and about 400,000 if Grenzer and all other troops were included.[80] According to Wraxall, writing from Vienna, Austria seemed well prepared and confident at the eve of the war:

> This city, which less than four months ago, when I arrived here, presented a picture of general tranquillity, is now transformed into an Arsenal. The streets, as well as the public places, are crowded with cannon, ammunition, baggage, and all the apparatus of an approaching campaign. Every day, new regiments arrive; who, after being reviewed, continue their march towards Bohemia or Moravia. Nothing can convey a more striking idea of the greatness of the house of Austria, the magnitude of its resources, the extent of its dominion, and the number of provinces subject to Maria Theresa…[81]

Saxony

It was not unusual in European military history that after a war, especially after defeat, armies were reduced, either as part of the peace dividend or because of economical need. The British Army was drastically reduced after the Wars of the Spanish and Austrian Succession and also after the Seven Years War. The French army, too, shrank after the reign of Louis XIV to 150,000 men, still a formidable force in the European context but probably half of its size during the Nine Years War. Within the Empire, Bavaria and Saxony, both of which started the new century with huge ambitions and increased forces, had to cut their military budgets after defeats in the War of the Spanish Succession and Great Northern War respectively. While the Saxon army was cut by half to about 15,000 men, Bavaria was unable to keep more than 5,000 men within its ranks. After the Second Silesian War the Saxon army was also considerably reduced, and in the years up to the Seven Years War its numbers fell to less than 20,000. Considering its dramatic defeat at Pirna and the economical devastations caused by the Prussians it would have been no wonder if the post-war army had not been further reduced, especially because it seemed that the new government finally accepted its second rank status not only within Europe, but even within the Empire.

---

79 Seyfarth, *Unpartheyische Geschichte*, p.104.
80 Hochedlinger, *Austria's Wars of Emergence*, p.298.
81 Wraxall, *Memoirs of the Courts of Berlin, Dresden, Warsaw and* Vienna, Vol.I, pp.348-349.

However, contrary to this, military reform and the rebuilding of the army took priority under Prince Xaver's administration. This is a reminder of the importance that individuals can have on history. Xaver not only had been the commander of the Saxon forces recreated during the war and paid by France, he was also advised by Choiseul in 1758 that in order to persist against Prussia, Saxony should keep a strong army. Under Xaver the army was build up to 31,000 men again, consisting of the Garde du Corps, one regiment of Karabiniers, six regiments of cuirassiers, four of Chevauxlegers, the Leibgrenadiergarde, 12 regiments of infantry, and specialist troops.[82]

However, after Xaver handed over the government to Friedrich August III in 1769 and left for France, the *Landtag* (parliament) voted for an annual budget of only 2,100,000 thalers, 547,000 thalers short of what Xaver's forces really needed. A special commission, headed by the new army commander Johann Georg, the Chevalier de Saxe (1704-1774), illegitimate son of Augustus the Strong, was given the task of finding ways to cut costs without reducing the army. This was finally achieved by granting leave to a certain number of men in each regiment for a full year or nine months. In 1770 the payment for 5,491 men and 1,344 horses was avoided in this way, reducing the effective army size to just 25,000 men. In 1771 further men were given a full year furlough, without calling the former ones back or recruiting new men, so the army total decreased further to just 23,000 and in 1773 to 21,500. However, this system proved to be problematic. During a mustering in 1775 the question was raised what should be done with regard to the uniforms of all the 'One-year-vacants'. The men had been allowed to keep their uniforms to identify themselves as members of the army. They had to wear them at Sunday church services. However, many used them during work or even sold them so during the mustering it was found that the army needed more than 7,000 new uniforms for all the men on furlough. As this would have been expensive, the elector decided in 1777 to give up the system and release the men, turning a hidden reduction into a real one.[83]

Still, an army is always in need of recruits. In Saxony two different systems had been in use since the beginning of the century. One was hiring within and outside the state, but in an industrious country like Saxony the army with its two-thalers-per-month pay was not a very attractive alternative for most civilians. The protection of the economy and its skilled workers always had priority over the needs of the army, especially as men tricked into service or recruited by force tend to desert and leave the country. Friedrich II of Prussia used every possibility to lure Saxon craftsman into his country whose economy – in respect of the quality of its products – lagged behind that of Saxony. The archives in Dresden are full of petitions by fathers, wives and other relatives appealing to the elector to relieve a young man tricked or forced into the service, because he was an artisan or journeyman in an important craft – and nearly every craft was considered as such. In most cases these supplications were granted.

---

82   Otto Rudert, *Die Reorganisation der Kursächsischen Armee 1763-1769* (Leipzig: Self published, 1911).
83   Hoffmann, *Die kursächsische Armee*, pp.15-20.

Sketch of the embroidery for a Saxon general's uniform, 1764. (Anne S.K. Brown Collection)

The second means of recruitment was the so called *Landrekrutenstellung*; a kind of draft system.[84] In 1702 August the Strong attempted to establish military service as a general subject obligation and to draft the so called 'land-recruits' into the army. These were young men who actually were obliged to serve in the *Defensionsregimenter* – the militia which was only called for home defence. Now the elector tried to draft them into the regular units for service abroad which was not unusual at the time: indeed, the French army also used its militia as a recruiting pool. In Saxony, however, this form of recruitment provoked a great deal of protest from the estates and was dismissed because of the resistance of many cities and rural administrative bodies (*Ämter*). Progress was only sluggish. However, the elector-king maintained this method of recruitment and ordered the levying of *Landrekruten* (land recruits) over the next years. These complied more or less spontaneously with the need of the army, but did not take place haphazardly. However, especially in times of crises, when the army had to replace losses within a short period of time, this system did not prove to be really effective. It was precisely at these moments that the subjects felt it was arbitrary and, of course, news of high loses in unsuccessful campaigns and battles was not helpful. This led to major draft-evasion.

In the summer of 1742 for example, the army leadership was forced to launch two large levies of *Landrekruten* in order to raise 6,000 new soldiers to replace the losses of the Bohemian campaign, when they fought side by side with the Prussians, and many men starved because of supply problems. The Saxon hereditary lands were to provide about 70 percent of the levies, and in these regions alone about 3,400 young men fled abroad to evade service. In the late summer of 1745, another levy of 2,000 men was ordered to replace the losses of the Saxon regiments thinned out in the Battle of Hohenfriedberg.[85] The highest call in the eighteenth century was done in 1768, when the army called for 8,000 men. That year only 1,332 men fled, but there were reports coming in from all over the country that recruiting officers often met with violent resistance. The call was made on 8 February, but in the middle of March just 49 percent of the recruits had come in, still a quite impressive total. In the middle of May the quota had risen to 87 percent and in September the call was abandoned. Cities and *Ämter* which still owed the government recruits had to pay 50 thalers per head instead.

The problems seen with this measure reflected the limitations of sovereign penetration. Early modern government was always based on consent and support of the low-level administration which often fell between two stools. The city of Bautzen in Lusatia, for example, had to send 50 men, 29 of them from surrounding villages. As soon as the city council received the mandate it ordered the gates closed, so that no young man could flee the city.

---

84 Stefan Kroll, 'Aushandeln von Herrschaft am Beispiel der Landrekrutenstellung in Kursachsen im 18. Jahrhundert' in Markus Meumann and Ralf Pröve (eds), *Herrschaft in der Frühen Neuzeit. Umrisse eines dynamisch-kommunikativen Prozesses* (Münster: LIT, 2004), pp.161-194.

85 Stefan Kroll, 'Kursächsische Soldaten in den drei Schlesischen Kriegen', in *Sachsen und Dresden im Siebenjährigen Krieg* (=Dresdner Hefte 68), pp.35-41, here p.37.

However, only nine recruits were found, four of them being considered unfit for service. To comply with the mandate the council had to conduct its own forceful recruitment using a carrot-and-stick policy. Volunteers were offered bounties and citizen rights for their service, while on the other hand relatives of fugitives were threatened. In other cities mayors and councils acted more as representatives of their communities than agents of the elector. The mayor of Laucha refused to send any recruits and even assembled his community for armed resistance which brought him an eight-day jail sentence.[86]

In 1769 the government tried to regularize this system and presented the *Landtag* with the idea of an annual draft of 1,500 men. As a carrot for the estates the elector offered to disband the unpopular hiring within the electorate. However – as usual when the army demanded money or men – the estates reacted badly. After long negotiations they accepted the proposal only with the reservation that they might withdraw their approval in a future *Landtag*. But until the start of the War of the Bavarian Succession the annual draft of 1,500 men became the single method of recruiting men for the army. There were problems, however. In every year the quota was not fulfilled, which was not yet a problem in peacetime as the regiments were anyway not kept at full strength. Another problem was that the recruits were too small, not reaching the minimum height of 75 Saxon Zoll for the Guards (Zoll = inches, a Saxon Zoll is 2.36 centimetres; 75 Zoll is therefore 1.77 metres or five feet eight inches) or 73 Zoll (five feet six inches) for the infantry. There was such a lack of suitable recruits that it was finally decided to accept men with only 69 Zoll (five feet three inches), 17–20 years old. The height of a soldier was important in an age when soldiers had to handle a musket a little under five feet in length in close packed formations without the freedom to adapt loading movements to their physical requirements.

An additional problem was that the draft in early 1778, when war was in sight and rumours running up and down the country, was particularly bad. The draft of 1775 was – despite all problems – short only of 35 men, that of 1777 of 273 men, but that of 1778 brought in only half the required recruits, being short of 742 men. Now, when the army was really in need of men to prepare for war, it lacked more than 1,000 recruits from the drafts of 1777 and 1778. To close the gap each musketeer company was allowed to hire two men abroad, making for a total of 288 men. In October the *Landtag* finally demanded a reform of the system which gave more responsibility to the administrative bodies. The minimum height of recruits was further lowered to 68 Zoll (five feet two inches). Despite the negative news from Bohemia, that year's draft was a remarkable success. Nevertheless, the system was discontinued and the army in 1780 returned to the method of hiring through the captains.[87]

---

86   Kroll, 'Aushandeln von Herrschaft`, pp.176-177.
87   Hoffmann, *Die kursächsische Armee*, pp.39-83 claimed that the system failed because the eighteenth century was not ripe for a modern draft system which required the 'citizen in uniform'. That, however, is a view typical of the nineteenth and early twentieth centuries when military developments were viewed as a staged process and also ignored the fact that, beside other European powers, Prussia and Austria as the main protagonists of the war run similar draft systems successfully.

Saxon Infantry Regiment Prince Anton. While the date on the picture is given as 1720, the style of the uniform – especially the officer's bicorne, is late eighteenth century. (Anne S.K. Brown Collection)

To fill the ranks the elector also published a pardon for deserters in Spring 1778. This led to the curious case of Christian Krüger, who had deserted in 1767 from the Saxon service and gone to Bavaria, where he was hired by the Austrians. During May 1778 he deserted again and reported back in Dresden, asked for the pardon 'and pledged, as he is old and unhealthy at the chest, for being discharged, wants to go to his relatives near Torgau and there work for his living through his own hands work.'[88] However, the regiments also reported many deserters during the following weeks, especially

---

[88] SächsHStA Dresden 11338/11003/07 Journal derer von dem commandirenden Herrn General-Lieutenant Grafen zu Solms an das unter seinem Commando stehende Corps d'Armée ergangen Parolen und täglichen Befehle, nebst denen von den Regimentern hierauf eingereichten Anzeigen 1778, fol. 45.

Saxon Infantry Regiment Prince Xaver. Again, the date is wrong, as a Regiment Xaver only existed between 1763 and 1806. (Anne S.K. Brown Collection)

Landrekruten, a typical phenomenon before a campaign. Another problem was a lack of pack horses, needed for carrying food from the countryside to the regimental camps. Already in late June the commanding general complained that the regiments took wagons and carts from the villages by force, and abolished this practice.[89]

Another problem that hit army and soldiers in these years was a hike in prices; 1770 and 1771 had been extremely wet years, each with more than 200 days of rain and more than 50 of that heavy rain. This caused bad harvests and that in turn caused an enormous increase in prices, probably the highest in the eighteenth century. Food prices always fluctuated in the early modern

---

89 SächsHStA Dresden 11338/11003/07 fol.74.

age, due to the season of the year. Wheat and corn prices were highest in the summer, when storehouses began to empty, only to drop significantly after the harvest. However, in those years the annual average more than tripled in some areas. As Saxony, despite its developed economy, was like every eighteenth century European state an agrarian society, this increase in food prices affected everything. Prussia tried to profit from the situation and stopped food exports to its southern neighbour which always depended on imports. In 1773 Friedrich II was happy to report to his brother Prince Heinrich that in the year before more than 60,000 Saxon artisans had left the country for Silesia.

The army administration was doubly affected by this crisis. On the one hand it increased the existing problems of raising funds, on the other it was forced to endow soldiers who were unable to buy the monthly amount of 60 pounds of bread. Contrary to the prices the pay of the soldiers was remarkably stable since the creation of the army under Johann Georg III in the closing decades of the sixteenth century.[90] In March 1771 the war chest had to admit that it was unable to give further credit to the indebted regiments and also had troubles to service its own. Only a special credit of Graf Joseph Bolza, a manufacturer and financier living in Dresden since 1741, and the end of the hike in prices in 1773 saved the situation. Bolza later would be affected by the war as his textile factory in the Bohemian city Josephstal (Josefův Důl) – in which he had invested half a million thalers – was closed and turned into a hospital in 1778.

At the head of the army there was some change, too. In 1774 the Chevalier the Saxe, the last *Feldmarschall* of the army, died. He was not replaced. Direct command of the army was taken over by the elector. The army was now divided in four inspectorates, two for the infantry and two for the cavalry. Each one was headed by an inspector-general who had to inspect the troops during peacetime, control the muster lists, and was responsible for discharging those men whose time of service was over. The inspectorates were probably influenced by Prussia, where Friedrich introduced them after the Seven Years War.[91]

To improve the performance of the army and the coordination between several regiments of different arms, annual training camps were established. However, there was none in 1770 and, due to the economic problems, none in 1771 and 1772. In 1775 the army introduced new manuals for the infantry and cavalry. That of the infantry basically reduced movements. While the older 1751 manual followed the Prussian exercises and combined effectiveness with a certain amount of show, the 1775 one was more 'rational' in the sense that it reduced unnecessary or too complicated movements. Speed now came foremost and that manual probably was influenced by the experiences many officers had while part of the French army from 1758. The new manual was presented by a company of the Leibgrenadiergarde to the elector and following his approval all infantry regiments had to send their

---

90 Alexander Querengässer, *The Saxon Mars and his Force. The Saxon Army during the Reign of John George III 1680-1691* (Warwick: Helion & Company, 2020).
91 Hoffmann, *Die kursächsische Armee*, pp.83-89.

OPPOSING FORCES

Parade of a squadron of Saxon Garde du Corps in front of the Cathedral in Dresden, c.1780. (Anne S.K. Brown Collection)

majors and adjutants to witness further exercises and introduce the manual within their regiments. This principle of a 'model company' was also used by the Baron von Steuben to train the Continental Army in these years. In 1776, 908 copies of the new manual were printed and handed to the infantry officers of the army. The cavalry manual was also reworked. The chevauxlegers lost their bayonets and their carbines were shortened, finally converting them from mounted infantry to a real mounted arm, using the same manual as the cuirassiers. In 1777, 378 copies of the cavalry manual were printed.[92]

The artillery had to be completely renewed as most of the Saxon guns were taken by the Prussians during the Seven Years War. Between 1766 and 1771 169 guns were cast and reported to be of good quality after a firing exercise near Dresden. Officers were trained in the artillery school in Dresden and there were annual live-firing exercises near the capital.[93]

The cavalry was restructured, too. In 1770 regiments were organized in eight instead of four companies, but the new ones, being given to the regimental staff as new captaincies, could not be created out of a lack of funds. In the same year the squadron of Garde du Corps was enlarged into a full regiment by transferring the Karabinier companies of the cuirassier regiments. The

---

92 Hoffmann, *Die kursächsische Armee*, pp.96-105.
93 Hoffmann, *Die kursächsische Armee*, pp.108-110.

THE WAR OF THE BAVARIAN SUCCESSION 1778-1789

Parade of the Saxon Lifeguard Grenadiers in front of the Frauenkirche in Dresden, c.1780. (Anne S.K. Brown Collection)

uniforms did not change that much, expect for the chevauxlegers whose uniforms changed from red to bluish-grey in 1770. For some reason, the Regiment Sacken, which had to receive new uniforms only in 1771, ordered red ones again. When the other three regiments had to receive new coats in 1774, they also changed back to red.[94] Surprisingly, the Saxon army did not have any light cavalry between 1763 and 1791, when a regiment of hussars was created. Saxony was one of the first western states to introduce hussars from Hungary during the Great Northern War. Later on, while there was never an administrative union, Saxony at least used some pulks of Polish uhlans during the Silesian Wars and had satisfying experiences with them. But there were no uhlans after 1763 and light cavalry duty, like guard duty at the border, was within the responsibility of the chevauxlegers.

At least the horses were still imported from Poland. This was a complicated business. Since Prussia had taken over Silesia it increased duties for Saxon merchants and of course remounts for the army made no difference. The horses had to be taken a long way around through Hungary and Bohemia and the increased distance raised the price. Because of that, in October 1777 the elector published a mandate promoting horse breeding in Saxony and in 1778 the regiments Renard and Sacken received 'German' horses. However,

---

94   Wolfgang Friedrich, *Die Uniformen der Kurfürstlich/Königlich Sächsischen Armee 1763-1810* (Dresden: self published, 1997).

it quickly became apparent that a long tradition of horse breeding could not be copied within a few months and so in November Polish horses were again ordered for these regiments and their 'German' horses handed over to the cuirassiers.[95]

The capitulation of Struppen in 1756 not only saw the loss of 18,000 men, but also that of their weapons, so when the army was rebuild after 1763 it had to provide a huge number of muskets. The depots and arsenals also had been emptied during the Prussian occupation. In 1764 it was estimated that the army lacked 14,821 muskets, 12,273 carbines and 13,121 pistols. In the same year the army signed contracts with several weapon manufactures in the Thuringian town of Suhl. By 29 September 1766 they had to provide 9,584 muskets with bayonets, 1,686 carbines, 1,538 pairs of pistols and 204 rifles. We lack information about the infantry musket specifications, but it was probably designed after the Austrian model-1754 musket, as Saxony oriented itself on the Austrian model. The army seems to have been satisfied with the quality of the weapons and further contracts were signed so that by 1773 22,494 muskets had been delivered.

However, in 1774 a special commission headed by the Wolf Caspar Abraham von Gersdorff (1704-1784) discussed the introduction of a new musket model. The commission examined a Dutch and a Danish musket – taken probably because relatives of von Gersdorff served as ambassadors in The Hague and Copenhagen. In 1776 the commission presented a new model of smaller calibre (0.677 inches) with an improved pan to give better protection from the rain. However, this musket was tested for another two years and it was not until 19 June 1778 that the Suhl manufacturer Johann Wilhelm Spangenberg (1722-1795) received an order for 15,000 guns. Because the army was unwilling to dispose the older 1766-pattern muskets, some of them were not yet five years old, Christian Friedrich Klaffenbach, a manufacturer from Olbernhau, was given a contract to adapt 1,000 of the older guns as closely as possible to the new system. In 1782 the army ordered another 12,824 model-1778 muskets from Spangenberg. However, this gun was not in use during the War of the Bavarian Succession.

The uniforms of the infantry had been white since 1734. Until 1771 the waistcoats had been in regimental colours, changing in that year to white, too so regiments were now only recognized through the buttons and facings of the coat.

With war in sight at the beginning of 1778, Friedrich August III recognized the need to again reorganise the army, not least due to the shortage of manpower. All the four inspector-generals were asked to develop concepts for a restructuring of the infantry and cavalry and all four answered the call by 23 and 24 February, the proposals being approved by the cabinet on 4 March. All the infantry regiments were maintained, but the weak third battalions, consisting only of four companies, were dissolved and the men divided between the remaining two battalions. Each battalion now consisted of four companies of musketeers and one of grenadiers, with 124 men each.

---

95 Hoffmann, *Die kursächsische Armee*, pp.106-107.

Total strength of a regiment including staff added to 1,253 men. However, during mobilisation the grenadier companies of each battalion were detached to form a battalion with those from a second regiment (in theory that with the same facing colour to preserve uniformity). The remaining regiment now had a field strength of 1,006 men, the grenadier battalions of 497. This reorganisation required the assembly of the regiments in their main garrisons which was done by 1 May, easing the following general mobilisation.[96]

The reorganisation of the cavalry was somewhat more complex. The four junior cuirassier regiments – von Arnim, von Benckendorff, von Brenckenhoff and von Ronnow – were all disbanded and their men and horses distributed to the remaining eight formations, the Garde du Corps, and two regiments each of cuirassiers, chevauxlegers and dragoons. The main distinction between the later was their horses: the chevauxlegers were to be remounted with Polish horses, the dragoons kept the somewhat heavier German mounts which were bred in Saxony. The fourth companies of the dragoon regiments, however, were given Polish horses, too. This gave the Garde du Corps a strength of 423 men and all the other cavalry regiments 669 men and 600 horses.[97]

During the war the Saxon army – following the example of the Prussians in Prince Heinrich's army – formed a light battalion from volunteers of all infantry regiments under the command of *Hauptmann* von Stieglitz, to be used as advance guards. Additionally, a Jägerkorps under the command of *Major* Hans Rudolf von Bischoffswerder (1741-1803) was created at the outbreak of the war. Bischoffswerder was colourful figure. Born in Saxon he joined the Prussian cuirassiers in 1760 and fought at the Battle of Freiberg, taking his leave after the end of the war, returning to Saxony and becoming chamberlain at the Prince of Kurland.[98] His Jägerkorps was created by calling up hunters and forest officers within the country to serve, bringing their own rifle with them (the same method used, when a permanent rifle corps was created in 1809). It was formed in four companies with a total of 498 men. It was filled up with picked men from the army, approved crack shots still armed with a musket and bayonet. The corps was clad in completely green uniforms with black casquets, an unusual headdress for the Saxon army.

---

96 Hoffmann, *Die kursächsische Armee*, pp.123-124.
97 Hoffmann, *Die kursächsische Armee*, pp.125-128.
98 Johannes Schulze, 'Hans Rudolf von Bischoffswerder', in Historische Kommission für die Provinz Sachsen und für Anhalt (Hrsg.), *Mitteldeutsche Lebensbilder Vol 3 Lebensbilder des 18. und 19. Jahrhunderts* (Magdeburg: self-published, 1928), pp.134–155.

OPPOSING FORCES

Saxon *Major* Hans Rudolf von Bischoffswerder, seen here in later life. (Public Domain)

4

The War

Beginnings

On 16 January 1778, 10,000 Austrian soldiers crossed the border into the Upper Palatinate and Lower Silesia. They met with no resistance, enabling Joseph II to write: 'All the world seems to be quiet and satisfied'.[1]

But Joseph was wrong. To the contrary, Friedrich II on the same day wrote to *General der Infanterie* Friedrich Bogislav von Tauentzien (1710-1791):

> As it easily could happen, that the march will be made in spring, I wanted to inform you about it and instruct you, to make your arrangements in advance and make preparations within the regiments so that, when the order comes, all preparations are made and nothing is lacking. What they lack to full strength, they should take from the cantons.[2]

The king was making his preparations. However, he overestimated the Austrian strength, writing to his envoy in Paris four days later, that they counted 20,000 troops, 122 pieces of artillery and 146 supply wagons.[3] In the following days he also received a memorial from the Saxon envoy in Berlin, Friedrich August von Zinzendorf, forwarding the Saxon claims for the Bavarian inheritance.

The Austrians also expected a Prussian attack. In the spring of 1778 Emperor Joseph together with Lacy, Loudon and Archduke Maximilian inspected the country of Northern Bohemia along the Elbe River, during which Lacy presented his first concepts for a defence of that country, which resulted in the *Defensionsplan für das Königreich Böhmen* (defence plan for the Kingdom of Bohemia) written down in April. Lacy wanted to concentrate the main Austrian forces in a central position close to the border to block any Prussian attempt to cross, in a similar fashion as *Feldmarschall* Browne had done in 1756 at Lobositz. However, Lacy's focus was at the

---

1 Quoted in Mielsch, 'Die kursächsische Armee im Bayerischen Erbfolgekrieg', p.74.
2 PCF 40, Nr. 25.874, p.38.
3 PCF 40, Nr. 25.881, p.42-43.

Bohemian-Silesian border as it was not yet expected that Saxony would enter the war or at least allow the passage of Prussian troops. The Western Army close the Isar Mountains would be commanded by Loudon and consisted of 80,000 men with 250 cannon. Further to the southeast stood the Elbe Army under the nominal command of the Emperor and Lacy, consisting of 100,000 men and 436 guns. The passages of the mountains and all tactically important positions were to be covered by redoubts, while fortified camps were constructed at Hohenelbe (Vrchlabí), Arnau (Hostinné), Jaromiersch (Jaroměř) and Smierschitz (Smiřice). *Feldzeugmeister* Carl Reichard Baron of Ellrichshausen (1720-1779) was in charge of the construction works. Additionally, the fortifications of Olmütz (Olomouc) and Eger (Cheb) were improved. Joseph was still in a good mood and made daily inspections of his brigades, but kept the troops in their cantonments and had them rest. The construction work was done by 3,000 workers.

On 17 April the Emperor and his brother Archduke Maximilian together with *Feldmarschall* Lacy went to Prague, where they met Laudon and Duke Albert of Saxe-Teschen (1738-1822), youngest son of Augustus III of Saxony and Poland and so an uncle of the Saxon elector. He had entered Austrian military service in 1759 and a year later became *chef* of a regiment of cuirassiers. In 1765 he became *Feldmarschall* and governor of Hungary and in 1766 married an Austrian archduchess, so his ties with Vienna were probably stronger than those with Dresden. He was respected and admired by the Empress, who granted him the principality of Teschen: precisely that Teschen where the peace would be signed in 1779. Albert was supposed to command the army in Moravia, while Joseph would personally lead that in Bohemia. This choice hurt Laudon, who was a much more experienced soldier than Albert, but it was probably made due to the duke's social status which was superior both to that of Lacy and Laudon, who were of lesser nobility. Lacy, Laudon and *Feldmarschall* Andreas Graf Hadik (1711-1790) all were designated as corps commanders under the Emperor. However, this plan was soon to be changed. The majority of the Austrian forces were now moved into Bohemia and formed two armies there, one commanded by the Emperor with Lacy at his side, the second one commanded by Laudon. Only 12,000 men remained in Bohemia.[4]

Following the secret treaty of 2 April 1778, the Saxon army was mobilized, too.[5] On 6 April all regiments were ordered to concentrate at the capital, which was already garrisoned by two infantry regiments. Only the Garde du Corps, the Leibgrenadiergarde and the two infantry regiments Kurfürst and Prinz Clemens remained immobile under the command of *Generalleutnant* Volpert Christian Riedesel zu Eisenbach (1708-1798). The mobile corps was to be commanded by *Generalleutnant* Friedrich Christoph zu Solms-Wildenfels (1712-1792). Born in 1712 in Königsberg in Prussia, he started his career in Swedish and later on Hessian service, before entering the Saxon

---

4 Reimann, *Geschichte des Bayerischen Erbfolgekrieges*, pp.88-90.
5 SächsHstA Dresden 11237/1370 Marschbefehle für Kompanien der Regimenter Friedrich Christoph Graf zu Solms-Wildenfels, Edler v. Lecoq, und Carl Maximilian Prinz von Sachsen, u. a. nach Frauenstein und Falkenhain.

THE WAR OF THE BAVARIAN SUCCESSION 1778-1789

Austrian generals, about 1780. (Anne S.K. Brown Collection)

army in 1742. He fought in the Second Silesian War and also commanded Saxon troops in French pay in the Seven Years War after the humiliation of Pirna. In 1759 he was promoted to *Generalleutnant* and commanded the Saxon infantry. After the war, he became chef of an infantry regiment in 1764. He definitely was an experienced officer.[6]

In early May the army sent advanced patrols of dragoons into Upper Lusatia to Löbau, Kottmarsdorf, Nieder-Oderwitz, Eckartsberg and Ostritz, while the Kurland Chevauxlegers sent 30 men to the Bohemian border near Schandau to guard the Elbe River. Another four companies of infantry with 80 horse and two guns were sent to the passes near Altenberg and Breitenbrunn, another four companies with 110 horse and two guns to Gottleuba, Gießhübel and Schandau and finally four companies, 160 horse and two guns farther west to Frauenstein and Marienberg, which was the longest, but least endangered sector of the border.[7]

The garrison of the fortress Königstein was to be strengthened up to 800 men, for which the line infantry regiments were ordered to send 350 semi-invalids who were in turn to be replaced with *Landrekruten*.[8] This measure also underlines, that a certain quantity of men unfit for duty were kept in the regiments, which seems to have been providing a basic amount of social safeguarding for deserving veterans. The regular invalid units were used to guard the magazines, many of them being established in Lusatia at Spremberg, Hoyerswerda, Görlitz and Zittau.[9]

On 5 May the army received its artillery from the Zeughaus in Dresden: sixty 4-pounder regimental guns, twelve 12-pounder guns (six heavy and six light) and eighteen 8-pounder howitzers. A further eight 4-pounder regimental guns, two 12-pounder guns, two 8-pounder guns, two 8-pounder howitzers formed the artillery reserve park for a total of 122 guns, to which another 10 were added at the end of the month.

The army was organized in brigades and concentrated in two corps around Dresden, one near to Pirna, one at Wilsdruff on the old Kesselsdorf battlefield.[10] Here the regiments were further exercised, not in larger groups but by battalions, also doing live shooting.[11] However, Regiment Solms

---

6 Schuster and Francke, *Sächsische Armee*, p.171.
7 SächsHStA Dresden 11338/11003/07 Journal derer von dem commandirenden Herrn General-Lieutenant Grafen zu Solms an das unter seinem Commando stehende Corps d'Armée ergangen Parolen und täglichen Befehle, nebst denen von den Regimentern hierauf eingereichten Anzeigen 1778, fol.36-41.
8 SächsHStA Dresden 11338/11003/07 Journal derer von dem commandirenden Herrn General-Lieutenant Grafen zu Solms an das unter seinem Commando stehende Corps d'Armée ergangen Parolen und täglichen Befehle, nebst denen von den Regimentern hierauf eingereichten Anzeigen 1778, fol.11, 15.
9 SächsHstA Dresden 11237/ 1382 Die in Ansehung des Mobilgemachten und in Campagne befindlichen Chur-Sechßischen Corps d'Armeé ergangenen Anordnungen und was dem anhaengig betr., fol.1-45.
10 SächsHstA Dresden 11237/1379 Bayerischer Erbfolgekrieg, without fol.
11 SächsHStA Dresden 11338/11003/07 Journal derer von dem commandirenden Herrn General-Lieutenant Grafen zu Solms an das unter seinem Commando stehende Corps d'Armée ergangen Parolen und täglichen Befehle, nebst denen von den Regimentern hierauf eingereichten Anzeigen 1778, fol.14.

THE WAR OF THE BAVARIAN SUCCESSION 1778-1789

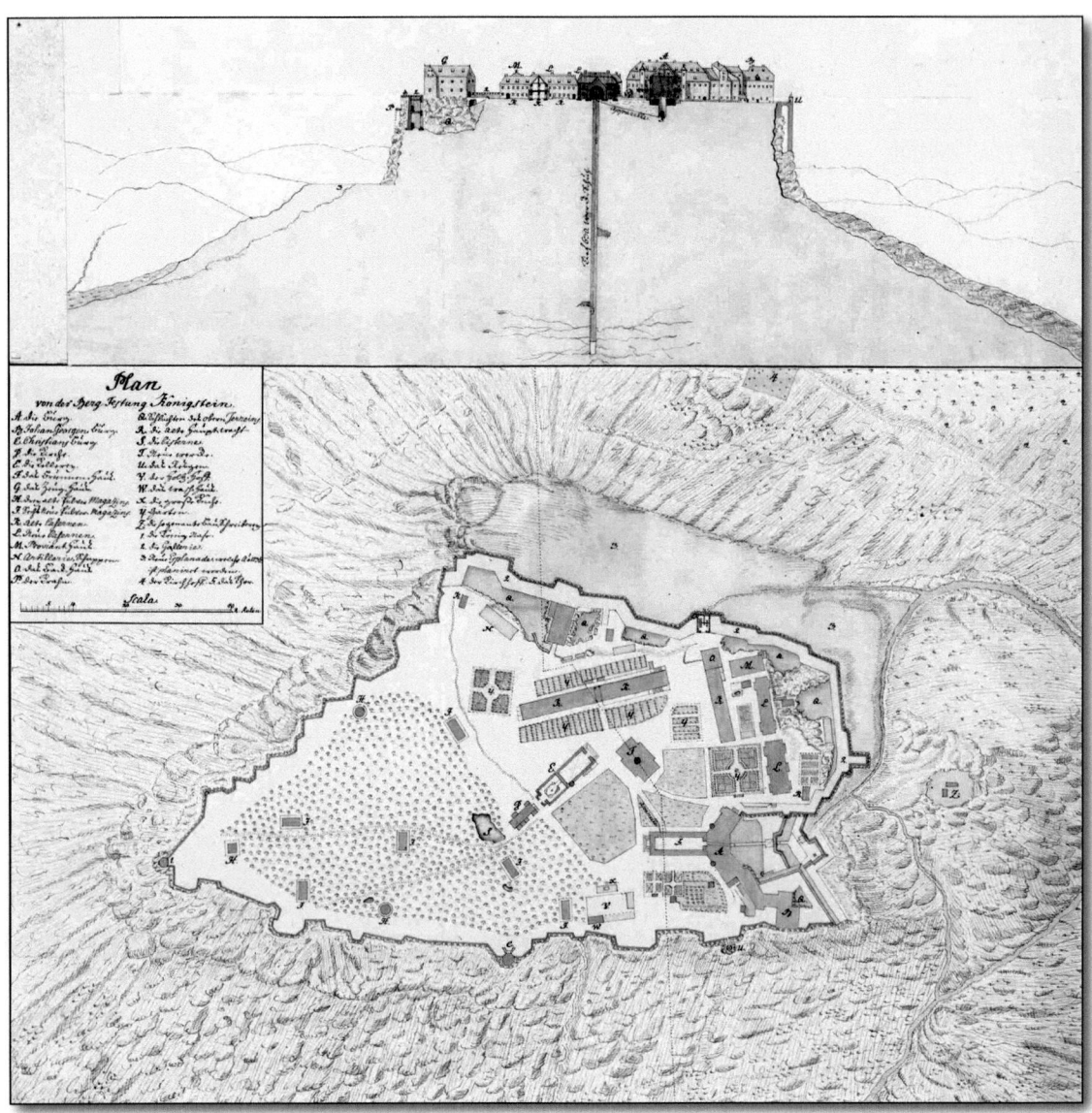

Plan of the Saxon fortress of Königstein. Situated on a steep table hill, the fortress was nearly impenetrable by storm. (Public Domain)

lamented bad powder, 'which during the firing damages the men'.[12] On 7 June the commanding general also ordered the artillery officers attached to the battalions to bring the horses for the regimental guns to these exercises, 'so they get used to the firing'.[13]

---

12 SächsHStA Dresden 11338/11003/07 Journal derer von dem commandirenden Herrn General-Lieutenant Grafen zu Solms an das unter seinem Commando stehende Corps d'Armée ergangen Parolen und täglichen Befehle, nebst denen von den Regimentern hierauf eingereichten Anzeigen 1778, fol.17.

13 SächsHStA Dresden 11338/11003/07 Journal derer von dem commandirenden Herrn General-Lieutenant Grafen zu Solms an das unter seinem Commando stehende Corps d'Armée ergangen Parolen und täglichen Befehle, nebst denen von den Regimentern hierauf eingereichten Anzeigen 1778, fol.15.

The capital was put into a state of defence. Its garrison consisted of the two infantry regiments mentioned, the Leibgrenadiergarde and the Garde du Corps, all in all six battalions and four squadrons. In the case of a surprise attack by the Austrians the fortress was expected to be able to defend itself at least a week, waiting for Prussian support.[14] Improvements on the fortifications of Dresden and the construction of new redoubts around the capital started in May and were continued throughout the war, but met with increasing resistance by the Ämter later on, who were more and more unwilling to send workers and material.[15]

The Austrian preparations were well recognized in Saxony, however the *Amtmann* (district magistrate) from Dippoldiswalde, a border county south of Dresden, reported to the elector on 13 May: 'The [Austrian] field guards placed along the border are ordered under threat of life and limb, neither to touch the Saxon border, nor to offend a Saxon subject in any way'.[16] These and other accounts by civilian officials along the border give the impression that Dresden was well informed about troop strength and movements and the establishment of magazines in Bohemia. The *Amtmann* of Plauen for example reported on 3 June that the garrison of Eger (Cheb) was strengthened by 300 Jäger from Tyrol and that another 300 were expected.[17] The mayor of Zittau was even able to give a description about the enemies weapons, reporting on 29 June that 'near Gabel 260 Sharpshooters, who carry rifles with two barrels and two lock plates, marched in'.[18] In late June first reports reached Dresden that Austrian officers with small escorts, or even no escort, crossed the border to survey the terrain and even interview Saxon peasants, causing the Prussians to claim that they had violated the border. However, many of the detailed reports received in Dresden were based on accounts of Saxon subjects who had crossed the border.

Prussia, too was busy preparing for war. Friedrich started for Breslau on 6 April accompanied by the Hereditary Prince of Brunswick Carl Wilhelm Ferdinand (1735-1806). The latter was a veteran of the Seven Years War, where he fought in Northern Germany under the command of his uncle Ferdinand of Brunswick (1721-1792) at Hastenbeck, Minden and Warburg. In late April Friedrich moved the regiments belonging to his army to Glatz, very close to the Bohemian border, while Heinrich's troops were located between Magdeburg and Halle. The prince himself still had his headquarters in Berlin.

14　Schuster and Francke, *Sächsische Armee*, pp.172-173.
15　SächsHstA Dresden 11237/1375 Defensions-Veranstaltungen in und um der Gegend Dreßden Anno 1778. 1779. 1780. 1781.
16　Sächs HStA Dresden 10025/ Loc. 6412/05 Die von den Bewegungen und Verteidigungs-Anstalten der Kayserlich-Königlichen Truppen, sowohl als von den durch selbige in hiesigen Landen verübten Feindseligkeiten eingegangenen Anzeigen betr. Anno 1778, fol.5.
17　Sächs HStA Dresden 10025/ Loc. 6412/05 Die von den Bewegungen und Verteidigungs-Anstalten der Kayserlich-Königlichen Truppen, sowohl als von den durch selbige in hiesigen Landen verübten Feindseligkeiten eingegangenen Anzeigen betr. Anno 1778, fol.67.
18　Sächs HStA Dresden 10025/ Loc. 6412/05 Die von den Bewegungen und Verteidigungs-Anstalten der Kayserlich-Königlichen Truppen, sowohl als von den durch selbige in hiesigen Landen verübten Feindseligkeiten eingegangenen Anzeigen betr. Anno 1778, fol.120.

THE WAR OF THE BAVARIAN SUCCESSION 1778-1789

Camp of the Saxon army outside Dresden, 1778. The picture shows the camp of the army on the heights to the west of the city. The camp streets are clearly distinguishable. At the end of each street a collection of different wagons can be seen, together with sutler tents and huge fires. (Plate 26 from Otto Richter, *Atlas zur Geschichte Dresdens* (Dresden: Stengel & Markert, 1898)

THE WAR

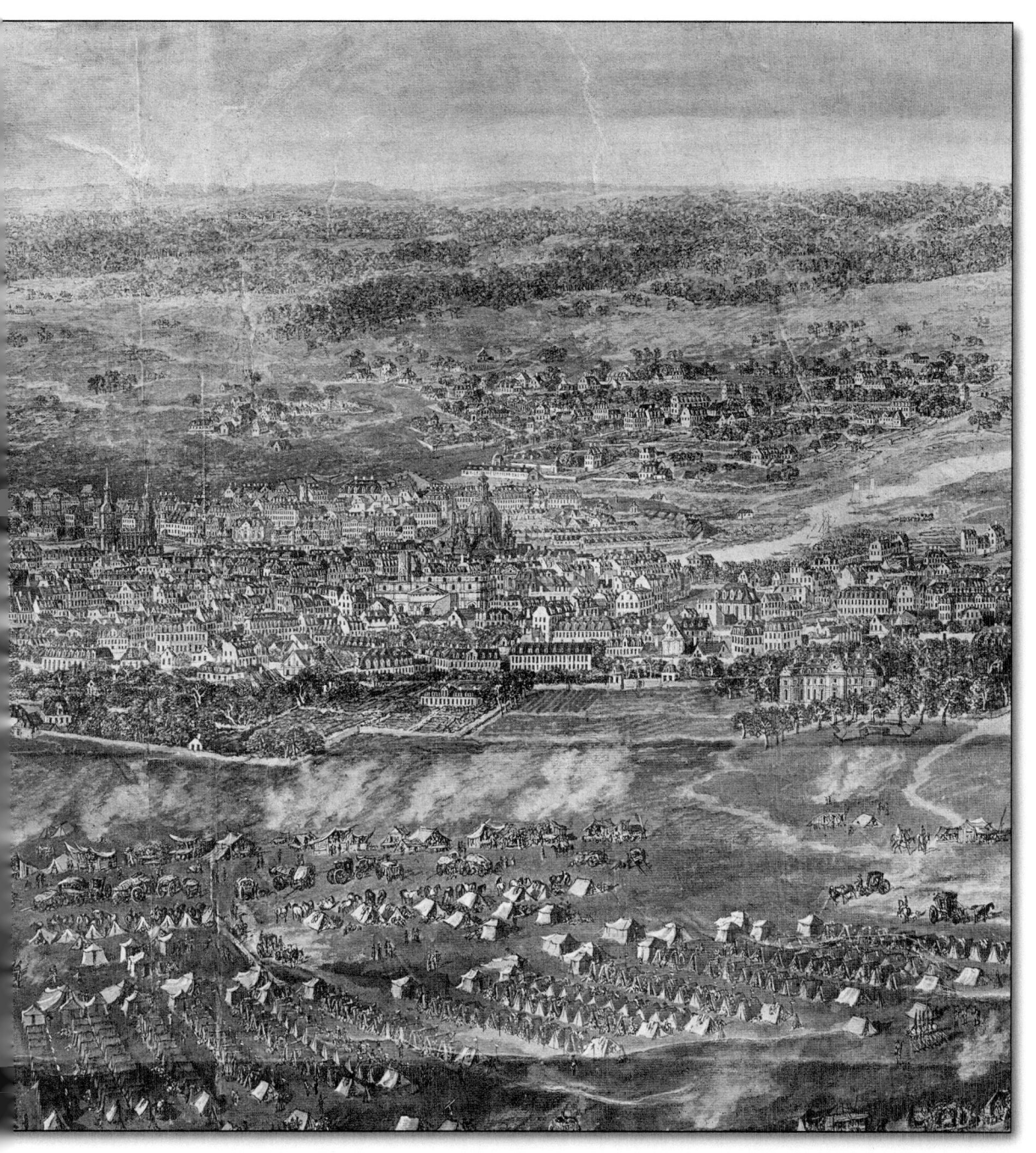

THE WAR OF THE BAVARIAN SUCCESSION 1778-1789

Prince Heinrich of Prussia, c.1779. (Anne S.K. Brown Collection)

Joseph moved his headquarters at the end of April to Brandis (Branýs nad labem), a small town to the North of Bohemia. Austrian light troops were sent to the border to check the movements of Prussian and Saxon troops. A special focus of the Austrians was on the passes beyond the Lusatian border town of Zittau. The concentration of Möllendorfs corps at Cottbus in late May led the Austrians to expect them to cross the border there.[19] They built a fortified camp at Gabel (Jablonné v Podještědí), a small town with a castle, 800 houses and a medieval wall. The Austrians now shifted the majority of their troops in Moravia into Bohemia, creating their main army between Jaromer and Königgrätz. This was the best position to block an advance into Bohemia from the direction of Glatz. This rearrangement left Duke Albert, seconded by the aging Hadik, with only a small army in Moravia. In fact, he would not play any substantial role in the coming conflict. As soon as the Prussians invaded Bohemia, Albert had to send nearly all the rest of his troops northward, leaving only a small corps under *Feldmarschalleutnant* Jacob Marchese di Botta (1729-1803) in Moravia.

At the end of June diplomatic negotiations between Berlin and Vienna were closed. On 3 July Prussia declared War on Austria. Friedrich later wrote in his history:

> The negotiations in Berlin were broken off on July 4th [sic – the actual date was earlier] and on the 5th all troops began to march. In order to better conceal their intentions, the Silesian army cantoned in an angular position between Reichenbach, Frankenstein and Neisse. From this position it was impossible for the enemy to guess whether the king's troops would turn to Moravia or Bohemia.[20]

The declaration was handed over to the Austrian envoy Graf Cobenzl.

The Operations of the Prussian Main Army

According to Friedrich's plan, one of the two Prussian armies had to fix the Austrian forces, but stay on the defensive, while the other one was to make a flank movement, trying to get behind the Austrians, take their magazines and cut their communications. If the Silesian army had to face them, Prince Henirich would be able to threaten Prague.[21] The Prussian main – or Silesian – Army started the campaign. In the middle of June a corps of 20 battalions and 28 squadrons under *Generalleutnant* Johann Jacob von Wunsch (1717-1788) prepared a fortified camp at Wiesau (Łączna) close to the border.

Wunsch was a rare exception among the Prussian generals. The son of a simple skinner he was born in Württemberg and served in its army during the Turkish War of 1737 to 1739, rising to the rank of *Leutnant*, which was easier there than in Prussia. However, seeing his path for further promotion blocked because of his low birth he shifted to the Bavarian army, where he

---

19   Reimann, *Geschichte des Bayerischen Erbfolgekrieges*, p.93.
20   Volz (ed.), *Die Werke Friedrichs des Großen*, Vol.5, pp.105.
21   Reimann, *Geschichte des Bayerischen Erbfolgekrieges*, p.81.

was made a captain and served in a hussar regiment which did service in the Low Countries, where Wunsch fought at Rocoux and Lauffeldt. With the beginning of the Seven Years War, he volunteered for the Prussian army, following a call of his patron, the Italian-born Ludwig Marquis von Angelelli de Malvezzi (1716-1797), who raised a *Freibatallion* from Saxon citizens. Wunsch rose to the rank of *Oberstleutnant* (1758) and was allowed to raise an own *Freibatallion*, to which a second one was added in 1759, so both formed a regiment and Wunsch became its colonel and in the same year *Generalmajor*. He fought a major skirmish action Torgau in late 1759 and was awarded with the Pour le Merite. In the same year he belonged to the corps of *Generalleutnant* von Finck, which was encircled and forced to surrender at Maxen. Wunsch unsuccessfully had tried to break through the Austrian lines and went into captivity. However, his brave attempt saved his head, when the affair was examined by a court-martial after the war as Wunsch was the only general of Finck's corps to be exonerated. As his regiment was disbanded in 1763, he was given the former regiment von Finck. In 1771 Wunsch was promoted to *Generalleutnant*. This was really an unusual career, because Wunsch embodied everything Friedrich disliked and wanted to get rid of in his army: non-noble birth, a background in the unbeloved *Freibatallions*, and involvement in a shameful capitulation. In fact, Wunsch owed much of this career to Prince Heinrich, who became a kind of patron to him from 1758 on. However, it was not before Friedrich's death in 1786 that his military ascent was followed by a social one: in 1787 he was ennobled by the new king Friedrich Wilhelm II. This also demonstrates impressively that Friedrich II might have been willing to make use of his general's talent, but still saw him as a social outsider. Wunsch was going to be a leading figure in this conflict.

The remainder of the Silesian Army started its march to the fortress of Silberberg (Srebrna Góra) at the beginning of July. Silberberg was a dominating height behind the fortress of Glatz, being able to protect Silesia in case this place was taken by the enemy. Friedrich had recognized its importance during the Seven Years War and ordered the construction of a fortress there in the years afterwards. However, on 4 July the king took 40 squadrons and moved them to Wunsch's camp. His corps was now designated as the advance guard and moved further to the west, to Lewin (Lewin Klodzki). On the same day the Prince of Brunswick moved the troops from Silberberg (30 battalions and 33 squadrons), now forming the left wing of the army, in two columns to Glatz. Because of the huge baggage train the army moved only slowly.

On 5 July the Prussian advance guard under the personal command of the king crossed the Bohemian border and entered Náchod, westwards of Glatz. The main army followed close behind, but was still slow, because artillery and wagons had to pass small roads and mountainous terrain. In Náchod the Prussians established a field bakery on the market and a hospital at the castle.[22] The town was forced to pay a ransom of 24,000

---

22 Seyfarth, *Unpartheyische Geschichte*, pp.166-170.

Friedrich II in the campaign of 1778 by Bernhard Rode. (1725-1797). (Bode-Museum, Berlin)

florins; nearby Braunau (Broumov), which was also occupied by the Prussians, had to pay 30,000.

On the afternoon of the 5th, Friedrich sent a hussar patrol under the command of *Oberst* Friedrich Wilhelm von Götzen (1734-1794) on a reconnaissance mission to Skalitz (Česká Skalice), the next town further west. The Prussians captured an Austrian officer. On the 6th Friedrich himself led a cavalry patrol to the Elbe as far as Chwalkowitz (Chvalkovice).

On the next day Austrian and Prussian troops again reconnoitred to Skalitz. According to the Prussian account, the Austrians, 2,000 strong, moved further east to the small village Kleny, when the king ordered Goetzen to chase them of with the Zeiten Hussars, which he did, capturing two officers and 40 men. Imperial accounts just mentioned a patrol of the Hussar Regiment Wurmser under the command of a captain – hardly amounting to anything like 2,000 men – being forced to retire in the face of overwhelming Prussian resistance.[23]

Friedrich later gave a plain description of his intentions:

---

23   Seyfarth, *Unpartheyische Geschichte*, pp.173-175.

The plan of campaign which the king had devised was very different from that which he had to carry out. He wanted to take the war to Moravia, leave about 20,000 men to cover the county of Glatz and the Landeshut passes, bypass the position at Heidenpiltsch, which was probably feasible, give battle to the Austrians and, if he had won, send a detachment of 20,000 men across the March straight to Pressburg, to occupy the Danube bridge there, cut off all supplies from Hungary to the Imperialists and undertake patrols from Pressburg against Vienna. This would have forced the court to withdraw some of its troops across the Danube to cover the capital and protect itself. This weakening of the armies in Bohemia would have given Prince Heinrich a free hand and facilitated all the operations of his army.[24]

According to Friedrich's history he immediately had to abandon this plan for two reasons. First, the Austrians only faced his main army with 10,000 men, so he had to expect that the majority of their forces, concentrated at Jaromir and estimated to consist of 80,000 men, would enter Silesia which was only covered by weak forces. The second reason was that the elector of Saxony expected an invasion of his country before Prince Heinrich's army appeared and Friedrich feared that in this case, Saxony might switch sides. All these reasons are hard to comprehend. Friedrich knew that the Austrian army was building up strength in north-eastern Bohemia, so it is not easy to understand why he expected them to block his route south if his movements offered them the possibility of cutting his line of communication. A successful invasion of Saxony was also doubtful. At the beginning of July Heinrich's army was still en route to Dresden but to force a shift of the Saxon alliance would have required a swift march by Laudon's army which was as far away from the Saxon capital as Heinrich's was and would have had to cross more difficult territory.

During June the Austrians had completed the arrangements of their two armies in Bohemia. Duke Albert had moved the majority of his forces to Königgrätz. At the beginning of July the army established a camp in battle order at Kukus (Kuks), to the north or Jaromer, formed in two lines. This position it never left.[25]

Friedrich claimed that these threats forced him to cross the border into Bohemia right between the two Austrian armies, take Nachód and so force the Emperor to send troops from his main army to support Laudon. Another 10,000 men under *Generalleutnants* Joachim Friedrich von Stutterheim (1715-1783) and Paul von Werner (1707-1785) were sent south to block an Austrian corps of similar size in the camp at Heidenpiltsch (Bílčice), covered by the Mohra River.

On 8 July Friedrich himself at the head of 50 squadrons of dragoons and hussars started a reconnaissance in force.[26] He found the Austrian positions

---

24 Volz (ed.), *Die Werke Friedrichs des Großen*, Vol.5, p.105.
25 Seyfarth, *Unpartheyische Geschichte*, pp.177-178.
26 According to Seyfarth, *Unpartheyische Geschichte*, p.175. Frederick himself mentioned the 7th, but in this case Seyfarthh seems more reliable, as he dated the first skirmish as occurring on the 7th, for which he had several sources.

at Königgrätz well-fortified with redouts and trenches eight foot deep and 16 foot wide, supported by palisades and chevaux de frise, in short 'more like a fortress than like a field fortification'. The southern bank of the Elbe River was higher than the northern one, adding to the protection of the defenders. The river itself was in flood. All Elbe crossings were defended by triple redoubts. On the wooded mountaintops the enemy had erected barricades; behind was a reserve of 40 battalions, which could quickly come to the rescue wherever the Prussians might be bold enough to venture an attack, provided that the attackers had first succeeded in gradually penetrating the numerous redoubts and fortifications with their 1,500 guns. The main difficulty, however, which added to all the others and made the Elbe crossing completely impossible, was this: the river bed is bordered from Jaromer to the high mountains on both banks by cliffs 12 feet or more high, which could only be crossed on the existing bridges. And it was precisely there that 'a lavish abundance of fortifications prevented any advance',[27] wrote Friedrich in his history of the war. The king's reconnaissance party moved so close to the Austrian fortifications that they were able to exchange musket and carbine shots. Friedrich seems to have been impressed, because for several days he remained more or less inactive.

In the meantime, the Austrian light troops started their operations. They were commanded by *Feldmarschalleutnant* Dagobert Sigmund von Wurmser (1724-1797). Born in Strasburg he started his career in French service and in 1742 took part in the invasion of Bohemia under the Duc de Belleisle (1684-1761). During the Seven Years War he commanded a French hussar regiment and gained experience in small warfare. In 1762 he raised his own regiment of light troops, but, as it became clear that France would abandon the war, Wurmser and his regiment were taken over into the service of Maria Theresia, where he became a *Feldwachtmeister* (equal to major general) and *Reichsgraf* (Imperial count). His regiment was disbanded in 1763, but he got a regiment of hussars in 1773 and another one in 1775 when the previous one was disbanded. In 1778 he became a *Feldmarschalleutnant* and was going to be Austria's most active field commander during this conflict.

On 14 July Wurmser ordered *Oberstleutnant* Peter von Quasdanovich (1738-1802) with the Carlstadt Hussars from their quarters in Alt Pleß (Starý Ples) to Zwol (Zvole), closer to the River Aupa (Úpa), a tributary of the Elbe which unites with it at Jaromir. Here they destroyed a bridge spanning the river and harassed Prussian advance guards. Wurmser himself took five regiments of cavalry and one of Croats and moved them further east to Schestowitz (Šestajovice) to deflect the enemy's attention from Quasdanovich's party. The Austrians moved at night and surprised a Prussian advance guard made up of Bosniaks at Wesselitz (Veselice). Next, the Austrians also dispersed a field guard of Prussian cuirassiers, raising alarm in the enemy's camp. When Quasdanovich reported his orders fulfilled – in the meantime he was attacked by Prussian infantry and also fired upon by artillery – Wurmser retreated, seeing his mission fulfilled.[28] Both sides only took a few losses.

---

27   Volz (ed.), *Die Werke Friedrichs des Großen*, Vol.5, pp.107-108.
28   Seyfarth, *Unpartheyische Geschichte*, pp.183-185.

Reconnaissance in force, small raids and counter action were going to define the conflict in this region, while the main armies remained in camp.

The Austrians soon received information that Náchod and Braunau had been forced to pay ransoms and give up hostages, and wanted to pay the Prussians back. On 16 July a major raiding party of light troops crossed the border into Silesia and occupied the towns Liebau (Lubawka) and Schoemberg (Chełmsko Śląskie), which had to pay a ransom of 30,000 florins and also provide hostages. The Austrians retired quickly, also taking some cattle with them. To avoid further raids in this direction, Friedrich sent a small corps under the Prince of Anhalt to block the road to Trautenau.

Small parties of both armies met each other every day. On 23 July the Prussians started a bigger raid against Wurmser's camp at Schestowitz. With a mixed force of infantry and cavalry under the command of *Generalmajor* Michael Konstantin von Zaremba (1711-1786) and *Generalmajor* Georg Ludolf von Wulffen (1719-1792) they raided to the north of the Metau and Aupa Rivers, while a second force under *Generalmajor* Leopold Ludwig von Lossow and the Prince of Anhalt raided south of the Metau. The Prussians pushed back the Austrian field guards at Slawentin. When Wurmser arrived at the battlefield with the Barco Hussars, he immediately counterattacked and drove the Prussians back to the small village of Rohenitz (Rohenice). Here he had to stop his pursuit after he detected three more Prussian battalions with six guns and a howitzer in a small forest behind the village, which started firing at his horsemen. However, he also received support and decided to attack the enemy's left flank. But as soon his cavalry had turned the Prussian flank, he detected a second line of infantry behind the first, and on the height of nearby Slawietin (Slavětín nad Metují) were another eight battalions and guns which started firing at them. The Austrians halted their advance, enabling the two Prussian lines at Rohenitz to unite with each other and retreat to Slawietin. Wurmser moved his troops to the Metau river and so forced the Prussians to retreat to their camp at Skalitz. Both sides admitted to having suffered about 40 casualties.[29]

Very often Austrian and Prussian reports are at odds with each other. When Prussian raids were unsuccessful, their reports claimed that they have been unspectacular, while the Austrians underlined their success in chasing them off. If the Prussians achieved a minor success, Austrian reports tended to imply that nothing had happened at all. The lack of original reports on the part of the Prussians makes it difficult to reconstruct the events, but even a contemporary like Seyfarth noted the discrepancy. True to the title of his book which claims to offer an *Unpartheyische Geschichte* (non-partisan history), he tried to quote reports from both sides, which underlines this discrepancy and makes it a really valuable source. To give an example of these contradictory reports, the Imperials claimed a minor success on 30 July when some Warasdiner hussars and Jäger crossed the Elbe between Arnau and Königinhof and attacked a Prussian field guard at the Katharinenberg (Catherine mountain). According to them the Prussians retreated so quickly

---

29   Seyfarth, *Unpartheyische Geschichte*, pp.195-201.

that they were only able to take 12 prisoners. The Prussian report, meanwhile, said that the field guard of 20 men had been attacked by several hundred pandurs, but was quickly supported by the Prince of Anhalt, who was able to repel the enemy's attack.[30] On the same day, the Austrians reported an attack of three Prussian battalions under Wunsch's personal command against Neustadt (Nove Mesto nad Metuji). Wunsch is reported to have broken down the old gate with gunfire and ordered a half battalion to attack the town. The Prussians entered the gate, but were soon repelled. However, no Prussian report makes mention of any movement against Neustadt![31]

The Prussian king hoped to be able to entice the Austrians from their strong position or to outfox them through clever feints. He put a corps in front of the forces camping near Jaromir which started feint attacks against Königinhof (Dvůr Králové nad Labem) and Hermanitz (Heřmanice nad Labem), two possible crossing points on the Elbe close to Jaromir, in order to turn the attention of the Austrians to the south. In the meantime, he wanted to lead his main army across the border farther north, cross the Elbe at Werdek (Verdek), and march for the high grounds of Switschin, from where he was able to divide the opposing forces. For this he stationed 25 battalions and 60 squadrons at Wölsdorf (Vlčkovice v Podkrkonoš) to feint the crossings. In preparation of the manoeuvre the Prussians undertook a couple of open or hidden reconnaissance movements. Cavalry patrols were sent out and raiding parties moved along the northern bank of the Elbe River. During these movements the Prussians spotted a fortified camp with seven battalions at the village Prausnitz (Dolní Brusnice) which they had to pass on the way to Switschin, and another one on the heights to the rear, manned by four battalions. In the face of these forces, which quickly could be supported by additional infantry and cavalry from the camps nearby, a crossing of the river at Werdek appeared too risky. However, this failure also revealed an amazing failure of Prussian intelligence. It seems that Friedrich – who knew since the beginning of the year that the Austrians were collecting forces in Bohemia – had never taken measures to establish a network of spies to keep him informed of the Austrian defensive precautions. This appears especially surprising as the king was well aware from the later stages of the Seven Years War that the Austrians preferred defensive fortified positions and it also reveals a certain arrogance at the part of the king, who expected to occupy an operational position of vital importance unprotected by the enemy's forces. However, Friedrich's main intention still was to fix the Austrians in front of his army to allow his brother to attack their flank or take Prague.[32]

After the march to Switschin failed, the corps at Wölsdorf appeared to be in danger as it had to face the main Austrian forces. Friedrich recognized it and raised its strength to 40 battalions. *Generalleutnant* Christoph Carl von Bülow (1716-1788) was sent with 30 squadrons and a couple of battalions to Smirschitz (Smiřice) to threaten the fords between Jaromir and Königgrätz, while *Generalleutnant* Friedrich Gotthelf von Falkenhayn (1719-1786) was

---

30   Seyfarth, *Unpartheyische Geschichte*, pp.207-208.
31   Seyfarth, *Unpartheyische Geschichte*, pp.208-209.
32   Reimann, *Geschichte des Bayerischen Erbfolgekrieges*, pp.119-120.

sent to Chalkowitz (Chvalkovice) to the north of Jaromir. Wunsch was sent back to Náchod to cover the line of communications and the Prince of Anhalt took possession of Pilnikau (Pílnikov) with 12 battalions and 12 squadrons so as to keep an eye on the Austrian forces at Switschin.

Because his plans so far had been frustrated, Friedrich in retrospect claimed that his manoeuvring at least enabled the undisturbed employment of his brothers' forces:

> During these troop movements in Bohemia, the Emperor's army was completely self-absorbed. The fear of being attacked by the hour prevented the thought of sending reinforcements to Field-Marshal Laudon; so Prince Heinrich reached Dresden without any resistance.[33]

This is a self-praising exaggeration as Laudon never intended to start a major invasion of Saxony. Austrian light troops harassed the Saxon border, but Laudon's main force was as 'self-absorbed' – to use the king's words – as Joseph's main army.

At the same time there was some fear in Berlin that the Austrians might send a flying corps to occupy the city, as they had done twice during the Seven Years War. However, Friedrich wrote confidently to his minister the Baron von der Schulenburg – who feared for the safety of the state treasure in the city – on 13 July that he expected that 'my brother and I will give the Austrians so much to deal with that they will lose interest to make an invasion of Berlin'.[34]

The Operations of Prince Heinrich's Saxo-Prussian Army

In the meantime, the army of Prince Heinrich, concentrated near Berlin, had entered Saxony, its advance guard with 13 battalions, 30 squadrons and 40 guns under *Generalleutnant* Wichard von Möllendorf (1724-1816) reached Dresden on 1 July and prepared camp on the eastern side of the Elbe River. The prince followed with the bulk of his forces six days later and established his headquarters in the Scloss Übigau, a few miles to the north of the city.

Heinrich was the younger brother of Friedrich and, according to the king, the only field commander during the Seven Years War who had not made any mistakes. However, Heinrich was probably well aware of his own qualities and did not hesitate to criticize his brother for flaws in his strategy and tactics. He did so in an essay published in 1753 under the pseudonym 'Maréchal Gessler' and repeatedly during the Seven Years War, for example after the Prussian defeat at Maxen which Friedrich blamed on *Generalleutnant* Finck, whereas Heinrich faulted the hasty operations of his brother who failed to support his general. Heinrich himself was probably more cautious and systematic in his operations and while he repeatedly gained independent commands it was not until the final month of the

---

33 Volz (ed.), *Die Werke Friedrichs des Großen*, Vol.5, p.109.
34 PCF 41, no, 26546, p.258.

The Schloss Übigau served as Prince Heinrich's headquarters during June 1778. (Public Domain)

conflict that he fought his first – and only – major battle as a commander at Freiberg, where he defeated the Reichsarmee and made effective use of columns. While his own behaviour towards his brother could be cool from time to time, right up to provocative, Friedrich repeatedly showed his affection for him and after the war assigned him to important diplomatic missions, for example to St Petersburg, where Heinrich negotiated the details of the first Partition of Poland with the Empress Catherine. During his stay in Russia Catherine also offered him the principality of Walachia as an independent principality. Later he was also offered the governorship of the American colonies by George III, shortly before the outbreak of the revolution, while during the war Baron von Steuben recommended the Prince as a possible American president or even king to Alexander Hamilton. However, none of these fancy plans came into fruition. Heinrich stayed in Prussia, where ironically, he spent most of his time in the palace of Rheinsberg, which was erected by Friedrich in his youth. Heinrich's court assembled critics of his brother and especially those officers disliked by the king. The prince openly demonstrated his own view by creating a small gallery with paintings of historical military heroes neglected by his brother and also erected an obelisk in 1790 to honour those Prussian officers of the Seven Years War who, according to his view, had been underappreciated by Friedrich.[35] However, Heinrich also shared some distinctive similarities with his brother. Married since 1752 to Wilhelmine of Hesse-Cassel (1726-1808), he spent most of his life separated from his wife and never had children with her. As is presumed to be the case with Friedrich, Heinrich

---

35 Jürgen Luh, *Heinrichs Heroen. Die Feldherrengalerie des Prinzen Heinrich im Schloss Rheinsberg* (Karwe: Edition Rieger, 2007).

preferred male companionship but was willing and able to live out his penchant. In the 1770s Christian Ludwig von Kaphengst (1740-1800), an officer in the Prussian army, was his favourite. While Heinrich was small and slender, Kaphengst was a Teutonic whopper who physically and psychologically dominated the prince and was able to make his fortune out of this relationship, even forcing the prince to cut his own and his wife's budget. Kaphengst also became his adjutant, but it is unclear how much influence he had over Heinrich in the field.

A few days after Möllendorf's arrival, the corps of the Prince of Anhalt, coming down from Halle, also arrived at the Saxon capital. Here, Saxon pioneers had built a pontoon bridge. The Prussian army crossed the river on that bridge and the stone bridge in Dresden, uniting with the Saxon army. Only a grenadier battalion and 10 squadrons of hussars were left behind to cover the other side of the river. On 10 July Prince Heinrich officially took over the command of the Saxon army, which increased his forces to 75,000 men. All the men received white feather plumes as symbols of recognition. The army was formed into four corps. The main force consisted of 35 Prussian battalions and 50 squadrons. The second, Saxon, corps was formed of 16 Battalions and eight squadrons, commanded by *Generalleutnant* Friedrich Christoph zu Solms-Wildenfels. The third corps under the command of the Prussian *Generalleutnant* Dubislaw von Platen (1714-1786) was made up off 11 Prussian and 10 Saxon battalions and 20 Prussian and 16 Saxon squadrons. The fourth corps under Möllendorf was entirely made up of Prussian troops, 13 battalions and 40 squadrons.

On the same day news of first Austrian incursions reached the prince's army. Austrian light troops had crossed the border in Lusatia and occupied the border town of Zittau and Herrenhut – a community founded during the Thirty Years War by Bohemian exiles – and demanded contributions, 200,000 guilders from the former, 20,000 florins from the later.[36] To deal with them, *Generalmajor* Carl von Podgursky (1720-1781) was sent with five battalions – three Prussian and two Saxon – and two regiments of cavalry from Prince Heinrich's army.

Because he lacked light infantry – Heinrich only had two of the *Freibataillone* – the prince created four more battalions from volunteers, which were to be commanded by *Oberstleutnant* Franz Casimir von Kleist (1736-1808), *Oberstleutnant* Otto Wilhelm von Schlieffen (1727-?) and the *Obristwachtmeister* (majors) Carl Friedrich von Klinkowström (1738-1816) and Wolf Heinrich Ernst von Klüx (1728-1805). Kleist with his battalion, the Freiregiment von Hard, and 400 Czetteritz-Hussars was sent to Freiberg and Chemnitz, to cover the border there.

---

36   SächsHStA Dresden 10025/ Loc. 6412/05 Die von den Bewegungen und Verteidigungs-Anstalten der Kayserlich-Königlichen Truppen, sowohl als von den durch selbige in hiesigen Landen verübten Feindseligkeiten eingegangenen Anzeigen betr. Anno 1778, fol. 160-169. More detailed: SächsHStA Dresden 11025/ 05806/01 Die von den Emperorlich Königlichen Trouppen der Stadt Zittau im Jahr 1778 auferlegte Kriegs-Contribution, und die zu deren Tilgung, auch Wiederaufnahme dasiger Stadt, geschehenen Vorschläge betr. Anno 1778.

Musketeer, Infanterie Regiment Deutschmeister Nr.4, in the uniform introduced for the Austrian army in 1767.
(Artwork by Alexandr Chernushkin © Helion and Company 2023)

Trooper, Austrian Chevauxleger Regiment Löwenstein Nr.18.
(Artwork by Alexandr Chernushkin © Helion and Company 2023)

Jäger, Austrian Deutches Feld-Jäger Corps. Disbanded in 1763, this unit was re-raised for the War of the Bavarian Succession. (Artwork by Alexandr Chernushkin © Helion and Company 2023)

Lancer, Prussian Bosniaken-Corps. An independent regiment since 1771, the Bosniaks took Nr.9 in the sequence of Prussian hussar regiments. (Artwork by Alexandr Chernushkin © Helion and Company 2023)

Musketeer, Prussian Freiregiment von Münster Nr.4. Raised in 1778, a single battalion had joined the Prussian forces in the field by the end of that year. (Artwork by Alexandr Chernushkin © Helion and Company 2023)

Trooper, Saxon Kürassier Regiment von Arnim.
(Artwork by Alexandr Chernushkin © Helion and Company 2023)

NCO, Saxon Infanterie Regiment Prinz Clemens.
(Artwork by Alexandr Chernushkin © Helion and Company 2023)

Jäger, Saxon Jägercorps Bischoffswerder. See p.72 for more details of the raising of this unit.
(Artwork by Alexandr Chernushkin © Helion and Company 2023)

Saxon troops on the march. (Anne S.K. Brown Collection)

Henrich received reports that the Austrians had made many preparations to defend the border. They had created abatis blocking every pass and covered them with light troops, which could quickly be supported by parts of Laudon's army. Henrich feared suffering heavy casualties, unless he could keep the Austrians in the dark about his real crossing point. He therefore started a major feint movement.

On 17 July Möllendorf's advance guard began its march to the border, taking an easterly direction and reaching the old mining town of Freiberg the same day. Crossing the border to the south of this city was the preferred way since late Medieval times, even if the Elbe River provided better possibilities for logistics. The first Prussian vanguards under *Generalmajor* Alexander von Knobelsdorff (1723-1799) reached Komotau (Chomutov) on 20 July. However, this was just a feint to delude the Austrians about Heinrich's real intentions. The prince marched the bulk of his army on 18 July, taking a more easterly road, and set up camp at Frauenstein. The Saxon corps covered his left flank. According to Seyfarth, Heinrich was surprised to find Komotau nearly uncovered by troops. Reconnaissance reports informed him, that the major Austrian concentration was at Aussig (Ústí nad labem) and Leitmeritz (Litoměřice). This forced the prince to change his plan, following an older idea of crossing the border in Lusatia.[37] In fact, the Austrians at Aussig only numbered between 12,000 and 15,000 men.[38]

Möllendorf's troops reached Frauenstein on 23 July. The Saxons in the meantime had gone back to Dippoldiswalde, further to the northeast, leading the whole army on a flanking march back to the Elbe, where they established camp again on 23 July to the north of the Müglitzbach. Here, the Saxon army formed their own light battalion of 200 which was also given two light field guns.[39] Four days later the army crossed the river over a newly built pontoon bridge at Zschieren. Heinrich had made up his mind. An invasion of western Bohemia was too dangerous for his army. Crossing the border on the eastern bank of the Elbe brought him closer to the army of his brother and lowered the risk that he might become isolated on the other side. Nevertheless, his ruse had its effect, because the news of Prussian hussars operating near Komotau forced the Austrians to send troops to the western bank of the Elbe.

One battalion, four guns and two howitzers had already crossed the Elbe and, under the command of Knobelsdorff, were ordered to join Podgursky's detachment. The infantry marched to Rathewalde, while the whole cavalry of the army took the road for the castle and town of Stolpen. The castle had been a Saxon fortress until 1764. In the Seven Years War it was occupied by Prussian troops who dismantled part of its fortifications. On the 29th the prince wanted to cross the border, but bad roads slowed the march down. However, the vanguard under *Generalleutnant* Wilhelm Sebastian von Belling (1719-1779), consisting of Prussian hussars, a grenadier battalion and the Saxon light battalion, crossed the border the Same day. The detachment of *Generalmajor* Podgursky, having chased off the Austrian light troops, also neared the border at Dürhennersdorf. Möllendorf, who had covered the army's rearguard at Maxen – those unlucky fields, where the Prussians lost a whole corps in 1759 – also crossed the Elbe on that day.

On the 30 July Heinrich continued his march further east, aiming for Rumburk, a small town right behind the border and close to Dürhennersdorf, where Podgursky's detachment waited. Rumburk was defended by a small rearguard of the Austrian army, which took up a stiff resistance, capturing a captain and 10 troopers of a Saxon chevauxleger regiment. The Austrians finally retreated and, during the next day, the Saxo-Prussian army cautiously crossed the border in three columns: Möllendorf near the Elbe, Podgursky to the east in the direction of Zittau, and the prince with the main forces in between. The mountains in this area were and are difficult terrain to cross. The landscape is strewn with small but steep round hills, separated by small valleys. Apart from the few fields cultivated around the villages, most of the landscape was overgrown by woods. It was an ideal place for ambushes and the Prussians already knew that Austrian light troops were operating in this area.[40]

---

37 Seyfarth, *Unpartheyische Geschichte*, p.450.
38 Reimann, *Geschichte des Bayerischen Erbfolgekrieges*, pp.117-118.
39 Mielsch, 'Die kursächsische Armee im Bayerischen Erbfolgekrieg', p.94.
40 Reimann, *Geschichte des Bayerischen Erbfolgekrieges*, pp.125-127.

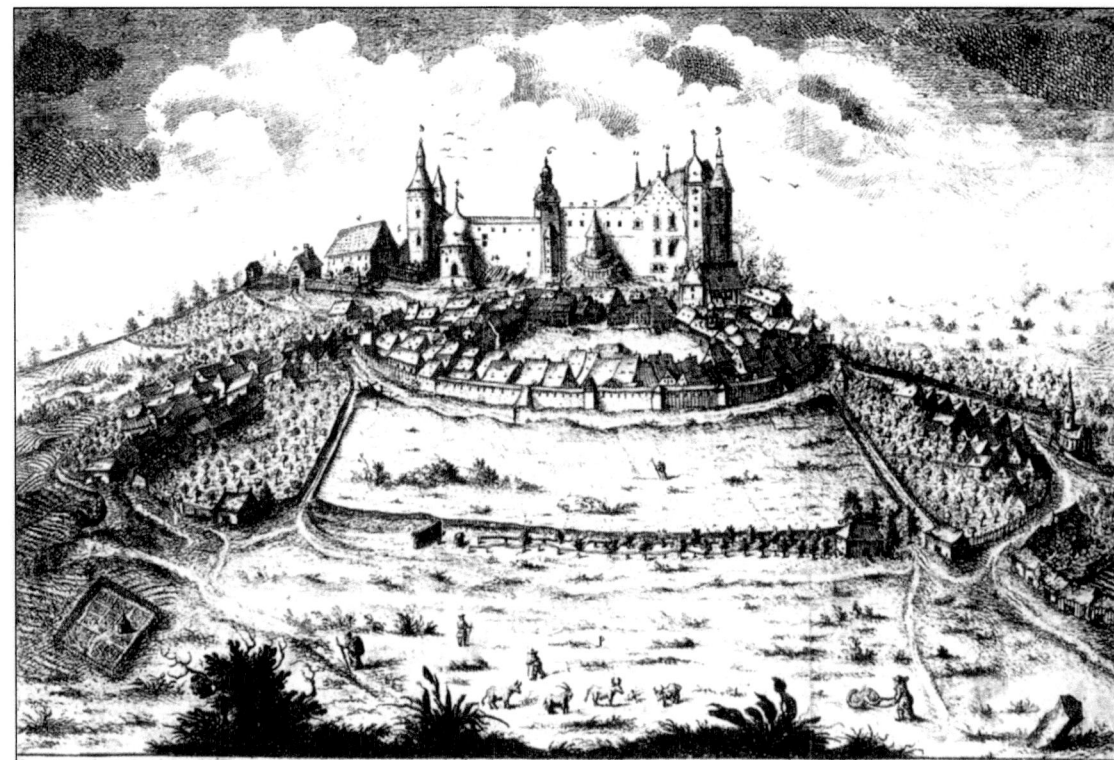

Stolpen castle, about 1750.
(Public Domain)

On 1 August Belling's vanguard met another Austrian detachment made up of four battalions (two each of the regiments Geisrück and Caprara) and a regiment of hussars under *Generalmajor* Joseph Nikolaus de Vins (1732-1789) which came up from Böhmisch Leipa (Česká Lípa). Podgursky had to march in the direction of Zittau, where the Saxon territory formed a small bulge into Bohemia, cross the border behind de Vins and cut him off. However, the passes near Rabenstein had been blocked by the Austrians, so the troops came too late. Only a detachment of 20 hussars under *Oberstleutnant* Carl Ludwig von Knobelsdorff (1724-1786) reached the outskirts of Kromdorf and witnessed Austrian teamsters hurrying back. They belonged to a detachment under Austrian *Oberst* von Bossi, retreating from Tollenstein hill to the southeast, after digging in their guns. In a minor skirmish 20 Prussian hussars chased off double that number of Austrians, capturing half of them. The Prussians now took Groß-Mergthal, a small village to the south of Krompach, and so cut of the Austrians retreat. However, their forces were weak and it would have taken Bossi's infantry little effort to push their way through, before Prussian infantry would have been able to arrive. However, demoralized through the defeat of the day before and fearing encirclement, his men started to disperse.

Generalmajor Joseph Nikolaus de Vins. (Public Domain)

Heinrich ordered Knobelsdorff to march on to Zwickau (Cvivkov) further west, to finish off de Vins, who was blocking Belling further to the north. However, Knobelsdorff had to wait for further reinforcements. In the meantime, Saxon troops under *Generalmajor* Jean Louis LeCoq (1719-1789) had attacked de Vins' infantry and forced them to retire. LeCoq pursued them and captured three guns and 162 prisoners. When Knobelsdorff had assembled 500 hussars he started his march but found Zwickau already occupied by Belling, de Vins having retreated to Gabel (Jablonné v Podještědí) further to the east. Here he met with the corps under *Feldmarschalleutnant* Sámuel Graf Gyulay (1723-1802), numbering 8,000 men. Knobelsdorff and Belling decided to attack these troops the next day and returned to their detachments. It was a rainy night, and the pickets of the Prussian vanguards were constantly disturbed by the flood of Austrian stragglers sneaking back to their ranks protected by the night and the woods. This raised constant alarm, so that Belling had to send out his infantry and ordered it to keep ready.

On the next day Belling and Podgursky together with Saxon light troops under Captain von der Golz continued their advance to Gabel. After a short time, a reconnaissance reported Austrian infantry in front of Knobelsdorff's men, belonging to Bossi's command. The Austrians, who still sought to find their way to Gabel, immediately retreated into nearby woods. The Prussians fired some cannon shot after them but decided to continue their march, while a quarter of Knobelsdorff's were detailed to chase off the Austrians in the woods. As soon as this was done, two Austrian deserters came running for the Prussian column and reported that the woods were full of demoralized Austrian troops who would surrender as soon as the Prussians came close, as they had been without rations for five days. At the same time, Belling, after hearing the cannon shot, also learned of this rabble, attacked the woods with three squadrons of hussars, while Knobelsdorff charged the other end. Contrary to the report of the deserters, the Austrians did not give up without a fight and for about an hour both sides skirmished with each other. At the end of the day the Prussians and Saxons – who had detected some further Austrian stragglers farther north – captured Bossi, 24 officers, 1,500 men, three colours and three guns. When the news of this disaster reached

Guylay, he immediately abandoned Gabel.[41] It was a promising start for the campaign, but in the end, it proved to be its biggest battle. Belling received the Order of the Black Eagle and some of his officers the Pour le Merite, *Hauptmann* Stieglitz of the Saxon light battalion was promoted to *Major* for his brave conduct during the fighting, which was not a real battle, but rather a series of skirmishes between the Saxo-Austrian troops and the dispersed Austrians of de Vins' detachment.

Belling was now redirected to Zittau from where he was to attack Grottau, which, however, was taken by a second detachment under von Knobelsdorff. Prince Heinrich tried to concentrate the majority of his forces there. The prince and his brother corresponded nearly every day, sometimes exchanging more than one letter. Both expressed their respect with regard to the terrain and their fear of ambushes by light troops. However, Heinrich estimated that Laudon, commanding the Isar-Army, would not expect him to take the route via Rumburk and Gabel. Having taken the later he left the most difficult part of the border mountains. While the terrain in front of him was still hilly, it did not provide for the same obstacles.[42]

Friedrich once more gave an exaggerated account of Heinrich's achievements:

> The Imperials were not prepared for this trick: it threw all their plans of defence upside down. In a hurry, Field Marshal Laudon left the position at Aussig and Dux and, what is even more surprising, his fortifications at Leitmeritz together with the magazine there. General Platen quickly used this error. He took Leitmeritz with the magazine and an Austrian pontoon bridge, advanced on Budin to the Eger and pushed his vanguard to Welwarn, which is only three miles from Prague. Terror and dismay spread throughout the city; the high nobility who had gone there fled, and Prague remained desolate for days. After Field Marshal Laudon, as reported, had given up the entire left bank of the Elbe, he only felt safe again in Munich Grätz, near Jung-Bunzlau. As the enemy feared everything for the Emperor's army, which Prince Heinrich could attack if he wished, Laudon occupied with strong detachments the whole course of the Iser, which flows between rocks and swamps. In Upper Silesia, the Prussians had overwhelmed and almost entirely destroyed two Imperial dragoon regiments in their camp at Heidenpiltsch.[43]

The king – in retrospect – claimed the war to be won by this stage. However, while the Prussians had penetrated the border and Heinrich had even achieved a minor success, the Austrian army was neither beaten nor driven out of its main positions, nor was the allegedly panic-stricken Prague taken by the Prussians.

---

41 Wilhelm von Knobelsdorff, *Zur Geschichte der Familie von Knobelsdorff* (Berlin: Unknown Publisher, 1857), Vol.3, pp.151-153; Mielsch, 'Die kursächsische Armee im Bayerischen Erbfolgekrieg', pp.94-95.
42 Reimann, *Geschichte des Bayerischen Erbfolgekrieges*, pp.140-141.
43 Volz (ed.), *Die Werke Friedrichs des Großen*, Vol.5, p.109.

THE WAR OF THE BAVARIAN SUCCESSION 1778-1789

Alexander Friedrich von Knobelsdorff, shown in later life as a *Feldmarschall*. (Public Domain)

On 16th July a man reached the king's headquarters at Wölsdorf, claiming to be the secretary of the Russian envoy at Vienna Prince Dmitri Michailowitsch Galizin (1721-1793). In reality he was the Austrian diplomat Johann Amadeus Franz von Thugut (1736-1818), an experienced man who for a long time had served as Austrian internuncio (envoy) at Constantinople, winning the Bukovina for Austria in the Treaty of Küçük Kaynarca that ended the Russo-Turkish War of 1768–1774, even though Austria was not even involved in this conflict. His mission to Friedrich was unofficial. Thugut was not sent by Joseph II, but by the Empress Maria Theresia. 'He delivered a letter from the Empress-Queen to the King', wrote Friedrich in his history of the war:

> We only reproduce its content. The Empress expressed her sorrow at the discord and confusion that had arisen, her concern for the person of the Emperor, the desire to find a middle ground towards mutual reconciliation, and asked the king to discuss these various points. Thereupon Thugut spoke up and said to the king that an understanding would be easy if one dealt honestly with one another. The intention of the Austrians was to bribe the king with favourable offers to refrain from supporting the Elector Palatine. To this end, Thugut assured that his court would not only not oppose the possible succession of the king in the margraviates of Ansbach and Bayreuth, but would also offer Prussia his assistance in exchanging these margraviates for border lands of Brandenburg, such as Lusatia or Mecklenburg, if he believes that this is to his advantage.[44]

Friedrich replied by pointing out that he had a legal and undeniable right of succession in Ansbach and Bayreuth, unlike Austria in Bavaria. He also rejected the idea that actions taken for the benefit of Austria were the same as in the interest of the Empire. Austria should relinquish a part of Bavaria. In his history of the war he also wrote that he demanded that 'precautions must be taken to prevent future acts of such violent despotism from shaking the peace and the foundations of the German Empire'.[45] What he wanted to suggest to Thugut by these words he does not explain, but he probably gives a hint that his later idea of a *Fürstenbund*, or league of princes, found its roots at this time. To demonstrate his peaceful intentions to Maria Theresia, Friedrich offered a treaty. The Empress should return Bavaria to Carl Theodor with the exception of Burghausen, the Bavarian Salines (salt mines), and a part of the Upper Palatinate. The Danube should be free for shipping and the blockade of Ratisborn lifted. The succession of the Wittelsbachs should be guaranteed, Saxony paid off, and the rights of all Habsburg fiefdoms within Saxony yielded. The Duke of Mecklenburg, who also had a small claim on the Bavarian inheritance, should be compensated with a vacant Imperial fief. Prussia's succession in Ansbach and Bayreuth would not be challenged by Vienna, and Russia and France would act as guarantee powers. These articles were immediately written down.

---

44   Volz (ed.), *Die Werke Friedrichs des Großen*, Vol.5, pp.110.
45   Volz (ed.), *Die Werke Friedrichs des Großen*, Vol.5, pp.110.

Thugut offered to be secretary, but the king, not trusting either his style or his intentions, wrote them himself. Surely the Empress-Queen would have gained much by accepting it. The Russian court had not yet explained [their intentions]; France advised Austria to make peace; but his advice made little impression on the fiery, impetuous character of the young Emperor and the imperious Prince Kaunitz.[46]

While Friedrich negotiated, the campaign of his brother also slowed down. Gideon Ernst Baron von Laudon (1717-1790) was probably Austria's best field commander. However, his career was a path of trial and tribulation. While he claimed to have had Scottish ancestors, the roots of his family in Livonia date back to the fifteenth century. At the age of 15 he entered Russian service in 1732, fought in the War of the Polish Succession and took part in the siege of Gdansk in 1732. After fighting in the Russo-Turkish War of 1736-1739 he left the Russian army in anger and went to Berlin to offer his services to Friedrich II, who briskly declined. In 1742 he joined the Austrian army as a captain of Franz Baron von der Trenck's (1711-1749) famous Pandurs. Service with the Grenzer gave him vital experience but did not offer many possibilities for promotion as officers of the light Balkan troops were generally despised as substandard. Conversion to Catholicism did not help him. However, successful activities of the light troops under his command finally led to rapid promotions during the Seven Years War. In 1758 he became *Generalmajor* and led the successful raids against a Prussian supply train at Domstadtl which forced a frustrated Friedrich II to abandon his siege of Olmütz – his last major incursion into Bohemia until 1778. For this achievement Laudon was promoted to *Feldmarschalleutnant*, but while his reputation was growing, he was never able to get rid of the mark of a 'Croat Officer'. While Laudon won his laurels in the field, his rivalry with Lacy – the staff officer – rose, especially as criticism of *Feldmarschall* Daun's cautious operations grew and there were rumours that he might be replaced. Laudon added further laurels at Hochkirch in 1758, where he won the Cross of Maria Theresia, and especially one year later, when he commanded the combined Austro-Russian army that gave Friedrich his most severe thrashing at Kunersdorf. In 1760 he forced a Prussian corps under *General der Infanterie* Heinrich August de la Motte Fouqué to surrender at Landeshut, but was later beaten by Friedrich at Liegnitz, a defeat he blamed on Daun and especially on Lacy, who he now recognized as an enemy. In 1761 he commanded his own army in Silesia, where he was able to take Schweidnitz (Świdnica) but not to force Friedrich out of his entrenched camp at Bunzelwitz (Bolesławice). In the following year his enemies won the upper hand at court and Laudon did not receive a new command. However, in 1766 he became a member of the *Hofkriegsrat*, in 1769 general commander in Moravia and in 1778 *Feldmarschall*.[47]

---

46 Volz (ed.), *Die Werke Friedrichs des Großen*, Vol.5, p.110.
47 Franz Persendorfer, *Feldmarschall Loudon. Der Sieg und sein Preis* (Vienna: ÖBV 1989). This is one of the few biographies available. However, Pesendorfer's book is written for the popular market and not without its flaws.

Laudon really was wrong-footed by Heinrich's surprising invasion as it did not follow the usual routes taken by the Prussians so far, who in their former campaign had either crossed to the south of Freiburg just as Heinrich had threatened, close to the Elbe, or further southeast over the Silesian border. Taking Gabel put Heinrich on Laudon's flank and further undermined the Emperor's confidence in him. In letters to his mother, Joseph argued that Laudon even lacked the support of the majority of his generals. It seems that he was on the brink of relieving him of his command.[48]

Two protected camps were now in front of Heinrich's army: Münchengrätz (Mnichovo Hradiště) and Turnau (Tornov). The Prussian prince carefully deployed his forces: advanced parties on his right flank extending it as far as the Elbe, while on the left under Podgursky and Knobelsdorff occupied Reichenberg (Liberec) to cover the army from an attack by the Austrians in Turnau. The two generals occupied the country between the city and the nearby impassable Isargebirge and covered it with abatis and by flooding some of the defiles. The Prussians carefully put some advance guards to the south of Reichenberg to take possession of a tactically important hill and then rested for a couple of weeks. But the great attack against the Austrian flank, for which Friedrich had hoped for so long, did not occur.[49]

In the meantime, the right flank of Prince Heinrich's army was covered by a corps under *Generalleutnant* von Platen which still stood on the northern side of the border, covering Saxony around Pirna. On 28 July Saxon pickets near Langenhennersdorf – in sight of the fortress of Königstein – were attacked and pushed back by Austrian light troops. In another skirmish further west, the Austrian were repulsed at Häßlich, close to the old battlefield of Maxen. On 30 July another Austrian force of approximately 500 men attacked a Saxon company of 100 men of the regiment Prinz Maximilian at Berggießhübel. The Saxons retreated fighting without taking any casualties. On 8 August von Platen finally marched his troops south, crossing the border at Nollendorf. His vanguard occupied Leitmeritz on the 11th while his main force bypassed Teplitz (Teplice) and rested on the old battlefield of Lobositz on the 14th. Here Platen established a camp. He sent out his light troops to requisition food from the countryside and remove redoubts and river obstacles at the Elbe so that this river could be opened as a line of communication. On 10 September the Saxon infantry regiment Le Coq was sent to Aussig to cover a pontoon bridge which enabled the army to cross the Elbe.

Operations in August

In early August, Thugut returned to Friedrich's camp. His offer for peace was also made known to Joseph and the Prussian king, who always claimed to have distrusted Thugut, suspected the answer was being dictated by the young Emperor and Kaunitz, not Maria Theresia:

---

48 Reimann, *Geschichte des Bayerischen Erbfolgekrieges*, pp.138-140.
49 Reimann, *Geschichte des Bayerischen Erbfolgekrieges*, pp.129-131.

Thugut travelled to Vienna with this document and then returned with a heap of insidious proposals that Prince Kaunitz had provided him with (August 10). Besides, he [Friedrich] did not like dealing with a man of Thugut's stamp. As a result, he sent him to Braunau, where he could confess his guile to his ministers, Count Finckenstein and Hertzberg. They sent him back to Vienna after a few days without having achieved anything (August 15). The whole content of these negotiations was communicated to the ministers in France and Russia, in order that they might be convinced of the unselfish attitude of Prussia and not be misled by the misrepresentation which the ministers of Vienna would give them.

The Empress Queen honestly desired peace. She knew the martial ambitions of her son, the Emperor, and feared the loss or weakening of her authority. But her minister, Prince Kaunitz, was of little help to her. With the instinct of a courtier, he preferred to associate himself with the Emperor, whose youth opened up brighter prospects for his family than with the aging Empress, from whom he could no longer expect any favours. After all, it is the fate of all human affairs that small interests decide the biggest questions![50]

In fact, the secret negotiations between the Empress and the Prussian king put a further strain on Maria Theresia's relationship with Joseph which already was out of balance due to the war. An infuriated Joseph threatened to leave Vienna and permanently settle at Aachen – a move which in fact would have seriously weakened his position as Emperor, as he would not have been more than a high-ranking guest of that city. The Wittelsbach Emperor Charles VII had had a similar experience in Frankfurt after being chased out of Munich by the Austrians in 1744. Maria Theresia called for the Grand Duke of Tuscany, Leopold, her second-born son, and sent him to Bohemia to cool down the mood of his brother. 'The success of this meeting was a rupture between the two brothers who had hitherto lived on the best of terms', wrote Friedrich later on. He followed this with another very polemical and sententious explanation of Joseph's character which totally ignored Friedrich's own former conduct as a king and conqueror of Silesia:

> The young Emperor's enthusiasm for war came from the wrong notions he had formed of fame. He thought it was enough to make noise in the world, seize provinces, extend his dominion, and command armies to gain fame. He did not feel the value of justice, equity and prudence. It is so necessary that the rulers have clear concepts of everything! Equally wrong were his military views. He thought that the mere presence of the Emperor in the army was enough for it to reap rich laurels. Experience had not yet been able to teach him how much work and trouble it takes to pluck even a small laurel leaf. He had often heard it said that a general had to be on the alert, and so he saw it as his duty to ride constantly through his camp from right to left wing, never leaving the entrenchments, even when there was skirmish or forage under his cannon.[51]

---

50   Volz (ed.), *Die Werke Friedrichs des Großen*, Vol.5, pp.111.
51   Volz (ed.), *Die Werke Friedrichs des Großen*, Vol.5, pp.111-112.

At least this last comment could not be denied. Joseph, who prepared this campaign in the hope of presenting himself as the legal successor to the warrior-king Friedrich, was unable to stand the stress of responsibility inherent in command of such a large army. When Heinrich's army passed Gabel and Platen's command took Leitmeritz, Joseph considered abandoning north-eastern Bohemia.[52]

While in the end there was no real need for the Austrians to leave their defensive positions, and it was even political advantageous not to invade Silesia or Saxony – a move which could have changed the opinions of Paris and Petersburg irretrievably in favour of the Saxo-Prussian coalition, the campaign so far offered no real possibility for the Emperor to distinguish himself and a significant part of the Austrian officer corps was dissatisfied that the huge and well-drilled army was not used to better effect.

In the meantime, the small war raged on a daily basis. On 6 August the Austrian hussar regiment Wurmser destroyed a Prussian supply train of 240 wagons on its way to Náchod. The Austrians claimed to have burned all the wagons. The Prussian reports mention the attack, but give no number of the wagons destroyed. If the Austrian reports are correct, this was probably one of the more important skirmishes of the month.

After the final breakdown of the negotiations, Friedrich once more tried to find a way to outflank the Austrians and probably make contact with his brother's forces. Again, it is quite astonishing that the king had no idea about how far the Austrian defensive line extended upwards of the Elbe River, towards the border. To find out he had to send another reconnaissance in force party under the Prince of Anhalt. His vanguards found the heights behind Hohenelbe (Vrchlabí), a town at the foot of the Riesengebirge, covered by only two Austrian battalions. After receiving this intelligence, Friedrich was optimistic about forcing a crossing of the Elbe – which was not very wide there – and pushing the small Austrian force back. This would enable him to unite his forces with those of Prince Heinrich and force the Austrians out of their fortified positions, as he would now outflank them. Heinrich, however, appeared more and more unsuited for his command. In the letters to his brother, he complained about the physical stress of campaigning. He also said he could trust none of his generals, except for Möllendorf, and felt forced to undertake every important reconnaissance himself, adding further stress to his weakened condition.[53]

However, the Prussian troops in the meantime suffered serious problems due to bad logistics and sickness. The late summer of 1778 was wet and cold and the fact that the army remained immobile in the same camp for a lengthy period did not help to improve the good health of the soldiers. Sickness did not spare general officers and so, for example, Knobelsdorff had to ask to be relieved and go for Zittau on 2 September. Most of the Saxon regiments were reduced by half.[54] The critical situation was described by Saxon general Bennigsen in a letter to minister von Stutterheim:

---

52   Reimann, *Geschichte des Bayerischen Erbfolgekrieges*, pp.149-151.
53   Reimann, *Geschichte des Bayerischen Erbfolgekrieges*, pp.152-153.
54   Mielsch, 'Die kursächsische Armee im Bayerischen Erbfolgekrieg', p.96.

> If we not leave our positions for other reasons than those of the plan of operations, we will be forced to do so soon for a lack of forage. It is not to be seen, how we could maintain ourselves in Bohemia without winning a major battle. The enemy probably will not leave his position, if he is not forced through action to do so, and it seems that the operations in this campaign are arrested by peace negotiations or other unknown reasons and that one will not undertake much, so it will be impossible to stay in Bohemia during the winter, but it seems very probably that we will take our winter quarters in Saxony.[55]

Immobility further troubled the armies as they were only able to feed themselves from the countryside for a short time. Both Prussian armies in 1778 were considerably larger than those operating there in the three Silesian Wars when they faced similar problems. The countryside was thinly populated so the logistical apparatus was forced to cover growing distances between the army camps and magazines or areas from where it was possible to obtain food. From a logistical point of view, it appeared to be a mistake that the Prussians did not take the Bohemian cities on the Elbe directly behind the border, Aussig and Tetschen (Decín), and so open the river as a line of supply. Saxony had collected 11 barges and smaller boats in May 1778, together with a crew of 49 men.[56] Depending on its size, a barge was able to transport the equivalent of between 30 and 60 wagonloads and that with much more speed than the teamsters who had to pass terrain, of which Prince Heinrich after the skirmish of Krompach said that it had 'not yet been entered by a wagoner much less an army'.[57]

Poor logistics and a lack of supplies also hampered Friedrich's plan to outflank the Austrian positions through Hohenelbe:

> Beautiful as this plan was, its execution presented great difficulties. Firstly, the Elbe could only be reached through ravines and defiles, and a great deal of artillery had to be carried along these paths, which was extremely difficult. The second was provisioning the army. If you crossed the Elbe, you could only take bread up to 5 miles from the river; another transport would have been forbidden due to the lack of horses.[58]

On 26 August Friedrich decided to attack the Austrian positions at Hohenelbe, defended by *Feldzeugmeister* Josip Siskovics (1719-1783). Siskovics was a very experienced commander, veteran of many battles of both the War of the Austrian Succession and the Seven Years War and the first Habsburg officer of Croat origins awarded the Military Order of Maria Theresia.

In his history of the war Friedrich claimed that he distrusted the intentions of his brother, alleging that he was too cautious and that this in turn forced

---

55 SächsHStA Dresden 10026/01099/12 Briefe und Berichte des Generallieutenants von Bennigsen an den Kabinettsminister von Stutterheim, without fol.
56 SächsHStA Dresden 11338/11004/15 Ausfertigungen das Commando des mobilen Corps betreffend, without fol. However, these boats were apparently used for a single transport only.
57 Schuster and Francke, *Sächsische Armee*, p.177.
58 Volz (ed.), *Die Werke Friedrichs des Großen*, Vol.5, pp.112.

him to keep his plans more secret – an illogical solution, because how should a general considered cautious be moved to act, if he was not clear about the intentions of a movement? According to Friedrich's history, it was difficult to persuade Heinrich to advance:

> He resented any hearty pounding, and his health was rather poor. All these obstacles, which the king realized, led him to play it safe and to keep his plan secret without abandoning it. So he did not want to break up his camp near Wölsdorf before the whole area from the Elbe to the Silesian border had been purely foraged, especially since the Austrians had forced the inhabitants to flee across the Elbe with all their cattle. In this way he made it at least impossible for the Austrians to keep any significant force on his frontiers and to disturb his troops in their quarters during the winter.[59]

The whole argument seems a little confused. However, on 15 August Friedrich started to shift the bulk of his army to the northwest, unmolested by the Austrians, who appeared unmovable. Friedrich moved one Prussian corps under the Crown Prince Carl Wilhelm Ferdinand of Brunswick to the heights of Dreihäuser (Třídomí) and a second one commanded by his nephew and legal successor Prince Friedrich Wilhelm to nearby Pilnikau, while the king himself marched with 40 battalions to the village of Leopold (Rudník). From these dispositions the Prussians advanced carefully westward. Prince Friedrich Wilhelm was to feint a crossing of the Elbe close to Hohenelbe, while the bulk of the army would cross further to the north, ever deeper into the Riesengebirge. However, the Prussians faced enormous difficulties to move their supply wagons, and especially the heavy guns, through the rocky roads, needing three days for three miles from Trautenau to Hermannseifen (Rudník v Krkonoších).

'The guns, with their wide gauge, could not get through the narrow rocky paths. They were eagerly awaited, but did not arrive',[60] wrote Friedrich in his history of the war and this was not just a mere excuse for his failure, as he also wrote in a letter to Prince Heinrich of the 28th August that he was unable to speed his march because of his problems with the artillery. In the meantime, the Austrians extended their fortifications. The Prussians waited. The weather turned cold and wet again. The Austrians prepared for battle, but once more Friedrich hesitated in the face of the formidable Austrian preparations:

> The loss of this precious time, wasted in fruitless efforts, was so advantageous to the Austrians that they were able to deploy their whole army and guns on the mountains beyond Hohenelbe. With that the whole plan became obsolete; for anything dared against a feeble corps becomes foolhardy when attempted against a numerous army, especially when it is in an almost impregnable position. Howitzers, the only type of gun that can be used against an enemy high position, were needed to throw back this force, and the howitzers were not

---

59   Volz (ed.), *Die Werke Friedrichs des Großen*, Vol.5, pp.112-113.
60   Volz (ed.), *Die Werke Friedrichs des Großen*, Vol.5, p.114.

there. Furthermore, one had to cross the Elbe by bridges and march in front of a broad front which would have destroyed the troops before they could form battle formation. In addition, Siskovich's corps had to be driven off the slopes of the Karkonosze mountains beforehand, otherwise it would have fallen on the attackers' flanks. It stood on Mount Wachura; his expulsion was therefore a prerequisite. Prince Heinrich also had to take part in the operation by giving any sign of life in the rear of the imperial army and advancing against the nearby Iser; but he would not make up his mind.[61]

This later charge is also reflected in the correspondence between the king and his brother in these days, where the king accused his brother of crushing his plans and being idle. But even if one recognizes the frustration and the oddly cautious attitude of the king himself, one wonder that he entrusted the command of his second major army at the theatre to a man, whom he blamed, at the time and later on, for failing to carry out his orders. Friedrich's history in many ways is a plea of self-defence in which he distributes blame to everybody else with hindsight, but the tone of the letters he wrote to his brother during these days was often much harsher than the downright muted – but not hidden – critique offered in that work.[62]

Friedrich then gives his readers an idea about his intentions, had the crossing succeeded:

> If all the obstacles had not materialized, the plan, as I said, was to drive Siskovich out of his position, then position 45 heavy howitzers behind Hohenelbe and from there bombard the part of the enemy army that was opposite our right. The intention was then to cross the Elbe by a ford which had been discovered near a monastery, and after forcing the enemy to leave his position, to position himself between Branna and Starkenbach, on the flank of the troops encamped at Neuschloss. But then the Austrians had only a choice: to rush there to attack the Prussians in a good position, which, however, took time, or to leave the whole process to our victorious troops.[63]

However, even this seems to be very doubtful. The Austrians – whom Friedrich correctly faulted for failing to use his flank march to attack his weak rearguard at Mölsdorf with their main army – would never have attacked the Prussians in a strong position. And even if the crossing of the Elbe line offered a certain advantage to the Prussians, this did not put the Austrian positions in jeopardy, as the hilly countryside to the south would have offered the Austrians sufficient possibilities to establish another line of defence.

On 25 August a major skirmish took place, when Wurmser attacked a Prussian rearguard of five battalions, three cuirassier and two dragoon regiments near Burkersdorf. Wurmser attacked them with two hussar regiments in the front and with a third one at the left flank, while the Austrian

---

61 Volz (ed.), *Die Werke Friedrichs des Großen*, Vol.5, p.114.
62 Schöning, *Der Bayerische Erbfolgekrieg*, pp.172-174.
63 Volz (ed.), *Die Werke Friedrichs des Großen*, Vol.5, p.114.

infantry was marching up. The cavalry of both sides exchanged carbine fire, according to Seyfarth 'so lively, that it was like infantry fire'.[64] Wurmser brought up some guns and forced the Prussians to retreat. This enabled him to attack their right flank. The Austrian gunners fired canister at the Prussian cavalry and also drove them back. Then they pursued their beaten foes to Trautenau, where they found a fortified Prussian camp at the Galgenberg. Here they also found superior Prussian forces, so Wurmser decided to withdraw. It was the last clash between the two armies in this month.

Operations During September

Lack of rations and unsanitary living conditions in cold, wet weather created a deadly mix and soon the hospitals were filled with sick. Prince Heinrich tried to spread his troops farther to the rear, but this was of little help by now. He also extended his left flank by pushing a mixed Saxo-Prussian detachment to Märzdorf (Martinice). He now enveloped the Austrian camp in Turnau from the north and east. If Heinrich hoped to trick the Austrians out of Turnau he was disappointed. At the beginning of September, they increased their forces there, now in turn threatening to cut of the troops in Märzdorf with a bold march. On 10 September Heinrich therefore decided to break up the camp there and had the detachment turn back to Gabel.[65]

At the same time the prince had also shifted a part of his army to his right, marching it closer to the Elbe River at Leitmeritz. Here he passed the Elbe on 12 September, while Möllendorf took over command of the troops remaining on the eastern bank. The rainy weather had turned the roads into a quagmire, slowing down the march of men and wagons. At Wernstädt 400 Prussian wagons were blocked by bad roads. Heinrich sent back Belling with some hussars, who was able to save all but 80. Those with horses that were too weak, or with axels broken, had to be burned.[66] The Austrian magazine, which the Prussians had captured at Leitmeritz, was evacuated by boat to Dresden. On the other hand, the Austrians later found more than 1,000 howitzer shells, 3,800 rounds of canister and 100 destroyed powder wagons on the road to Leitmeritz. All the munitions were collected and brought to the Arsenal in Prague.[67]

With his extended lines the army of Prince Heinrich was inviting attack, but Laudon stood inactive at his camps. Apart from a detachment covering the border close to Zittau, now under the command of the Prince of Anhalt-Bernburg, the Prince until 14 September moved his whole army over the river, establishing a camp at Tschischkowitz (Čížkovice). From here he at least was able to better supply his troops, either by the Elbe or by foraging in Western Bohemia, which was nearly unprotected by troops. Already on the 14th a Saxon detachment under *Generalmajor* Christian Wilibald von Goldacker

---

64 Seyfarth, *Unpartheyische Geschichte*, p.241.
65 Reimann, *Geschichte des Bayerischen Erbfolgekrieges*, pp.160-161.
66 Seyfarth, *Unpartheyische Geschichte*, pp.543-545.
67 Seidel, *Versuch einer militärischen Geschichte*, Vol.II, pp.181-182.

(1721-1801) raided the country as far west as the town of Eger (Cheb). He had some minor skirmishes with enemy light troops but accomplished his mission. Another raiding party under the Prussian *Generalmajor* Johann Ludwig von Grünberg (1726-1799) was sent out on the 19th.

At the end of September, however, the Austrians started to concentrate an increasing number of their light troops on the western bank of the Elbe which moved their way around Prince Heinrich's flank and threatened his lines of communications, moving close to the Saxon cities Annaberg and Marienberg. They even tried to capture the former but were repulsed. Heinrich now feared for his flank and on 20 September decided to terminate the campaign and leave Bohemia. The army crossed the border, harassed by Austrian light troops which on 24 September attacked the baggage train of a Saxon column under *Generalmajor* Ernst Friedrich von Carlsburg (1711-1786), capturing his personal baggage and seven other wagons. While crossing the border, the Saxon corps was reinforced with the newly created Jägercorps.

The corps of the Prince of Anhalt-Bernburg at Gabel also retreated behind the border and the Prince took command over the Saxon troops from the sick Graf von Solms.[68] This corps was made up of eight Prussian and 12 Saxon infantry regiments, plus four Saxon cavalry regiment and two regiments of Saxon chevauxlegers. On 11 September it covered the mountain passes near Oybin and then marched back in three columns and established a fortified camp around Eckartsberg near Zittau. The city itself was put in a state of defence in case of a second Austrian attack. The Austrians pushed forward some of their light troops but did not cross the border.[69]

The western part of the Saxo-Bohemian border was only slightly protected by the Saxon dragoon regiment of von Sacken. With the other side of the border free of Prussian troops, Austrian light troops started to raid Saxon cities in the Erzgebirge. The freikorps of generals Sauer and Otto harassed the settlements close to the border, burning villages, taking hostages and collecting contributions. The Saxon dragoons were unable to prevent these actions as their widely dispersed pickets were too weak. The regiment assembled at Chemnitz, where it was supported by a regiment of infantry coming down from Dresden.

Friedrich also abandoned any idea of staying in Bohemia after his failed crossing of the Elbe. He ransacked the countryside and prepared for winter quarters. In his history of the war the king, who never hesitated to suck an occupied territory dry, gave another cynical comment about the behaviour of the Austrians: 'As usual, there was foraging, always on the banks of the Elbe and under the enemy cannon, without the Emperor and his troops doing the slightest thing, indeed without a man daring to cross the Elbe to prevent the unfortunate peasants from falling under their noses the forage was taken away.'[70] In fact just a few sentences later Friedrich described how his troops on their march back to Silesia were attacked by a few Austrian

---

68   Mielsch, 'Die kursächsische Armee im Bayerischen Erbfolgekrieg', p.100.
69   Reimann, *Geschichte des Bayerischen Erbfolgekrieges*, pp.161-163, 166-168.
70   Volz (ed.), *Die Werke Friedrichs des Großen*, Vol.5, pp.114.

Pandurs. A bigger party under Wurmser followed the column of Ferdinand of Brunswick, but the prince decided to turn about and face the enemy who quickly retreated.[71]

The Prussians established a series of small camps at the foot of the Riesengebirge, protecting the retreat of their artillery. Wurmser tried to attack Brunswick in his position but was repeatedly beaten off with ease. 'His conduct', Friedrich wrote of Brunswick, 'would have been a credit to any other officer who would have done the same'.[72]

In the third week of September Friedrich's army crossed the mountains back into Silesia. On the 21st Wurmser unsuccessfully tried to attack the Prussian rearguard, after his light troops had won a minor skirmish the day before. However, he advanced while a Prussian brigade still covered a height close to the camp and was easily able to beat the Austrians off. At the end of September, the Prussians were back in Silesia and Brunswick took over command. Friedrich was well aware that there was still a good month for campaigning left and in his history of the war he claimed that he expected the Austrians to conduct a winter campaign into Silesia:

> The campaign had come to a rapid conclusion. It was only the end of September and the season for military operations was by no means over. One had to assume, therefore, that the enemy would not let it go at that, but that after the strict defensive which he had observed during the campaign he was still up to something and was probably even planning a winter campaign. Two main points of attack came into consideration for an Austrian invasion, firstly a powerful attack against the Hereditary Prince and secondly an advance through the Lusatian Passes. The fact that at the head of the armies stood a young, ambitious Emperor, anxious to distinguish himself by some brilliant blow, seemed to justify the plans which were expected of him, and in any case required careful consideration. The enemy's possible plans against Upper Silesia seemed the easiest to carry out. He had large magazines in Olmütz and could easily transport his provisions. In addition, he only had to drive the Prussians out of Troppau to force them to leave the Oppa and retreat to Kosel and Neisse. It was more difficult to penetrate Lusatia. There stood 20,000 men under the Prince of Bernburg; the Imperials had no magazines near Lusatia; In the area of Schluckenau, Gabel, Rumburg and Friedland food was scarce, so that it would have been difficult for the enemy to store up enough supplies to feed a larger force. After all, since he had all the vehicles in Bohemia at his disposal, he was able to set up warehouses in that area with the present and at great expense in order to prepare for an invasion, which, however, would have had great difficulties because of the fortified position on the Eckartsberge.[73]

However, this subsequent comment demonstrated once more that Friedrich had lost his capability to read the intentions of his enemies, a major quality of a good general and one that so often distinguished him in his former three encounters with the Austrians. Now it seems that he not only misinterpreted

---

71 Reimann, *Geschichte des Bayerischen Erbfolgekrieges*, pp.158-160.
72 Volz (ed.), *Die Werke Friedrichs des Großen*, Vol.5 pp.116.
73 Volz (ed.), *Die Werke Friedrichs des Großen*, Vol.5, pp.117.

Joseph's character, which might be excusable as the young Emperor presented himself to Friedrich in the way described by him when they met before the war, but that he was unable to adopt his opinion on the basis of the experiences he had made in the late campaign.

In October, Friedrich moved a considerable part of his army into Upper Silesia. The small war of raiding and counter raiding in the Riesengebirge continued, with neither Wurmser nor Wunsch being idle. Wurmser tried to attack isolated Prussian regiments or battalions in their quarters. On 7 November he surprised the Fusilier Regiment von Thadden, killing its colonel during the fighting, and on 20 November the Austrians attacked the Grenadier Battalion von Hausen, which repulsed the attack.

Upper Silesia

A sideshow to these operations was Upper Silesia, guarded by weak Prussian forces under *Generalleutnant* Johann Paul von Werner (1707-1785), a veteran hussar officer. At the beginning of July both sides started raids across the border. The Prussians took Weidenau (Vidnava), the Austrians Leobschütz (Głubczyce), demanding money and hostages. On 15 July Prussian hussars entered Hotzenplotz (Osoblaha), where they took 1,500 thalers. At the end of the month, 400 Prussian light horse raided Zuckmantel (Zlaté Hory), taking a contribution, and skirmished with Austrian troops.[74]

In the meantime, Werner received reinforcements under *Generalleutnant* von Stutterheim. The united forces marched to Lobenstein (Úvalno) from where detachments were sent into the surrounding countryside and captured Hungarian wine worth 100,000 guilders. Then they marched to Troppau (Opava), where they were faced by an Austrian corps under *Feldmarschalleutnant* von Botta. However, on 11 August the Prussians were able to surprise and destroy an Austrian advance guard of two dragoon regiments (Württemberg and Modena) and some infantry near Glomnitz (Hlavnice). Another attempted attack on Botta's camp four days later remained inconclusive. However, the Prussians raided deep into Moravia, took 1,800 guilders as contribution from Jägerndorf (Krnov), while Troppau had to supply 6,000 bushels of grain, 2,500 bushels of oats, 1,600 bushels flour in barrels, 13,648 hundredweight of hay, and 480 three-scores of straw.[75]

This forced Joseph to send further reinforcements to Botta. In early October, however, Friedrich shifted 16 battalions and 15 squadrons into Upper Silesia to prepare an attack into Moravia. He also feared that the Austrians, who held Jägerndorf at the border, might attack Kosel or Neiße. The king was able to drive the enemy out of this village, which was soon fortified, as was Troppau farther north. Both fortified camps could be used as a starting point for a new offensive in the spring.[76]

---

74 Seidel, *Versuch einer militärischen Geschichte*, Vol.III, pp.3-4.
75 Seidel, *Versuch einer militärischen Geschichte*, Vol.III, pp.10-16.
76 Reimann, *Geschichte des Bayerischen Erbfolgekrieges*, pp.185-187.

With both armies shifting more troops into this region, the number of daily skirmishes increased considerably. Most of these encounters were fought by cavalry parties. On 25 November a major skirmish occurred, when four Austrian battalions (two of Regiment Migazzi, one each of the Regiments Anton Colloredo and Khevenhüller) under the command of *Generalmajor* Carl Conrad Baron von Stein reconnoitred the Prussian field fortifications at Jägerndorf. Stein's force was soon detected. The Prussians deployed three battalions and six squadrons in the nearby village of Comeise, with more troops staying at Jägerndorf. Covered by some woods and the hilly terrain, the Austrians were able to hide their weak numbers and to attack a Prussian redoubt. Their artillery set fire to the village of Weißkirch (Kostelec). A Prussian battalion of the Regiment von Thüna (previously Renzel), which was quartered there, moved against the heights, where the Austrians had placed their artillery, while von Stutterheim moved his troops out of Jägerndorf. The following skirmish was quite confused, according to the reports. The Austrians claimed to have repulsed several Prussian attacks. The Prussians claimed that the battalion of Regiment von Thüna was attacked by the Austrian infantry, but stood firm and in turn was able to storm the height, where the Austrian guns were placed. Here it was once more attacked by the Austrians, but Stutterheim now moved three of his battalions against his enemy's flank and totally routed the Austrians. The Austrians reported the loss of 200 dead and wounded, the Prussians said that they made 70 prisoners and found an additional 350 men on the battlefield, giving their own losses as 144 dead and 205 wounded.[77] As the weather soon turned cold, it was the last major action in this theatre in 1778. The Prussians still sent out raiding parties, which, apart from money and supplies, also demanded linen for making new shirts.

The Prussian campaign of 1778 in fact was a major failure. Nowhere had the Prussian been able to force the Austrians to a major battle and all the raiding, while doing serious harm to the local population, remained inconclusive for the war as a whole. A Prussian report of that time placed the blame on bad maps and insufficient knowledge of the terrain:

> We made war in a country, which was made for chicanery. The enemy knew every mountain there, if scalable or unscalable, or possible to bypass, each rock, bluff, ravine or valley and everything they did not know was shown to them by every peasant, who at the same time was a spy. We did not get knowledge of the terrain by the best maps, but through tedious investigation and inspection of it. Every peasant betrayed us, when we wanted to do something during the day. They hide in the woods and report to the enemy.[78]

The low intensity of operations was also reflected in the low numbers of prisoners. Just about 1,400 men were reported as being transported through Saxony to Prussia. These were only those taken by Prince Heinrich's army,

---

77　Seyfarth, *Unpartheyische Geschichte*, pp.390-404; Seidel, *Versuch einer militärischen Geschichte*, Vol.III, pp.69-71.
78　Seyfarth, *Unpartheyische Geschichte*, p.620.

THE WAR OF THE BAVARIAN SUCCESSION 1778-1789

A wounded Prussian hussar mourns his dying horse, c.1776. (Anne S.K. Brown Collection)

but still this number is low.[79] All parties of war signed a convention on 28 December, agreeing to exchange all the hostages taken, no matter if their villages and towns had paid their ransoms. Outstanding sums were nullified.

Regarding the treatment of military prisoners Prussia and Austria agreed to continue conventions signed in 1741 and 1756, which obliged both to take care of prisoners. However, all costs for feeding and clothing the men had to be taken over by the original employer after exchange. All prisoners taken so far were to be exchanged in February, but contrary to the previous conventions mentioned, later exchanges would happen on an annual instead of a monthly basis. According to a new convention a field marshal was worth 3,000 prisoners or 15,000 thalers, a general 2,000 and 1,000 respectively, a colonel 130 prisoners or 650 thalers, and an ensign five men or 25 thalers. NCOs down to sergeant were worth two men and from 10 to 30 thalers, and an individual soldier was worth five thalers.[80] Unfortunately we only have the numbers of Saxon prisoners exchanged in February: 35 men, 30 from cavalry units, four from the infantry and one jäger.[81] Another paper mentions 40 men for which 977 thalers 23 groschen and 8 pfennige had been paid.[82] This sum included not just the ransom, which would have been no more than 200 thalers as none of the men was above the rank of corporal, but food, clothing, and payment which continued during the time.

The Prussian army in Silesia was distributed along a long frontier, covering all the major passes an invading army might use for an advance. Friedrich expected an incursion into Lusatia, where the border was comparably easy to cross, so that the Austrians would split his two armies. The fact that Möllendorf on his retreat to Bautzen was attacked by Austrian forces seemed to confirm this fear, but the Prussians soon found out that the Austrians had not prepared any magazines for an army in this area. As it already started getting cold in the mountains, the king decided to put the majority of his forces in Silesia into winter quarters further from the border.

When these fortification works were finished the king travelled to Breslau in the middle of November to make plans for the next campaign. In the meantime, he also prepared a political solution. The Empress Catherine was still offering help as soon as her relations with the Turks calmed down. To accelerate this process, Friedrich asked France for help. Within a short time the French induced the Ottomans to release Russian merchant ships, which had been taken into custody in Constantinople, and to accept a Russian protégé as the new khan of the Crimean Tartars. As soon as these matters were settled, Catherine on 2 October had her ambassadors in Vienna and

---

79 SächsHstA Dresden 11237/1374 Den March und die Verquartierung derer Kayßerl: Königl: Kriegs-Gefangenen, sammt deren Escorte von Dresden über Meißen Torgau und Jüterbogk in die Churbrandenburgischen Lande und was dem anhängig betr.: Anno 1778.
80 SächsHstA Dresden 11237/1373 Acta Die zwischen denen zu dem Auswechßelungs-Geschäffte ernannten Kayserl: Königlen und Königl: Preußischen bevollmächtigten Commissarien geschloßene Convention in Betreff derer auszuwechselnden Kayserl: Königl: Königl: Preußischen und Chur Saechßischen Kriegsgefangenen und zu erlaßenden Geißeln und was dem anhaengig betr. Anno 1779, fol. 30-45.
81 SächsHstA Dresden 11237/1373, fol.90-91.
82 SächsHstA Dresden 11237/1373, fol.103-104.

Ratisbon declare that the Empress-Queen should admit to the legal claims of the Imperial princes respecting to the Bavarian inheritance which was illegally taken by Austria. If she would not comply, Russia would have no other choice but to support the King of Prussia with an auxiliary corps.

The Russian declaration was a serious threat as the majority of Austria's army was stationed in Bohemia and there were no prospect of successfully facing a Russian attack in Galicia. According to Friedrich's history:

> This declaration had the effect of a thunderbolt in Vienna. The unexpected event disturbed and confused Prince Kaunitz, who had not foreseen anything, was ashamed of being surprised and did not know who to blame. His son, ambassador at Petersburg, was young and inexperienced, and devoted more to pleasure than to duty. He had informed his court neither of the state of the negotiations with Constantinople nor of the Tsarina's attitude towards the King of Prussia.[83]

Joseph, so reluctant during the campaign, now demonstrated a certain stubbornness and convinced his mother to raise an additional 80,000 recruits. However, Austria lacked the funds to pay for these troops and also had trouble raising credits in foreign countries. Therefore the Empress was also looking for French mediation, which put the court of Versailles in a favourable position. Being in any case unwilling to get involved in this conflict, the position as mediator proposed by both belligerents offered the possibility for France to wield influence within the Empire.

The Empress also knew about the importance of Russia and, about the same time that Catherine sent her instructions to her envoys in the Empire, Maria Theresia and Kaunitz on 27 September 1778 sent a declaration to St Petersburg. Friedrich later on considered himself lucky that Maria Theresia had not sent this declaration earlier, because it might have discouraged Catherine to put pressure on Austria.

Friedrich in the meantime sent letters to Jean-Frédéric Phélypeaux, Comte de Maurepas (1701-1781), Louis XVI's leading minister, declaring his readiness for peace, but also considering the terms acceptable to him, declaring – as he did later in his official history – that his main interest was the preservation of the Imperial constitution and the defence of the legal claims of the Elector of Saxony and the Duke of Zweibrücken. Maurepas sent detailed instructions to the French ambassador in Vienna, Jacques-Laure Le Tonnelier, Bailli de Breteuil (1723-1785), who, however, found Joseph unwilling to accept his proposals. Maria Theresia, however, accepted the French offer.

In the meantime, while the diplomatic channels were intensively pursued, new military preparations were also made to back up diplomatic pressure with force. A Russian army of 30,000 men commanded by Prince Nikolai Wassiljewitsch Repnin (1734-1801) reached Breslau at the end of the year. Repnin himself met Friedrich on 18 December and they discussed plans how to make effective use of the Russian support. According to his own

---

83　Volz (ed.), *Die Werke Friedrichs des Großen*, Vol.5, p.119.

history, Friedrich suggested an attack into Galicia which was covered by few Austrian troops and from where the Russians could quickly advance into Hungary. Friedrich wrote, he also offered 'to send in a corps of his troops, and to abandon all the riches of those provinces to the greed of the Russian generals'.[84] Contrary to this account, a plan for the campaign of 1779, written by the king, called for Russian support of his campaign in Moravia: this appears sensible, because if Friedrich really wanted the Russians to attack Galicia, he would have prevented Repnin from marching his corps into Silesia. An attack on Galicia or even Bohemia might have offered a bigger prospect of success, but it would also have strengthened Russia's position in East Central Europe, which was not in Friedrich's interests.

Repnin, however, was well aware that Russian participation in a campaign in Moravia would only help the interests of the King of Prussia. He knew, how much hope Friedrich pinned on their help and presented him their bill in advance. Friedrich had to learn quickly that military support from the Russians was not to be had for free or for the cheap promise of benefits at someone else's expense, and this explains his infuriated account of the Russian reaction to his proposal:

> This proposal was rejected out of ignorance and an even more insatiable thirst for enrichment. According to the contract, the Russians were to provide an auxiliary corps of 16,000 men. They charged an excessive price for it, out of all proportion to the service that could be expected from them. That would have cost the king 3½ million thalers a year, plus subsidies of half a million for a war against the Turks, which Russia was waging poorly. Indeed, as if these were not oppressive and excessive conditions enough, Prince Repnin also insisted that the king, in the event that the Turkish war called him back to Poland with his auxiliary corps, should undertake to escort him back with 16,000 Prussians so that he would not be disturbed by the Austrian troops in Lodomirien on the way. The pinnacle of ridicule, however, was his demand that the Prussians should take care of their own food and pay for their needs everywhere in cash. From such conditions it was clear that the tsarina did not seriously want to help the Prussians; they stifled the feeling of gratitude one should have had for their help. Such proofs of friendship could only be ascribed to Catherine's desire to interfere in German affairs under this pretext in order to extend her influence in Europe. She acted out of vain lust for glory and not in the interests of her ally, nor the obligations she had assumed through their alliance.[85]

Friedrich correctly assumed that this high price was presented to him to put pressure on him to negotiate a peace. Always willing to make a fool of his allies as he did with his enemies, he claimed:

> The most dangerous and annoying of all these unpleasant things was the clumsiness and lack of insight of the Russian ministers. Count Panin was by no means well versed in the insidious tricks of Austrian diplomacy. The traps set for

---

84   Volz (ed.), *Die Werke Friedrichs des Großen*, Vol.5, p.122.
85   Volz (ed.), *Die Werke Friedrichs des Großen*, Vol.5, p.122.

him had to be constantly pointed out. If one hadn't always kept an eye on him, Prince Kaunitz would have played with him as he pleased.[86]

That Friedrich was no longer master of the diplomatic negotiations he did not attribute to his own weakness, but rather to the 'weakness' of the court at Versailles and the 'ignorance' of St Petersburg. However, the proposal for a peace which was presented by Breteuil to Repnin in January 1779 he still saw as a sign of his own triumph, as the terms were nearly the same as those that he had presented to Thugut in August, except for the clause by which he had to assign his claim for Julich and Berg to the Duke of Zweibrücken.

Neither Saxony nor the Duke of Zweibrücken were satisfied with this proposal: the former, because they expected a more substantial financial settlement, the latter, because, despite the political and military situation, he still hoped to inherit Bavaria without any losses. Friedrich was willing to renegotiate the proposal, recognizing the fact that any strengthening of the Wittelsbachs would be at the cost of Austria. However, this attempt was ill-received by Joseph, who declared that the Franco-Russian proposal was also an Austrian ultimatum and that he was willing to fight to the end, if Friedrich rejected it. The king, always claiming his intentions to be honest, presented himself as disappointed in his history of the war:

> Although nothing was more natural than to demand the complete surrender of an illegally occupied province, France and Russia wanted nothing more than peace, the former to get rid of the Emperor who demanded support, the later to not have to provide the Prussians with an auxiliary corps. They acted accordingly and urged the Prussian ministers not to create new obstacles to the general conclusion of peace. Hampered by two mediating powers, both of whom deserved the greatest consideration, the King of Prussia could not serve his allies with all the zeal he felt for them. He could not offend Austria, France and Russia at the same time, but he wanted to agree with the latter on the measures that were still to be taken. This delayed the meeting of the Peace Congress by a month; for so much time was needed to receive the answer from Petersburg.[87]

Of cause, this is a one-sided interpretation as Friedrich aimed for a total victory that would leave Austria with nothing. This was unacceptable to both France and Russia for two reasons, as it strengthened Prussia's reputation and influence within the Empire on the one hand and weakened the young Emperor on the other. To both, Austria still was an important ally – the Franco-Austrian alliance was still valid – and France was concerned that Joseph might turn his eye to Italy for compensation, while France was fighting Britain in America. There is a good case to believe that Friedrich was well aware of this, and the readers of his official history should keep in mind that his statements do not reflect his real view on events or personalities, but represent an attempt to defend his own conduct and his reputation. For this

---

86   Volz (ed.), *Die Werke Friedrichs des Großen*, Vol.5, pp.122-123.
87   Volz (ed.), *Die Werke Friedrichs des Großen*, Vol.5, p.124.

it was best to present Prussian setbacks not as his own failures, but as due to weaknesses, dishonesty and foolishness of his allies.

While the Austrians have been able to frustrate Friedrich's claims, there was criticism on their passive way of conducting war, too. Wraxall remembers the conversation with an Austrian officer at the palace of Prince Colloredo, who frankly criticized the conduct of the Emperor during the last campaign:

> 'Never', said he, 'since the accession of the reigning Empress, during eight-and-thirty years, have the Austrians exhibited so inglorious a spectacle to Europe, as in the campaign of 1778. We have indeed in former periods been more unfortunate; we have been defeated and put to the sword; but we have never yet, with superior numbers, at the beginning of the campaign, in the midst of our own territories, and possessing all the means of offensive war, submitted to be shut up and besieged within our lines. At the most disastrous period of the late war in 1757, after the defeat which we sustained at Prague, Daun would not have adopted to so humiliating a plan, though he might have been justified in pursuing it. If ever offensive operations were necessary in order to inspire the troops with ardor, they were so in the present campaign. It was indispensable, after a peace of fifteen years, to shew [sic] the Austrian soldier that he was not inferior to the Prussian, either in discipline, in courage or in leaders. But what has the Emperor done? He has impressed an indelible conviction on all his officers and soldiers, that whatever may be the justice of his cause, he feels his inability to maintain it in the field. He has tacitly admitted the Prussian superiority. From the inaccessible heights of Konigingratz, Joseph beheld the finest provinces of Bohemia plundered, without daring to make an effort for their defence. Frederic has carried of immense contributions, and deeply imprinted the terror of his arms in every village, and on every inhabitant. Was any exertion made to impede his retreat out of Bohemia, when loaded with plunder? None. He retired without our scarcely daring to molest him, and he will return far more formidable in the ensuing spring.
>
> But our misfortunes and our disgrace do not stop here. The pernicious presence of the Emperor has diffused them over every part of the military operations, and prevented our success, where, without his interference, it would have been equally certain and brilliant. Though the king was able to effect his retreat without confusion to Schatzlar, in sight of the Emperor and Marshal Lacy; Prince Henry of Prussia could not have retired with equal impunity into saxony, under the eyes of Laudohn. That able commander, who was encamped at Munchengratz; after effectually preventing the junction of the two armies, only waited for the favorable moment of action. He knew the impediments to Prince Henry's retreat, the ruined condition of his cavalry, the difficulty of dragging his artillery, and the impossibility of his making effectual resistance, if vigorously attacked. Laudohn [sic] had even formed all his dispositions for the purpose, issued his final orders, and was about to execute them on the following morning day-break. Our success must have been infallible. But, for our misfortune, his Imperial Majesty arrived from Konigingratz, in an open carriage, alone, on the evening before the destined attack. All Laudohn's plans were instantly reversed; we remained inactive; and Prince Henry, like the King his brother, closed the campaign triumphantly. It is thus that we are sacrificed, counteracted and dishonored. How can it be

otherwise? The Empress, we are not ignorant, only wishes for peace. The Emperor breathes war, but knows not how to conduct it, though he aspires to superintend all the operations in person. Prince Kaunitz fluctuates between both; desirous of repose, yet anxious to gratify a Prince whose passion is ambition, and who may soon become his sole master. Such is the actual state of our affairs'.[88]

Preparations for the 1779 campaign

Even while negotiating for peace, both Austria and Prussia anxiously faced the costs of another campaign year and had to prepare for it. The Austrians tried to expel the Prussians from Jägerndorf and Troppau, but hesitated to attack these fortified camps directly. After some undecisive cannonading they retreated. They sent 15,000 men under *Feldzeugmeister* Carl Heinrich von Ellrichshausen (1720-1779) to Engelsberg (Andělská Hora ve Slezsku), close to Jägerndorf. From here, the Austrians were able to outflank the Prussian camp and to start raids into Silesia as far as Neiße. However, the Prince of Brunswick soon got irritated by these incursions. He assembled his troops and attacked the Austrians in their camps, which they abandoned without any bigger fight. During their retreat they lost four guns and 50 prisoners.

Ellrichshausen now moved his troops father north to Zuckmantel (Zlaté Hory) and Ziegenhals (Głuchołazy) from where the Austrians again started raids into the flat country beyond the border, causing alarm in the nearby Prussian winter camps. Friedrich moved *Generalleutnant* von Wunsch from Glatz. Wunsch forced the Austrians out of Ziegenhals and followed them to Zuckmantel. However, the country here was undulating, benefiting the defender. The Austrians had strengthened their position with field fortifications and guns, and the high mountains around did not allow the Prussians to outflank this position.[89]

Wunsch decided that it was not reasonable to attack, and, as there was also no possibility to stay, he retreated back towards Glatz in the west. On his way he heard cannonading from the direction of Habelschwert (Bystrzyca Kłodzka) and accordingly changed his direction. He met 250 routed Prussian soldiers from the Regiment Luck. Their officers informed him that the Austrians had attacked the forces commanded by *Generalmajor* Prince Adolf von Hessen-Philipsthal (1743-1803), who had been left behind by Wunsch to cover his line of communications with two battalions. Habelschwert only had outdated medieval walls, which however were able to give good protection against an attacker lacking artillery. However, the Austrians had prepared scaling ladders. The Prussians, who had recklessly neglected guarding their camp, were totally surprised. The Austrians entered the town and quickly forced the prince's battalions to surrender. 'This shameful catastrophe can only be ascribed to the ignorance of the young prince, who took part in his

---

88 Wraxall, *Memoirs of the Courts of Berlin, Dresden, Warsaw and* Vienna, Vol.I, pp.212-215.
89 Reimann, *Geschichte des Bayerischen Erbfolgekrieges*, pp.209-210.

first campaign and should not have been entrusted with an independent command',[90] wrote Friedrich in his history of the war.

Moments later new gunshots could be heard. A second Austrian column had followed Wunsch and attacked a fortified blockhouse covered by a ditch in his rear, where he had posted 100 men to cover his retreat. The Austrians seemed to have had no problems in bringing howitzers over the mountains and they made good use of them. They set the blockhouse ablaze with a howitzer shot and forced the Prussian commander, *Hauptmann* Michael Wilhelm Capeller to surrender, before Wunsch was able to relieve him. Capeller later claimed that he tried to unite with Wunsch, after hearing the Prussian grenadier march beat from afar, but coming under the attack of Austrian hussars and light infantry he had no option but to lay down his arms. The Prussian general now quickly retreated to Glatz. According to Friedrich's account, Wurmser had no idea of the existence of the redoubt and, while he was able to take it, the time lost prevented him from surprising Glatz and so gain a strong foothold in Silesia. Capeller – so thought the king – through his gallant defence had saved the fortress. However, it is doubtful that Wurmser really wanted to take Glatz. The garrison of the fortress was weak, but its defensive works strong and with Wunsch still nearby a coup de main seemed unlikely and anything taking more time too risky.

Instead, Wurmser operated in the countryside nearby and caught up some small Prussian detachments, quartered in the villages. In his history of the war Friedrich speculated that Wurmser hoped to draw Prussian troops from their camps at Jägerndorf and Troppau and so weaken these positions and enable Ellrichshausen to mount a successful attack. Instead, the king himself took the Garde du Corps, the Gendarmes, the Regiment of Anhalt and several other battalions out of their winter quarters around Breslau and moved them to Reichenbach, where he arrived at 4 February, and then to Friedland (Mieroszów), which was well fortified. Austrian troops also had reached Waldenburg, close to the major fortress of Waldenburg (Wałbrzych). To drive them back the king sent a detachment under the Prince of Anhalt to Braunau (Broumov) and a second one under *Generalmajor* Johann Sigismund von Lestwitz (1718-1788) to nearby Scharfeneck (Ścinawka Górna), so he was able to march either to the direction of Glatz further east or towards Waldenburg further northwest. However, the Austrians quickly retreated once more, which is also proof of their weakness. Wurmser's small invasion was nothing more than a big raiding party and certainly not strong enough for a major siege operation or a battle. The Prussians followed them and the Prince of Anhalt was able to capture 50 Pandurs. On 16 February, Friedrich occupied Silberberg (Srebrnogórska). With most passes under the control of the Prussians, the Austrians now also vacated Habelschwerdt.[91]

The Austrian light troops continued to badger the Prussian border garrisons, but some of their actions seemed to aim more for glory than reasonable military results. Friedrich himself gave two anecdotes in his history of the war:

---

90 Volz (ed.), *Die Werke Friedrichs des Großen*, Vol.5, p.125.
91 Reimann, *Geschichte des Bayerischen Erbfolgekrieges*, pp.212-213.

During the night of the 7th it happened that a non-commissioned officer from the Wunsch regiment deserted and, in order to take revenge on his major, led the Austrian hussars into the village, where he picked up the major and five flags. So true is it that an officer can never be too alert to protect himself from ambush. Something similar happened a few months earlier to the Thadden regiment in Silesia, when it was stationed in the village of Dittersbach near Schmiedeberg. The hussars made a mock attack on a regiment's outpost while another squad broke through a garden and barn into the commander's house and stole three flags. However, they were evicted before he could get hold of the others. Such occurrences do not do the Prussian service credit, but with the multitude of officers who belong to an army, not all can be equally competent and vigilant.[92]

Prince Heinrich's Army During the Winter

In the first days of October Heinrich sent his troops into their winter quarters. He himself took his headquarters in the Palace of Großsedlitz to the South of Dresden. His Prussian troops took their quarters further south between Dohna, Pirna, Königstein, Gottleuba and Liebstadt, the majority of the Saxon army marching to Zittau.[93] Smaller detachments covered the border further west. During November the majority of Heinrich's cavalry was even sent back to Potsdam. Heinrich had no plan to do anything apart from protecting the border during winter, but his brother wanted to keep the pressure on the Austrians high. They exchanged letters for weeks and, at the beginning of February, Heinrich finally made a comment that illustrates their different attitude, when he claimed to know, 'that such difficult expeditions are among the first to succeed, but there are examples enough of the contrary'.[94]

There was no fighting during these months, and it was not before the beginning of February 1779 that Heinrich ordered the attack of a corps under Möllendorf into Bohemia, taking the route over Einsiedel. The prince had received reports that the Austrians had prepared for an invasion during the winter. They had even collected sledges to move their artillery.[95] Möllendorf's advance was intended to clarify these reports. For this Heinrich ordered the regiments in western Saxony to concentrate near Zwickau on 6 February. One day before, Möllendorf's vanguards chased back the Austrian patrols at the border to Laun. He marched on to Brüx, where he met another small Austrian force of Croats, which was beaten back by his cavalry. Six Prussian guns overwhelmed the Austrian artillery, and the infantry and the Saxon jäger entered the city playing 'janissary music'.[96] The Prussians made 350 prisoners and captured three guns. Brüx was taken at the same day, along

---

92 Volz (ed.), *Die Werke Friedrichs des Großen*, Vol.5, pp.125-126.
93 SächsHStA Dresden 11338/11004/16 Befehle des Prinzen von Anhalt-Bernburg an das sächsische Armeekorps während des Bayerischen Erbfolgekrieges, fol.36-65.
94 Schöning, *Der Bayerische Erbfolgekrieg*, p.272.
95 This was not unusual. The Saxon troops in Lusatia also prepared sledges: SächsHStA Dresden 11338/11004/16 Befehle des Prinzen von Anhalt-Bernburg an das sächsische Armeekorps während des Bayerischen Erbfolgekrieges, fol.66.
96 Seyfarth, *Unpartheyische Geschichte*, p.666.

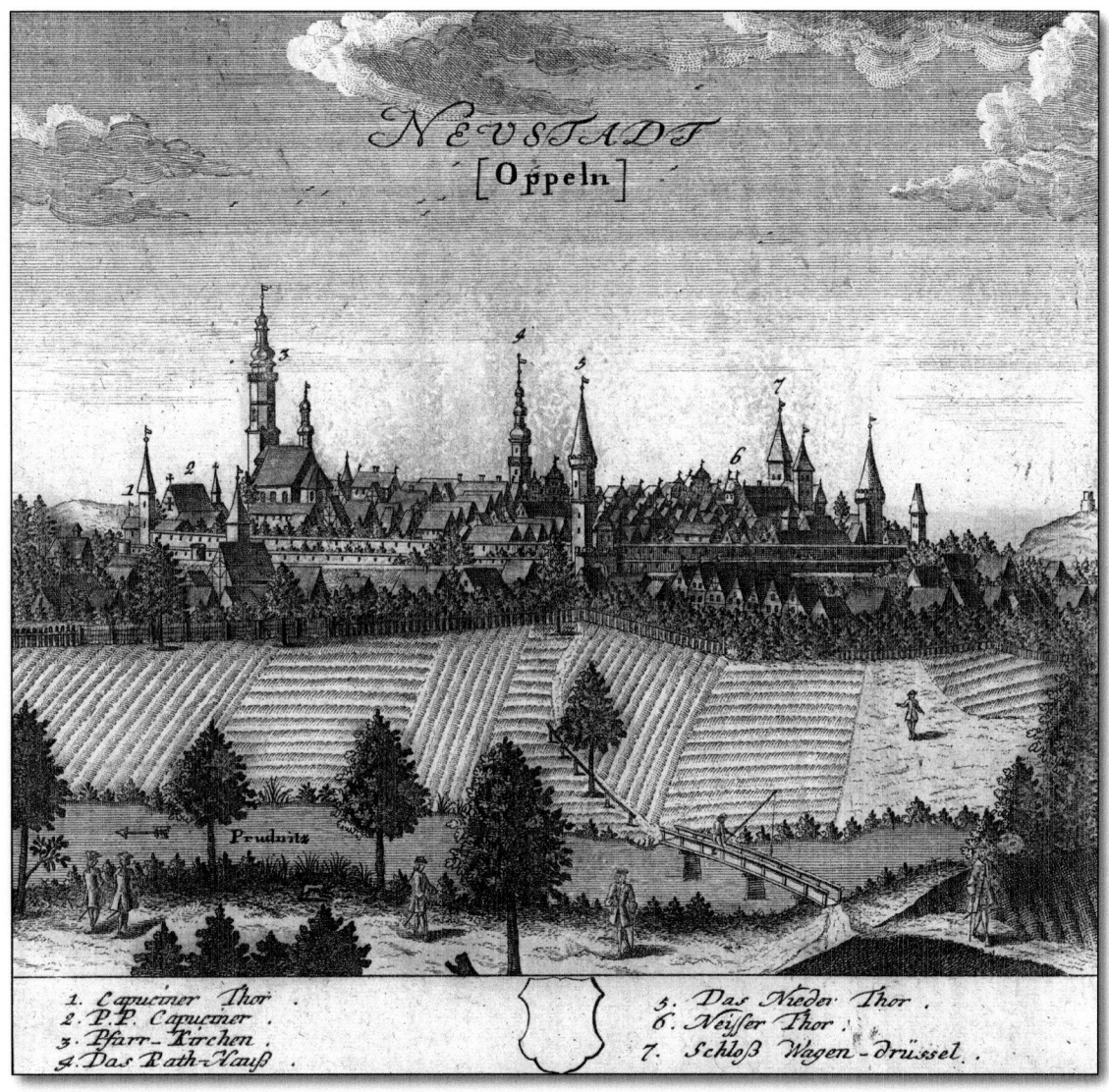

Neustadt in Schlesien, here in a picture from 1739. The double wall of Medieval times is well recognizable. (Public Domain)

with the Austrian magazine there. This gave the Prussians a good foothold in Bohemia, but the planned invasion was soon called off. Friedrich was satisfied with Möllendorf's small campaign and awarded him with the Order of the Black Eagle.[97]

In Silesia, Austrian *Generalmajor* Oliver Graf von Wallis (1742-1799) with a corps of 8-10,000 men tried to surprise Neustadt (Prudnik), which was garrisoned by Prussian infantry of the Regiment Prinz Heinrich von Preußen and the Grenadier Battalion Preuß. The town only had old medieval walls, but the Austrians did not risk a storm. Instead, they unlimbered 20 howitzers and bombarded the town, which soon caught fire. 240 houses burned down, but the Prussian garrison refused to surrender. When *Generalleutnant* von

---

97 Reimann, *Geschichte des Bayerischen Erbfolgekrieges*, pp.213-214.

Stutterheim, standing nearby, heard the cannon fire, he marched his troops to Branitz, cutting the Austrian line of communication. Other Prussian detachments standing nearby also started to concentrate in this area, finally forcing Wallis to retreat on 28 February, harassed by the Prussians. Friedrich – who in his earlier wars never recoiled from setting a town ablaze – accused Joseph II to have ordered the bombardment of Neustadt for diplomatic reasons:

> Since the Emperor considered the King of Prussia to be passionate and short-tempered, he imagined that by burning one of his cities he would irritate him so much that he would be more recalcitrant in the forthcoming negotiations and cause greater difficulties, and even break them off altogether out of a bad mood. But this disgraceful enterprise of the Austrians only turned out to their own disgrace.[98]

However, Friedrich was willing to honour the brave defenders with a Groschen for each man.[99]

---

98 Volz (ed.), *Die Werke Friedrichs des Großen*, Vol.5, p.127.
99 Schöning, *Der Bayerische Erbfolgekrieg*, pp.276-277.

5

The Peace of Teschen

Even as preparations for the new year's campaigning began, a courier from St Petersburg arrived in Breslau. His message informed the king that Catherine II agreed to his propositions so Repnin forwarded them to Breteuil in Vienna. Empress Maria Theresia was keen to accept them and at the beginning of March Repnin received a letter from Breteuil in which he was informed that the Empress wanted a ceasefire to start a conference. Friedrich received this news at Silberberg on 4 March. He immediately informed his generals to start negotiations with their Austrian counterparts in their districts and two days later returned to Breslau to talk with Repnin. The armistice started in Bohemia on 7 March, one day later in Moravia and Upper Silesia and on the 10th on the Saxon-Bohemian border. All troops were withdrawn from the border areas and put into winter quarters.

The peace conference was to be held at Teschen (Cieszyn). Besides Repnin and Breteuil, Riedesel was sent to represent Prussia, Zinzendorf Saxony, Hohenfeld Zweibrücken and Cobenzl Austria. Astonishingly, the ruling Elector of Bavaria, over whose possessions the war was officially fought, took no part in the negotiations.

The Austrian envoy Cobenzl was in quite a difficult position, because Vienna was split into two parties. Maria Theresia was willing to accept the Prussian proposals just for the sake of peace, but Joseph saw this as a kind of defeat he was not willing to accept. 'This created many difficulties for the mediating powers', wrote Friedrich in his history of the war:

> [A]lthough the Emperor well understood that if he openly thwarted a negotiation in which Russia and France were involved, he would have to deal with strong opponents. He hoped to achieve the same goal by veiled resistance, especially if he did not step forward himself but put forward another whom he could direct at his discretion. His choice fell on the Elector Palatinate, who, together with his ministers, was blindly devoted to the imperial court. But this new ruse was soon exposed.[1]

---

1 Volz (ed.), *Die Werke Friedrichs des Großen*, Vol.5, p.128.

At Teschen Cobenzl accepted the proposal which officially was forwarded by France. A quick peace seemed possible, but then Repnin received a letter from the Russian envoy at Ratisbon, informing him that Carl Theodor was unwilling and unable to pay Saxony any financial compensation. Instead, the elector claimed that he felt bounded to the treaty he had signed with Austria. He did not want to have his own interests discussed in a peace conference in which he did not take part. Friedrich supposed Joseph's guiding hand behind this:

> However, the Elector Palatine played the role prompted to him by the Emperor quite awkwardly. Breteuil and Prince Repnin easily discovered the true author of this new trick. Both adopting an authoritative tone, they declared with all the dignity of plenipotentiaries of great empires that all the contracting powers had already accepted the peace project proposed to them, and that they would therefore regard as an enemy anyone who disobeyed his first commitment. At these words, Cobenzl turned pale, the man from the Palatinate bowed, and couriers hurriedly left for Vienna.[2]

However, Carl Theodor was not the only 'minor' at the table, who was unwilling to accept the Franco-Russian proposal without further negotiations. The Saxons, 'whose greed was insatiable',[3] wrote Friedrich, wanted more money and Zweibrücken repeatedly argued that Bavaria could not be divided. Although these objections lengthened the negotiations, they were finally brushed aside by the major powers. Friedrich, who so often claimed to have started the war to protect the interests of the two minor Imperial estates, now claimed to have brought them to reason:

> The king had to intervene to prevent things from going on like this. With the help of the intermediaries, he managed, albeit with difficulty, to dampen the undue heat of the two ambassadors. He proved to the Saxons that without France, Russia and Prussia the elector would not get a penny from Austria, no matter how justified his claims might be, that he should therefore act sensibly and be content with the sums that had been obtained with great difficulty for him. Much the same was said to the envoy from Zweibrücken. He was told that after losing three quarters of Bavaria, his prince could be happy if he got two thirds back, not to mention that the king dropped the Brandenburg inheritance claims on Julich and Berg in his favour. The two envoys had scarcely been appeased when the Emperor's puppet, the Elector Palatine, reappeared and raised new objects. France was outraged and the envoy of Louis XVI in Munich struck a tone such as Louis XIV had allowed himself in the midst of his victories. Nevertheless the quarrels in Teschen continued, and the plenipotentiaries themselves began to despair of the success of their negotiations.[4]

---

2   Volz (ed.), *Die Werke Friedrichs des Großen*, Vol.5, p.129.
3   Volz (ed.), *Die Werke Friedrichs des Großen*, Vol.5, p.129.
4   Volz (ed.), *Die Werke Friedrichs des Großen*, Vol.5, p.129.

THE PEACE OF TESCHEN

The conference had taken more than six weeks, when on 20 April a courier from Vienna arrived, bringing the news of the Treaty of Ainali Kawak, which ended the diplomatic frictions between Russia and the Ottoman Empire. This weakened the hand of Joseph, who had always speculated on a further escalation of the conflicts, which would have deterred Russia from giving military support to Prussia.

As Friedrich wrote:

> The Russo-Turkish peace agreement is actually the point in time when the Teschen Congress began. The clockworks that the Emperor had secretly set in motion immediately stopped as if they had broken. The Elector Palatine and his plenipotentiary shrouded themselves in reverential silence; Count Cobenzl became more obliging, dropping his fraudulent proposals and speaking openly and honestly about what was the subject of the negotiations. All these favourable circumstances promoted the work so rapidly that within a fortnight there was general agreement, and the peace was concluded and signed on May 13, the birthday of the Empress-Queen.[5]

According to the treaty, Carl Theodor's rights were confirmed and the two Wittelsbach electorates of Bavaria and the Palatinate united into one. The succession of the Duke of Pfalz-Zweibrücken in both states was guaranteed. In fact, both electorates were officially united with Carl Theodor's death in 1799, becoming the third biggest state within the empire behind Prussia and Austria, getting ahead of Saxony. In fact, after he became King of Bavaria in 1805 Max Joseph tried to establish Bavaria as a power equal to the Hohenzollern and Habsburg states.

Austria gained the so called Innviertel, the Bavarian territories to the east of the small rivers Inn and Salzach. In return the Emperor guaranteed Prussia's right to succeed in the margravates of Brandenburg-Ansbach and Brandenburg-Bayreuth, both ruled by cadet branches of the Hohenzollerns that were expected to die out soon. In the end, both were united in 1791 under Christian Friedrich Carl Alexander of Brandenburg-Ansbach (1736-1806) as Ansbach-Bayreuth and soon after handed over to Prussia, while the margrave received an annual life annuity of 300,000 thalers.

Saxony made no territorial gains but received six million thalers from the new Bavarian elector which had to be paid in annual instalments of 500,000 thalers. Additionally, Austria quit the suzerainty of the barony (Herrschaft) of Schönburg, a small enclave within Saxon territory, to which the Saxon electors had tried for a long time to strengthen their access.

Probably the most important point of the peace was its guarantee through Russia which superseded Sweden, together with France the guarantor power of the Peace of Westphalia.

The treaty was finally signed on 13 May 1779, the birthday of the Empress, but it was not ratified by the Empire until 28 February 1780, while Joseph II

---

5   Volz (ed.), *Die Werke Friedrichs des Großen*, Vol.5, p.130.

THE WAR OF THE BAVARIAN SUCCESSION 1778-1789

Saxon Elector Friedrich August I. (Anne S.K. Brown Collection)

ratified it only on 8 March of that year. The Prussian troops immediately withdrew from the Bohemian territories still occupied by them.[6]

'This is how the German turmoil ended', wrote Friedrich in his history of the war:

> The whole world was prepared for a war lasting several years before they were settled. But what happened was a whimsical mixture of diplomatic negotiations and military operations. The reason for this lay in the two factions that divided the imperial court, one of which now gained the upper hand and now was suppressed by the other. The officers were in constant uncertainty; no one knew whether it was peace or war, and this awkward situation lasted until the day the peace was signed in Teschen. The Prussian troops appeared to be victorious over their opponents wherever they could actually fight, whereas the Imperialists retained the upper hand in everything that meant cunning, ambush, and cunning, in short, in everything connected with small-scale warfare.[7]

---

6   SächsHstA Dresden 11237/ 1382 Die in Ansehung des Mobilgemachten und in Campagne befindlichen Chur-Sechßischen Corps d'Armeé ergangenen Anordnungen und was dem anhaengig betr.

7   Volz (ed.), *Die Werke Friedrichs des Großen*, Vol.5, p.131.

6

Further Developments

But it is the fate of all human things that nothing succeeds perfectly. Mankind is destined to be content with the approximate. So what was the result of this war that set almost all of Europe in motion? For this time Germany was saved from imperial despotism. The Emperor had suffered a kind of defeat; for he had to give back what he had snatched from me. But what effects will this war have for the future? Will the Emperor become more cautious? Will everyone be able to cultivate their field in peace? Will peace be better secured as a result? We can only answer these questions with scepticism. Nothing is impossible in the future. Our eyes are too short-sighted to see through future coincidences. There is nothing left for us but to submit to providence, or rather to fate. They will determine the future as well as they determined the past and the infinite period before we were born.[1]

With these questions and speculations Friedrich II ended his history of the war. It is a clear attempt to defend his reputation. The king always tried to present himself as defender of German liberties against a despotic Emperor. This antagonism had a long tradition in German history. Similar arguments have been brought forward by the Princes of the Schmalkaldic League against Charles V in the sixteenth century and by the Protestant Union against Ferdinand II in the seventeenth century. It played into Friedrich's hand that Joseph's politics earned him the reputation of an enlightened despot. However, while the first three Silesian Wars had been fought to strengthen Prussia itself, irrespective of Austria, the War of the Bavarian Succession is a clear expression of the new rivalry between the two states and Friedrich clearly demonstrated that he would not allow Austria to significantly strengthen its own position or made territorial gains which could be understood as compensation for the loss of Silesia.

The peace however did not satisfy all signatories. Carl Theodor from now on proved to be very unpopular within his electorate and secretly negotiated with Joseph II to exchange Bavaria for the Austrian Netherlands, which

---

1 Volz (ed.), *Die Werke Friedrichs des Großen*, Vol.5, pp.132-133.

were closer to his home territory and to his heart. However, when these negotiations became public they just increased his unpopularity within a Bavarian population which had no interest in being swallowed by Austria. Joseph II, in contrast, was favourable to this idea and even recognized Carl Theodor's claim to the title 'King of Burgundy'. As the Southern Netherlands were not part of the Empire, their possession would have opened the opportunity of a crown to the Wittelsbachs, as the possession of the Duchy of Prussia – also outside the Empire – offered it to the Hohenzollerns in 1701.

However, this project was not only unpopular within Bavaria. Friedrich II too had no desire to see the Habsburgs consolidate their territorial power, and while Friedrich August III of Saxony accepted the fact that his country was only a second rank power within Europe and the Empire, he was unwilling to be surpassed by another rival dynasty. The project offered Friedrich II reason to assemble the imperial estates in a league directed against the policy of Joseph II. On 23 July 1785 Prussia, Saxony and Hannover joined in the Drei-Kurfürsten-Bund (League of the Three Electors). In quick succession 14 further minor estates, including Hesse-Cassel, Brunswick-Wolffenbüttel, Zweibrücken, Saxe-Gotha, Saxe-Weimar, Mecklenburg Baden and Ansbach joined the league, which now became known as Fürstenbund (League of Princes).[2]

Soon, however, greater developments in Europe soon ensured that the protagonists changed their focus. In 1781 Joseph II had signed a defensive alliance with Russia, initially with the intention of securing Russian support for his planned acquisition of Bavaria, as Friedrich always feared a military intervention by the tsardom. Catharine II of Russia for her part was not that interested in Imperial politics or to serve as a backer for Austrian interests. She had plans of her own and they provided for a separation of the European possessions of the Ottoman Empire. The 'Greek Plan' of the Empress Catherine promised Austria the recovery of all the territories lost in the shameful 1737-1739 war and additionally Bosnia, the Herzegovina, and Albania. Joseph was reluctant initially, fearing that a major military involvement of Austria at the Balkans would give Prussia a free hand in the Empire. However, because he was determined to assure himself of Russian support he agreed to this plan and in the following year deployed 200,000 men at the border with the Ottoman Empire and so forced the sultan to keep a sufficient part of his own troops at hand there, while the Russians under Potemkin occupied the Crimea. It was a perfect example of how military power could achieve an effect without the declaration of war.[3]

In 1786 Friedrich II of Prussia died. The Austro-Russian alliance and the still valid Franco-Austrian alliance saw Prussia politically isolated, but Friedrich's successor Friedrich Wilhelm II was unwilling to have his own

---

2   Still a very readable account: Leopold von Ranke, *Die deutschen Mächte und der Fürstenbund. Deutsche Geschichte von 1780 bis 1790* (Leipzig: Duncker & Humblot, 1871-1872).

3   Michael Hochedlinger, '"Herzensfreundschaft" – Zweckgemeinschaft – Hypothek? Das russisch-österreichische Bündnis von 1781 bis zur zweiten Teilung Polens', in Claus Scharf (ed.), *Katharina II., Russland und Europa. Beiträge zur internationalen* (Maynce: Philipp von Zabern, 2001), pp.183–225.

foreign policy influenced by this fact. When Austria aligned itself to Russia in its war with the Ottomans in 1787, the king saw this not as an advantage but as a risk, because territorial gains by Austria would better Austria's position. To weaken the rival power, Friedrich Wilhelm II supported rebellions within the Habsburg estates, especially the Southern Netherlands, Tyrol, Galicia, Dalmatia and Hungary.[4] Prussia itself became involved in the Dutch Rising in 1787. In this conflict the Prussians demonstrated their military capability and captured Amsterdam – a prize denied to Louis XIV during the Dutch War 1670-1678.[5] In the same year, turmoil also shocked the Austrian Netherlands, where Joseph's reform programs had not been popular. Already in 1787 Belgian militia mobilised against the Habsburg governor.[6] Under these circumstances an exchange of Bavaria with the Southern Netherlands appeared unattractive to Carl Theodor.

Austria meanwhile had a very bad start in the war with the Turks: the 1788 campaign proved to be a disaster, culminating in the shameful panic of Karánsebes, where an Austrian army disintegrated after rumours reached camp of the approach of an Ottoman army. Joseph II once more proved to be no leader of the calibre of Frederick the Great.[7] The Austrian ineffectiveness in this campaign contrasted markedly with its performance in the War of the Bavarian Succession and also the Prussian performance during the Dutch crisis. However, this picture had to be put in its proper context. The Dutch militias the Prussians faced were certainly a much less formidable foe than the Ottomans, whose military effectiveness must not be underestimated even in the late eighteenth century, and they were likewise less effective than the Dutch troops facing the Sun King's armies in 1672. On the other hand, Austria in the Balkans was forced to conduct an offensive which proved to be much more difficult than a defence in prepared positions. However, the army once more demonstrated its capability to adapt to different tactical circumstances. Instead of linear tactics it adopted the Russian system of mutually supporting squares, and under Laudon's experienced leadership in 1789 it was able turn the tables and to recapture Belgrade.[8] It was the old *Feldmarschall*'s last and greatest triumph.

The political context changed again in the early 1790s. The French Revolution of 1789 might not have been the major concern of the European powers, as it initially was considered as a French affair. But with the radicalisation of the Revolution, Austria and Prussia closed their ranks and on 27 August 1791 signed the Declaration of Pillnitz in which both parties

---

4 Wilhelm Bringmann, *Preußen unter Friedrich Wilhelm II. 1787-1796* (Frankfurt a. M.: Peter Lang, 2001).
5 Munro Price, 'The Dutch Affair and the Fall of the Ancien Régime, 1784–1787', The Historical Journal 38/4 (1995), pp.875–805.
6 Jan Craeybeckx: 'The Brabant Rovolution. A Conservative Revolt In A Backward Country?', *Acta Historiae Neerlandica* 4 (1970), pp.48-83.
7 Claudia Reichl-Ham, 'Der Türkenkrieg Josephs II.', *Pallasch. Zeitschrift für Militärgeschichte* 50 (2014), pp.5–31.
8 Michael Hochedlinger, *Krise und Wiederherstellung. Österreichische Großmachtpolitik zwischen Türkenkrieg und "Zweiter Diplomatischer Revolution" 1787–1791* (Berlin Duncker & Humblot, 2000).

declared their support for Louis XVI. It was characteristic for the growing political insignificance of Saxony that Friedrich August III, who was the host for this conference – Pillnitz being a castle close to Dresden – did not take part in the talks. What is often overlooked is the fact that the main points negotiated at Pillnitz did not consider the fate of Louis XVI, but rather the fate Poland and how Austria should end its war with the Ottomans. So while Friedrich Wilhelm II and Leopold II demonstrated unity with regard to the French revolutionaries, they remained rivals over the size of the pieces to be cut out of the Polish cake.

In the light of this background the Bavarian questions fell from the view of all the protagonists. Joseph II died in 1790 and his successor Leopold II in quick succession in 1792. In both cases Elector Carl Theodor took over the Imperial vicariate. It is an irony of history that in 1793 Prussia suddenly agreed to the idea of an exchange of the Southern Netherlands and Bavaria between the Habsburgs and the Wittelsbachs, because it was interested in getting Austria's approval of the Second Partition of Poland. Military events, however, thwarted this idea. Austria had been able in 1793 to push the French troops in Flanders back, but in 1794 the province was completely overrun by the French, as were all the Palatine territories to the west of the Rhine. All grand schemes for an exchange of countries and the creation of new crowns – which in some way bring to mind the grandiloquent reshaping of Napoleonic Europe – came to an end. When Carl Theodor finally died in 1799, he was succeeded by Maximilian IV Joseph, who in the turbulent Napoleonic area was able to consolidate and seriously increase Bavarian territory and gain for himself the crown his predecessor was peering at and which the Wittelsbachs were to wear until all the German dynasties, including the Hohenzollern and the Wettins, were to fall in the revolution of 1918.[9] However, at the moment Carl Theodor died, 110,000 Austrian troops stood in Bavaria and there was a serious risk that the Habsburgs might finally provide themselves with the inheritance they had to surrender in 1779. There were also new talks for an exchange with the Austrian Netherlands, which proved threatened and difficult to defend against French attack. However once more the international pressure was much too high. Austria was the last major continental power to face France in a war. Prussia had signed its peace at Basel in 1795 and Russia too was not willing to accept such an enlargement of Austria, which now could be regarded as a compensation for Polish territory not gained in the Second and Third Partitions of Poland.

---

9   Hubert Glaser, *Krone und Verfassung: König Max I. Joseph und der neue Staat* (Munich R. Piper & Co, 1980).

Conclusion

The general conclusion about the War of the Bavarian Succession is that it proved for the first time the weaknesses of the Prussian military system and a lack of vigour on part of Friedrich II due to his age. While there might be some truth in this, there are other important factors which influenced its outcome. One was the improved effectiveness of the Austrian army, which denied the Prussians a decisive battle, a tendency which had already been seen in the later stages of the Seven Years War. By pinning the Prussians down close to the border of Bohemia the Austrians denied them the option to draw resources from outside their kingdom. Without any financial support, Prussia's ability to wage war was limited from the beginning and a successful outcome depended on victories in the field.

It was the intention of this book to give a modern narrative and analysis of the War of the Bavarian Succession, that last clash between Frederick the Great and Austria in the eighteenth century. Rather than demonstrating a decline in Prussian military capability as it is often claimed for this conflict, it reflected inherent weaknesses of the Prussian military system during the king's reign in general. The economic and financial basis for keeping a disproportionally large army was weak and could only be maintained during peacetime; during a war Prussia was either compelled to win a quick victory, obtain substantial subsidies, or occupy territory from which to gain significant contributions. A combination of some or all of these factors came into play during the first three Silesian Wars, but none of them did so during the War of the Bavarian Succession. Prussia did not receive any subsidies from Britain or France, Saxony was now an ally whose territories had to be respected and not squeezed like a lemon, and the carefully prepared Austrian defensive positions in Bohemia and Friedrich's risk-averseness – which one might ascribe to his age or to the respect that his opponents won in the later stages of the Seven Years War – denied him the much-needed quick victory. Structurally the Prussian army also appeared stiff. While during the Seven Years War it underwent a clear learning curve, introducing more and heavier artillery and adopting the column formation, a lack of proper light infantry was a weakness Friedrich never really grasped. Stressing the need for harsh discipline – an attitude that even increased after the end of the Seven Years War – he generally despised light troops, the Austrian Croats and Pandurs as well as the Prussian *freibataillone*, as rabble: it seems he never really was able to appreciate their value during a campaign. Only the Prussian hussar regiments were increased, but their drill was regularised, to conform to the cuirassiers and dragoons, making them more effective in battle but less so for small warfare. So, in 1778 Austrian light troops once more, like in 1742, 1744 and 1758, were able to harass the Prussian supply system which in itself was another weakness of Friedrich's army.

One wonders, why an army that had extreme difficulties in operating in Bohemia a few dozen miles from its magazines – even if the border mountains were hard to cross – is still valued by military historians as the crème of mid-eighteenth century military, while the Russians – or the Chinese under the Quialong Emperor to stress a non-European example – moved armies of the same size over far greater distances, while France and Britain were able to project their power to other continents. That Prince Heinrich in command of an army of 80,000 men – even if one deducts a high percentage of casualties through sickness – was forced to withdraw from western Bohemia in 1778 merely because of the operations of Austrian light troops underlines this problem. All the other major European powers – Britain, France, Russia and Austria – showed themselves to be much more progressive with regard to the introduction of light infantry troops in the second half of the eighteenth century.

Pointing out the limitations of Prussian military effectiveness does not mean to deny its existence, however. Failing to force the Austrians to battle in 1778 and 1779 was due to the defender having been much better prepared for a Prussian invasion than in 1742, 1744 and 1756-1757, but on the other hand the Austrians were also unwilling to seek a chance to strike at the Prussians. Under other circumstances the Prussians of the late eighteenth century still demonstrated their power – as in the Dutch crisis – or their fighting capability, for example in the War of the First Coalition, when a Prussian army under the Duke of Brunswick was able to beat numerically superior French armies at Pirmasens (14 September 1793), Kaiserslautern (28-30 November 1793) or Biesingen (17 November 1793). In the later battle the odds were more than three-to-one against the Prussians and still they were able to beat back the French columns through the firepower of their artillery and a bayonet charge of the infantry.

Military effectiveness depended on many factors and victory was not only decided through numbers and capability, but also through the willingness or necessity of an enemy to give battle on favourable terms. All this had to be kept in mind if one wants assess Prussian military effectiveness in the eighteenth and early nineteenth centuries. The popular narrative – that it reached a peak in the Seven Years War, and that during the War of the Bavarian Succession the first cracks appeared pointing directly to the nadir of the crushing defeats at Jena and Auerstädt in 1806 – is an overly simplistic and teleological explanation which is still popular within the academic and popular literature as well, but it is deeply flawed. If this study of an allegedly less important conflict of the second half of the eighteenth century was able to demonstrate these flaws, I would consider that a major achievement.

The War of the Bavarian Succession differs from the more well-known Seven Years War in another important respect. In 1756 all major European powers were involved in alliance systems that were hostile to each other. The road to political negotiations led only through military results or military exhaustion. In the War of the Bavarian Succession, however, both Prussia and Austria relied on the mediation of the neutral great powers France and Russia from the outset. This hope inhibited military operations because the risk of defeat would have significantly worsened one's own negotiating position.

Regarding the alleged indecisiveness of the war, this is an assessment based solely on the outcome of the war itself and of the 1778 campaign. But judging decisiveness this way – as it is so often done in modern studies – is a deeply flawed approach, because the outcome has to be considered in terms of goals. On the operational level the Austrians appeared successful, as they denied Prussia the possibility of fighting a battle on Friedrich's terms or of moving deeper into Bohemia. There was criticism within the Austrian officer corps that the army did not seek the offensive itself and drive the Prussians out of the kingdom, but this was not the plan of either Lacy or Laudon. In operational terms the war was a defensive victory for Austria, even if the Prussian king tried to reverse this fact in his history of the war:

> The third accusation applies above all to the Austrian general who worked out the campaign plan. This plan in no way corresponded to the political situation of the court; for the Emperor had no ally from whom he could look for help. On the other hand, the King of Prussia could count on the support of the Russians, the troops of Hanover and other imperial princes. So it was not at all in the interest of the imperial army to limit its defence plan as narrowly as the banks of the Elbe. The defensive against Saxony and Lusatia was just as unwise as that of the Emperor against Silesia; for it is impossible to defend such extensive frontiers against an enemy who, if he penetrates with all his might at a single point, will overturn all the measures taken against him, and throw into confusion all the departments charged with frontier protection, since they have to withdraw hastily. This often happened in the Alps when the kings of Sardinia wanted to prevent the passage: the French always forced it. If they could not penetrate at one point, they found ways and means to advance elsewhere, as far as Piedmont and Turin. The Emperor's interest, then, dictated that he begin an offensive war, attacking the Prussians the moment they emerged from the Silesian mountains; for if he struck them, it was foreseeable that such a decisive blow would intimidate their allies and prevent any assistance from their side. But if he was defeated, he always found his fortified positions behind the Elbe, in which he was able to hold his ground, stop the further advance of the enemy and wage a defensive war, which would then have corresponded to all the rules of art.[1]

However, contrary to this analysis, Friedrich himself had not concentrated his troops for such a blow at a single point.

On the strategic level the roles had been reversed with Austria seeking territorial gains, while Friedrich just wanted to prevent this. In general, he

---

1 Volz (ed.), *Die Werke Friedrichs des Großen*, Vol.5, p.132.

achieved this aim so there is no reason to consider this conflict – from a Prussian perspective – as indecisive. The war aim – as in the Seven Years War – was the status quo ante and this was essentially fulfilled. However, there is another level which was important to eighteenth century rulers and which must not be ignored. Wars were fought for the reputation of the ruler. This was true of Friedrich, who later claimed to have started the First Silesian War with the 'ambition […] to make myself a reputation',[2] but also for Joseph II who tried to copy Friedrich in his martial habits. In this regard both rulers failed. Joseph was not, and would never become, a second Frederick the Great and despite the fact that the war was in rational terms a Prussian success, the fact that Friedrich was not able to win new battlefield laurels was definitely recognized by contemporaries and tarnished his reputation. Friedrich, however, tried to justify his conduct in the war by writing his own history of it and clearly put the blame on the mistreated Saxons, adding a final injury to his treatment of his unnatural allies:

> The Prussians, on the other hand, can be accused of lacking nerve and energy in their Saxon army; for she missed a single opportunity that presented itself when Prince Heinrich was at Niemes and the king at Hohenelbe. A march across the Iser was enough to force the Emperor to retreat. Then the Emperor found no better position for his army than behind the Bohdanech ponds or perhaps near Kutná Hora. In this case, however, half of Bohemia was lost to him, and the Prussians gained a decisive advantage over their enemies in this campaign.[3]

However, not even contemporaries found this very convincing.

The diplomatic dimension of the war is also important to its conduct and outcome. Right from the beginning the Austrians, especially Maria Theresia, who favoured peace, offered negotiations, while Friedrich hoped for the Russians to mediate in his favour. As Prussia's goals in the war were limited and indirect – denying Austria territorial gains – there was a greater willingness to rely on negotiations than to spend blood in risky attacks, a point that is not very often appreciated when this war is analysed in terms of a decline of Prussian military power or Friedrich in terms of an old tired general.

In a longer perspective the war also demonstrated the Prussian ambition to influence the processes within the Empire. While so far it had built up alliances to strengthen its own hand in conflict, the War of the Bavarian Succession clearly demonstrated Berlin's willingness to act as an antipole to Vienna. This policy was eased by Joseph's irrational politics which ignored the complex balances within the Imperial estates. It was quite an achievement to drive a generally loyal and pro-Austrian country like Saxony into the arms of Prussia, which had overtaken it during the last half century and bled it white just 15 years before. The conflict also demonstrated that second rank powers like Saxony tried to use the Austro-Prussian rivalry to their own advantages: if the Saxon gains were limited, so too had been their goals.

---

2   Volz (ed.), *Die Werke Friedrichs des Großen*, Vol.2, p.6.
3   Volz (ed.), *Die Werke Friedrichs des Großen*, Vol.5, p.132.

Appendix I

Order of Battle and Deployment of the Imperial and Royal Austrian Army, 1 July 1778

Commander-in-Chief Emperor Joseph II with headquarters in Mladějow northeast of Sobotka: Quartermaster-General of the Army GM von Kuhn;[1] Under-Quartermaster-General *Oberst* von Seeger; Chief of Artillery FML Freiherr von Rouvroy; Chief of the Engineering Corps FZM Graf Pellegrini.

Right Wing of the Army

Commander: FM Duke Albert of Saxe-Teschen with headquarters at Jaroměř; Deputy-commander, FM Graf Hadik; Chief of the Quartermaster General's Staff, *Oberst* Freiherr von Elmpt.

First Line
Cavalry Corps. Commander, GdK Freiherr von Jacquemin at Smiřitz.
Division FML Frieherr von Miltitz (Brigade GM Freiherr von Zezschwitz) at Chrudim, 12 squadrons.
Division FML Graf Almásy (Brigade GM Graf Hohenzollern) between Miletin, Königinhof and Miletin, Bürglitz, Siebojed, 14 squadrons.

Infantry Corps. Commander, FZM Freiherr von Elrichshausen at Jaroměř.
Division FML Graf Michael Wallis (Brigades of GM Graf Kinsky and GM von Alemann) from Předměřitz via Lochenitz to Semonitz on both sides of the Elbe, 10 battalions.

---

[1] When the army was formed, GM Pavlovsky, then GM Baron von Bechard, served as Army Quartermaster General. In place of the latter, at the beginning of June, GM von Kuhn was appointed.

Division FML Graf Patrik Olivier Wallis (Brigades of GM Graf Grisoni and GM Fürst Hohenlohe-Kirchberg) from Ples on the left bank of the Elbe via Jaroměř, Grabschütz, Wölsdorf, Schurz, Gradlitz to Königinhof, 10 battalions.

Second Line

Cavalry Corps. Commander, GdK Freiherr von Jacquemin at Smiřitz.[2]

Division FML Graf Wurmser (Brigade GM Freiherr von Wimpifen) at Librantitz on the left bank of the Elbe northwest of Hohenbruck and near Chrudim, 12 squadrons.

Division FML Freiherr von Barcö (Brigade vacant) von Dohalitz an der Bistritz via Sadowa, Maslowěd, Benatek, Hořenowes to Žíželowes, 14 squadrons.

Infantry Corps. Commander, FZM Freiherr von Elrichshausen at Jaroměř.[3]
Division FML Graf d'Alton (Brigades of GM Graf Kaunitz-Rietberg and
GM Graf Wenzel Colloredo) from Plotitscht, Břiza via Swěty, Nedelischt, Chlum, Habřina to Neznaschow, seven battalions.

Division FML Freiherr von Drechsel (Brigades of GM Freiherr von Neugebauer and GM Graf Anton Esterházy) from Ertina via Littitsch, Salnei, Kaschow, Siebojed to Liebthal, eight battalions.

Other Forces

Detached Brigade of GM Graf Wartensleben at Pardubitz and Němčitz, three battalions, 800 Scharfschützen and Jäger (approximately one battalion), nine squadrons.

At the outposts along the Prussian border, eight squadrons.

Under FML Graf d'Alton at Arnau, three battalions and two squadrons.

Artillery Reserve under GM Freiherr von Bärnkopp at Trotina, four battalions with 55 guns.

Stabsinfanterie, Stabsdragoner, Pioneers, at Jaroměř, two battalions, two squadrons.

Army Train under *Oberstleutnant* von Humbracht at Jaroměř, nine companies (3,946 men, 598 horses).

Fortress garrison of Königgrätz under GM Freiherr von Bechard, six battalions.

Total of the right wing of the army: 54 battalions, nine companies, 73 squadrons, 70,000 men, 19,000 horses, 223 guns.

Centre of the Army

Commander: FM Graf Lacy with headquarters at Wostružno west of Jičin; Chief of the Quartermaster General's Staff, *Oberst* von Renner.

---

2 That is to say, Jacquemin was in command of the cavalry of the first and second lines.
3 That is to say, Elrichshausen was in command of the infantry of the first and second lines.

Vanguard Corps
Commander FML Graf Samuel Gyulai (Brigade GM Freiherr von Kiss), from Reichenberg via Kunnersdorf, Radl, Böhmisch-Aicha and Oschitz to Wartenberg, six battalions, 400 Scharfschützen (half-battalion), 13 squadrons.

First Line
Cavalry Corps. Commander, GdK Marquis Voghera at Wokschitz near Jičin.
Division FML Freiherr von Brockhausen (Brigade GM Graf Richecourt) at Markwatitz, Unter-Bautzen and Řitonitz, 20 squadrons.

Infantry Corps. Commander, FZM Graf Siskovics at Jičin.
Division FML Freiherr von Stain (Brigades of GM Graf Fabris und GM Graf Clerfayt) at Jičin, Eisenstadtl and Libuň, nine battalions.
Division FML von Langlois (Brigade GM von Lübeck) near Wschen, Groß-Skal and Wiskeř, six battalions.

Second Line
Cavalry Corps. Commander, GdK Marquis Voghera at Wokschitz near Jičin.[4]
Division FML Graf Nostitz (Brigade GM Graf Blankenstein) from Liban via Wosenitz to Žerčitz, 20 squadrons.

Infantry Corps. Commander, FZM Graf Siskovics at Jičin.[5]
Division FML Graf Josef Colloredo (Brigades of GM Gazzinelli and GM von Terzy) between Podhrad and Přichwoj, Pudkosť and Dobschitz, 10 battalions.
Division FML von Lattermann (Brigade GM Karl Erbprinz von Hesse-Rheinfels) between Lamnitz and Stružinetz, six battalions.

Other Forces
Artillery Reserve under *Oberst* Penzeneter von Pentzenstein, at Brodetz, four battalions with 55 guns.
Stabsinfanterie, Stabsdragoner, technical troops, at Jičin, two battalions, two squadrons.
Army Train under *Oberst* von Krauß at Jičin, eight companies (3,705 men, 7,162 horses).

Total of the centre of the army: 43½ battalions, eight companies, 55 squadrons, 58,000 men, 14,500 horses, 203 guns.

Left Wing of the Army

Commander: FM Freiherr von Loudon with headquarters at Podkosť; Chief of the Quartermaster General's Staff, *Oberst* Zehentner.

---
4 That is to say, Voghera was in command of the cavalry of the first and second lines.
5 That is to say, Siskovics was in command of the infantry of the first and second lines.

Vanguard Corps
Commander, FML von Graeven (Brigade GM de Vins), from Niemes, Reichstadt via Gabel to Ringelshain, six battalions, 400 sharpshooters (½ battalion), 14 squadrons.

First Line
Infantry Corps. Commander, FZM Graf Pellegrini in Münchengrätz.
Division FML Count Nugent (Brigade GM Graf Brechainville) at Bakow, Zasadka east of Münchengrätz and Žďár, south-east of Loukow, six battalions.
Division FML Freiherr von Tillier (Brigades GM Graf Remigius Wallis and GM Graf Herberstein) at Nieder-Gruppai, Kosmanos and Jungbunzlau, nine battalions.

Cavalry Corps. Commander, GdK Graf Esterházy in Jungbunzlau.
Division FML Prinz Friedrich Josias von Sachsen-Koburg (Brigade GM von Sauer) between Podlazky and Katusitz on the right bank of the Iser west of Kosmanos, 18 squadrons.

Second Line
Infantry Corps. Commander, FZM Graf Pellegrini in Münchengrätz.[6]
Division FML Graf Franz Harrach (Brigade GM Freiherr von Reisky) between Münchengrätz and Fürstenbruck, six battalions.
Division FML Fürst de Ligne (Brigades GM Graf Thun-Hohenstein and GM Graf Arco) between Brezno and Dobrowitz near Jungbunzlau, then near Kloster, Haber and Maükowitz west of Münchengrätz, nine battalions.

Cavalry Corps. Commander, GdK Graf Esterházy in Jungbunzlau.[7]
Division FML Graf Josef Kinsky (Brigade GM von Haag) from Krnsko on the Iser west of Strenitz and Skalsko to Mscheno, 20 squadrons.

Corps on the Left Bank of the Elbe
Commander, GdK Fürst Karl Liechtenstein in Leitmeritz.
Division FML von Riese in Aussig: Brigade GM Graf Tige near Dlaschkowitz southwest of Lobositz and Modlan, northeast of Teplitz, 14 squadrons; Brigade GM Graf Hohenfeld near Brozan and Budin on the Eger, then near Türmitz on the Biela, six battalions; Brigade GM Graf Browne near Leitmeritz, Lobositz, Aussig and Schwaden, six battalions; Brigade GM Prinz Georg von Mecklenburg-Strelitz near Teplitz, six squadrons.

Other Forces
Artillery reserve of the left army wing at Brodetz, four battalions with 60 guns.
Stabsinfanterie, Stabsdragoner, technical troops, at Podkosť, two battalions, two squadrons.

---

6   That is to say, Pellegrini was in command of the infantry of the first and second lines.
7   That is to say, Esterházy was in command of the cavalry of the first and second lines.

Army Train near Podkosť, nine companies (3,706 men, 7163 horses).

Total of the left wing of the army: 54½ battalions, nine companies, 74 squadrons, 70,000 men, 20,000 horses, 252 guns.

Garrisons and Reinforcements

Fortress Garrison of Prague, GM von Hasslinger (later FZM Graf Guasco): six third battalions, one squadron (3,100 men, 230 horses).
Fortress Garrison of Eger, GM von Schönowsky: four third battalions (3,300 men, 33 horses).
In Bavaria under FML Freiherr von Gemmingen zu Straubing: six third battalions.
On the march from the Netherlands via Luxembourg, Günzburg to Regensburg (by Danube ships), Falkenstein, Cham, Waldmünchen, Bischofteinitz, Pilsen to the army in Bohemia: Brigades of GM Graf Rindsmaul and GM Graf d'Arberg, seven battalions, one dragoon regiment, two artillery companies, 34 field guns.

Total of the garrisons and reinforcements: 23 battalions, two companies, six squadrons, 25,000 men, 1,000 horses, 34 guns.

Corps in Moravia and Silesia

Commander: FML Marquis Botta; Chief of the Quartermaster General's Staff, *Oberstleutnant* Jenney.
Brigade GM Freiherr von Splenyi on the Mohra from Heidenpiltsch to Herzogswald, Butsch and Wigstadtl, six battalions.
Brigade GM von Knebel near Schönwald, one battalion, six squadrons.
Brigade GM von Kirchheim near Friedland, Zuckmantel, Jägerndorf, Troppau and on outposts, ½ battalion, six squadrons.
Brigade GM Graf Josef Mittrowsky between Bielitz and Teschen, two battalions, six squadrons.
Detached in Galicia: Brigade of *Oberst* Latour between Wieliczka and Bochnia, two battalions, two squadrons.
Artillery, six companies; Army Train, four companies.

Total of the corps in Moravia and Silesia 11½ battalions, 10 companies, 20 squadrons, 15,000 men, 5,000 horses, 56 guns.

Fortress garrison of Olmütz: seven third battalions (5,600 men).

Fortress garrison from Brünn (Spielberg) two third battalions (1,600 men).

The army under the supreme command of the Emperor Josef II, assembled in the theatre of war, on 1 July 1778 therefore had in all 195½ battalions,

38 companies, 228 squadrons with an effective strength of 250,000 men, 60,000 horses, 768 guns.

Of these were disposed:

In the army in Bohemia on both sides of the Elbe and Iser 129 battalions, 196 squadrons, 163,000 men, 36,000 horses, 712 field guns.

With the corps in Moravia-Silesia 11½ battalions, 20 squadrons, 12,000 men, 3,500 horses, 56 field guns.

Total strength of the fighting force 140½ battalions, 216 squadrons, 175,000 men, 39,500 horses, 768 guns.

Source: Oskar von Criste, *Kriege unter Kaiser Josef II: nach den Feldakten und anderen authentischen Quellen bearbeitet in der kriegsgeschichtlichen Abteilung des k. und k. Kriegsarchivs* (Wein: Verlag von L. W. Seidel & Sohn, 1904), pp.263-266.

Appendix II

Order of Battle and Formation of the Allied Prussian-Saxon Army on July 1, 1778

Commander in Chief: Friedrich II with headquarters at Silberberg.

First Army

First Line

Commander: GdI Erbprinz von Braunschweig between Reichenbach, Silberberg, Wartha, Patschkau, Frankenstein and Nimptsch.
Cavalry Division of GL von Bülow (Brigade GM von Prittwitz), 13 squadrons.
Infantry Division of GL Prinz Friedrich von Braunschweig (Brigades GM von Röder and von Zaremba), 15 battalions.
Infantry Division of GL von Ramin (Brigade GM Bornstedt), five battalions.
Infantry Division of GL von Stutterheim (Brigades of GM Graf Anhalt and von Schwartz), 10 battalions.
Division of GM von Dalwig (Infantry brigade GM von Rohr, cavalry brigades of GM von Podewils, von Arnim and von Pannewitz), five battalions, 20 squadrons.
Total: 25 battalions, 43 squadrons.

Second Line

Commander: GdI von Tauentzien between Nimptsch, Frankenstein, Wartha, Patschkau and Münsterberg, then between Ottmachau and Neisse.
Division GL von Thadden (Brigades of GM von Wulffen and Prinz von Preußen), five battalions, 20 squadrons.
Infantry Division GL von Falkenhayn (Brigades of GM von Erlach, von Billerbeck, von Keller), 15 battalions.
Division of GL von Rentzell (Infantry brigade von Flemming, Cavalry brigade von Thun), five battalions, five squadrons.

Cavalry brigades of GM von Bosse, 5 squadrons, GM von Lossow, 20 squadrons.
Total: 25 battalions, 50 squadrons.

Reserves

1st Reserve Corps: GL von Krockow, Cavalry Brigade GM von Apenburg, 10 squadrons near Neisse; Infantry Brigades of GM von Lestwitz, six battalions, and GM von Braun, four battalions, near Reichenbach, Münsterberg and the surrounding area.

2nd Reserve Corps: GL von Werner: Brigades of GM von Krockow, von Lehwaldt and von Lengefeld, 10 battalions, 10 squadrons near Neisse and the surrounding area.

3rd Reserve Corps: GL von Wubsch: Brigades of GM Pelkowsky, von Luck and Landgraf Hesse-Philippsthal, 11 battalions, 10 squadrons east from Nimptsch between the Lohe and Ohlau.
Total: 31 battalions, 30 squadrons.

Fortress garrisons in Silesia in Silberberg, Glatz, Neisse, Schweidnitz etc., about 15 battalions.

Total strength of the First Army in Silesia 96 battalions, 123 squadrons, 16 position batteries or including artillery, technical troops, train etc. about 115,000 men: effective, 80,000 men with 433 guns.

Second Army

Commander-in-Chief Prinz Heinrich von Preußen with headquarters in Berlin.

Prussian Troops

First Line

Cavalry Division of GL von Platen (Brigade GM von Seelhorst), 10 squadrons at Schönebeck, Frohse an der Elbe and Großsalze, then at Halle an der Saale.

Division of GL Prinz of Anhalt-Bernburg (Brigades of GM von Bohlen, von Reitzenstein, von Kalckstein), 10 squadrons, five battalions between Köthen, Bernburg, Ketzin, Brandenburg an der Havel and Bagow am Beetz-See, then in Berlin, Potsdam, Micheln north of Köthen, Beeskow an der Spree.

Infantry Division of GL Graf Hordt (Brigade GM von Lettow), five battalions in Berlin, Potsdam and Aken on the Elbe.

Infantry Division of GL von Kleist (Brigade GM von Schlieben), five battalions in Aken and Koethen.

Infantry Division of GL von Möllendorff (Brigades of GM von Eichmann and von Sobeck), 10 battalions between Aken, Köthen and Bernburg, then in Kalbe, Beeskow and Potsdam.

Cavalry Division of GL von Pomeiske (Brigades of GM von Marwitz and von Weyher), 20 squadrons in Berlin, Potsdam, Charlottenburg, near Großrosenburg at the confluence the Saale and Elbe, then at Bischofsee, Kunuersdorf etc., in the area of Frankfurt an der Oder.

Total: 25 battalions, 40 squadrons.

Second Line

Cavalry Division of GL von Lölhöffel (Brigade GM Graf Lottum), 10 squadrons in Berlin and at Buckow etc. west of Beeskow an der Spree.

Infantry Division of GL von Wolffersdorff (Brigade GM von Waldeck), six battalions in Berlin, then between Aken and Köthen, near Trebbichau etc.

Infantry Division of GL von Brietzke (GM von Haacke), seven battalions in Berlin, Bernburg and surroundings.

Infantry Division of GL Prinz von Nassau-Usingen (Brigade GM von Steinwehr and von Knobelsdorff), 12 battalions near Köthen, Bernburg, Kalbe, Storkow, Frankfurt an der Oder.

Cavalry Division of GL von Belling (Brigade GM von Posadowsky), 10 squadrons between Lebus and Frankfurt on the right bank of the Oder.

Total: 25 battalions, 20 squadrons.

Reserve Corps

Cavalry Division of GL von Lentulus (Brigades of GM von Czettritz and von Podjursky), 50 squadrons in Berlin, Fürstenwalde, between Frankfurt an der Oder, Müllrose and Beeskow.

Infantry Division of GL von Lossow (Brigades of GM von Petersdorff and von Zastrow), 11 Battalions near Spandau, Treuenbrietzen, München-Nienburg and Altenburg on the Saale, then at Fürstenwalde.

Total: 11 battalions, 50 squadrons.

Other Troops

Freiregiment von Hordt two battalions; Freibataillon von Politz one battalion.

Artillery train, provisions transport, field war chest, bakery and hospital in Berlin, then between Aken and Köthen.

The Royal Prussian troops therefore numbered 64 battalions, 110 squadrons, with 311 guns.

Electoral Saxon Troops

Commander: GL Graf von Solms with headquarters at Dresden

First Line

Cavalry Division of GL von Benkendorff (Brigade GM du Hamel), eight squadrons near Wilsdruff and Pirna.

Infantry Division of GL von Bennigsen (Brigades of GM le Coq and von Pfeylitzer), 16 battalions at Tharandt, Rabenau, Dippoldiswalde, Reinhardtgrimma, Possendorf and Großröhrsdorf.

Second Line
Division of GL Graf Anhalt (Cavalry brigades of GM von Goldacker and von Brüneberg), 16 squadrons at Kesselsdorf, Gorbitz, Plauen and Leuven; (Infantry brigades of GM von Karlsburg and von Zauthier), 10 battalions near Dresden, Lockwitz, Dohna, Pirna and Hohenstein east of Pirna on the right bank of the Elbe.

Other Troops
Detached corps, two battalions, four squadrons.
Artillery consisting of 122 guns at Gruna southeast of Dresden.
Garrison of Dresden under the command of *Oberst* von Gaudi, six battalions, four squadrons.
Total of the Electoral Saxon troops: 34 battalions, 32 squadrons, 122 guns.

Total of Second Army under the supreme command of Prinz Heinrich von Preußen: 98 battalions, 142 squadrons, 433 guns, with an effective strength of about 115,000 men, including the artillery, the technical troops, the Train, etc., to give 80,000 effectives with 433 guns.

Of this mass were under the immediate command of Prinz Heinrich in the Mark between Berlin and Brandenburg 18 battalions, 30 squadrons; under the command of GL von Möllendorff between Frankfurt an der Oder, Fürstenwalde, Storkow and Beeskow 11 battalions, 40 squadrons; under the command of GL Prinz von Anhalt-Bernburg in Magdeburg and Anhalt between Halle and Magdeburg 35 battalions, 40 squadrons; finally in the Electorate of Sachsen the Saxon army between Dresden, Pirna, Tharandt and Wilsdruff

34 battalions, 32 squadrons.

Total strength of the allied Prussian-Saxon army 194 battalions, 265 squadrons, 866 guns with an effective strength of approximately 230,000 men and a fighting force of 160,000 men with 866 guns.

Source: Criste, *Kriege unter Kaiser Josef II*, pp.267-269.

Appendix III

Composition of the Prussian Armies in 1778

First, or Main, Army

Grenadier Battalions

Schlieben Nr.1/13
Rautern Nr.2/16
Hausen N3.4/53
Ramecke Nr.5/20
Apenburg Nr.15/l8
Below Nr.17/22
Löben Nr.19/25
Eberstein Nr.23/26
Kowalsky Nr.29/3l

Preuß Nr.33/42
Scholten Nr.36/Gar.7
Görz Nr.37/38
Lölhöfel Nr.40/43
Oserowski Nr.51/52
Frankenberg Nr.54/55
Stehende Grenadier-Bataillon Hardt Nr.4
Stehende Grenadier-Bataillon Lentzke Nr.5
Stehende Grenadier-Bataillon Gillern Nr.6

Infantry Regiments

Kalckreuth Nr.1 (2 bns)
Stuttherhiem Nr.2 (2 bns)
Thadden Nr.4 (2 bns)
Braun Nr.13 (2 bns)
Garde zu Fuss Nr.15 (3 bns)
Buddenbrock Nr.16 (2 bns)
Billerbeck Nr.17 (2 bns)
Prinz von Preussen Nr.18 (2 bns)
Braunschweig Nr.19 (2 bns)
Schlieben Nr.22 (2 bns)
Rentzell (later Thüna) Nr.23 (2 bns)
Ramin Nr.25 (2 bns)
Woldeck Nr.26 (2 bns)
Kalckstein Nr.28 (2 bns)
Flemming Nr.29 (2 bns)

Tauentzien Nr.31 (2 bns)
Hohenlohe-Ingelfingen Nr.33 (2 bns)
Raumer Nr.36 (2 bns)
Keller Nr.37 (2 bns)
Falkenhayn Nr.38 (2 bns)
Erlach Nr.40 (2 bns)
Brandenburg-Schwedt Nr.42 (2 bns)
Anhalt Nr.43 (2 bns)
Schwartz Nr.49 (2 bns)
Krockow Nr.51 (2 bns)
Lengefeld Nr.52 (2 bns)
Luck Nr.53 (2 bns)
Rohr Nr.54 (2 bns)
Hessen-Philippsthal Nr.55 (2 bns)

APPENDIX III

Light Infantry
Freiregiment Hordt (2 bns)
Freiregiment Stein (2 bns)
Freibataillon Politz

Cuirassier Regiments
Roeder Nr.1 (5 sqns)
Arnim Nr.4 (5 sqns)
Pannwitz Nr.8 (5 sqns)
Podewils Nr.9 (5 sqns)
Gensdarmes Nr.10 (5 sqns)
Dallwig Nr.12 (5 sqns)
Garde du Corps Nr.13 (3 sqns)

Dragoon Regiments
Krockow (later Württemberg) Nr.2 (5 sqns)
Thun Nr.3 (5 sqns)
Wulffen Nr.4 (5 sqns)
Anspach-Bayreuth Nr.5 (10 sqns)
Apenburg Nr.7 (5 sqns)
Finckenstein Nr.10 (5 sqns)
Bosse Nr.11 (5 sqns)

Hussar Regiments
Leib Husaren Nr.2 (10 sqns)
Rosenbusch Nr.3 (10 sqns)
Lossow Nr5 (10 sqns)
Werner Nr.6 (10 sqns)
Bosniaken-Corps Nr.9 (10 sqns)

Artillery
Artillerie-Regiment Nr.1 (7 cos)
Artillerie-Regiment Nr.2 (7 cos)
Artillerie-Regiment Nr.3 (5 cos)
Artillerie-Regiment Nr.4 (5 cos)

Other Troops
Jäger zu Pferd (one company)
Garnison-Bataillon von Brehme

Second Army

Grenadier Battalions
Blomberg Nr.3/6
Owstien Nr.7/8
Bandemer Nr.9/10
Herzberg Nr.11/14
Brösicke Nr.12/13
Holstein Nr.21/27
Grollmann Nr.24/39
Kamecke Nr.28/32
Resdorf Nr.30/47
Brünow Nr.35/46
Stehende Grenadier-Bataillon Oldenburg Nr.1
Stehende Grenadier-Bataillon Meusel Nr.2
Stehende Grenadier-Bataillon Romberg Nr.3
Stehende Grenadier-Bataillon Bähr Nr.7

Infantry Regiments
Anhalt-Bernburg-Schaumburg Nr.3 (3 bns)
Saldern Nr.5 (2 bns)
Bevern Nr.7 (2 bns)
Hacke Nr.8 (2 bns)
Wolffersdorff Nr.9 (2 bns)
Petersdorff Nr.10 (2 bns)
Zastrow Nr.11 (2 bns)
Braunschweig-Wolfenbüttel Nr.24 (2 bns)
Knobelsdorff Nr.27 (2 bns)
Sobeck (later von Birckensee) Nr.30 (2 bns)
Brösigke Nr.34 (2 bns)
Brünow Nr.35 (2 bns)
Möllendorff Nr.39 (2 bns)
Lossau Nr.4l (2 bns)

THE WAR OF THE BAVARIAN SUCCESSION 1778-1789

Order of Battle of the Prussian First Army in 1778. (SächsHStA DD)

Wunsch Nr.12 (2 bns)
Steinwehr Nr.14 (2 bns)
L. Kalckreuth Nr.20 (2 bns)
Schwerin Nr.21 (2 bns)

Britzke Nr.44 (2 bns)
Hessen-Kassel Nr.45 (2 bns)
Pfuel Nr.46 (2 bns)
Nassau-Usingen (later Lehwaldt) Nr.47 (2 bns)

Cuirassier Regiments

Wiersbitzki Nr.2 (5 sqns)
Leibregiment zu Pferd Nr.3 (5 sqns)
Lölhöffel Nr.5 (5 sqns)

Hoverbeck Nr.6 (5 sqns)
Marwitz Nr.7 (5 sqns)
Leibkarabinier Nr.11 (5 sqns)

Dragoon Regiments

Lottum Nr.1 (5 sqns)
Posadowsky Nr.6 (10 sqns)
Platen Nr.8 (5 sqns)

Pomeiske Nr.9 (5 sqns)
Reitzenstein Nr.12 (5 sqns)

Hussar Regiments

Czettritz Nr.1 (10 sqns)
Podgruski Nr.4 (10 sqns)
Usedom Nr.7 (10 sqns)

Hohenstock Nr.8 (10 sqns)
Owstein Nr.10 (10 sqns)

Artillery

Artillerie-Regiment Nr.1 (3 cos)
Artillerie-Regiment Nr.2 (3 cos)

Artillerie-Regiment Nr.3 (5 cos)
Artillerie-Regiment Nr.4 (5 cos)

Source: Nafziger Collection 778XAA 'Prussian Army War of the Bavarian Succession 1778-1779', with details from Duffy, *Army of Frederick the Great* (Second Edition), pp.363-390.

Bibliography

Archival Sources

Geheimes Staatsarchiv Preußischer Kulturbesitz
HA Rep. 96, Nr. 66 H Schriftwechsel mit dem kursächischen Gesandten im preußischen Hauptquartier Friedrich August Graf von Zinzendorf und Pottendorf über den Bayerischen Erbfolgekrieg und den Frieden von Teschen.
Nr. 92 C 2 Bremer.
Nr. 92 D Czetteritz.
Nr. 92 H 4 Errichtung von Freikorps im Bayerischen Erbfolgekrieg.
Nr. 92 H 1 Ramin.
Nr. 92 H 2 Saß.
Nr. 92 G Moellendorf.
BPH Rep. 47 Nr. 536 Militärischen Angelegenheiten und Instruktionen während des Feldzuges 1778/79 im Bayerischen Erbfolgekrieg.

Sächsisches Hauptstaatsarchiv Dresden
10025 Geheimes Konsilium
Loc. 05806/01 Die von den Emperorlich Königlichen Trouppen der Stadt Zittau im Jahr 1778 auferlegte Kriegs-Contribution, und die zu deren Tilgung, auch Wiederaufnahme dasiger Stadt, geschehenen Vorschläge betr. Anno 1778.
Loc. 6405/02 Was während der über die kurbayerische Sukzessionsangelegenheit ausgebrochenen Kriegsunruhen wegen des Kommandos über die kursächsische Armee, derselben Delogierung, auch erforderliche Marschquartiere und Vorspanne geschrieben worden.
Loc. 6412/05 Die von den Bewegungen und Verteidigungs-Anstalten der Kayserlich-Königlichen Truppen, sowohl als von den durch selbige in hiesigen Landen verübten Feindseligkeiten eingegangenen Anzeigen betr. Anno 1778.
Loc. 6419/08 Die Winterverpflegung der königlich preußischen Armee aus hiesigen Landen.
Loc. 06426/05 Der Einmarsch der königlich preußischen Truppen in hiesige Lande und die für selbige gelieferten Verpflegungsbedürfnisse, auch gestellte Vorspanne.
10026 Geheimes Kabinett
Loc. 01099/12 Briefe und Berichte des Generallieutenants von Bennigsen an den Kabinettsminister von Stutterheim.
Loc. 03399/06 Beilagen und Noten zum Gesandtschaftsgeschäffte seit Rück-Kunft von Tschen nach Berlin 1779.

11237 Geheimes Kriegsratskollegium
- 1367 Nach dem Einmarsch preußischer Truppen in Sachsen ergangene Anordnungen zur Deckung des Bedarfs an Quartieren und Verpflegung.
- 1368 Durchmarsch eines Korps preußischer Truppen durch die Niederlausitz und Einmarsch der preußischen Armee in Kursachsen.
- 1369 Wegen des mobil gemachten und im Feld stehende kursächsische Armeekorps ergangene Anordnungen sowie Berichte und Vorträge des Geheimen Kriegsrats und Direktors des Feldkriegskommissariats von Schleinitz.
- 1370 Marschbefehle für Kompanien der Regimenter Friedrich Christoph Graf zu Solms-Wildenfels, Edler v. Lecoq, und Carl Maximilian Prinz von Sachsen, u. a. nach Frauenstein und Falkenhain.
- 1371 Nach dem Einmarsch preußischer Truppen in Sachsen ergangene Anordnungen zur Deckung des Bedarfs an Quartieren und Verpflegung.
- 1372 Wegen der in dem Gegenden um Dresden kantonierten, neuformierten und mobil gemachten kursächsischen Armee ergangenen Anordnungen.
- 1373 Acta Die zwischen denen zu dem Auswechßelungs-Geschäffte ernannten Kayserl: Königlen und Königl: Preußischen bevollmächtigten Commissarien geschloßene Convention in Betreff derer auszuwechselnden Kayserl: Königl: Königl: Preußischen und Chur Saechßischen Kriegsgefangenen und zu erlaßenden Geißeln und was dem anhaengig betr. Anno 1779.
- 1374 Den March und die Verquartierung derer Kayßerl: Königl: Kriegs-Gefangenen, sammt deren Escorte von Dresden über Meißen Torgau und Jüterbogk in die Churbrandenburgischen Lande und was dem anhängig betr.: Anno 1778.
- 1375 Defensions-Veranstaltungen in und um der Gegend Dreßden Anno 1778. 1779. 1780. 1781.
- 1376 Rückmarsch der preußischen Armee aus Sachsen nach dem Friedensschluss und die mit dem preußischen Feldkriegskommissariat wegen der erforderlichen Vorspanndienste geschlossene Konvention vom 20. April 1779.
- 1377 Wegen des mobil gemachten und im Feld stehende kursächsische Armeekorps ergangene Anordnungen.
- 1378 Rückmarsch der kursächsischen Truppen nach dem Friedensschluss in ihre angewiesenen Standquartiere.
- 1379 Bayerischer Erbfolgekrieg.
- 1380 Nach dem Einmarsch preußischer Truppen in Sachsen ergangene Anordnungen zur Deckung des Bedarfs an Quartieren und Verpflegung.
- 1381 Rückmarsch der preußischen Armee aus Sachsen nach dem Friedensschluss und die mit dem preußischen Feldkriegskommissariat wegen der erforderlichen Vorspanndienste geschlossene Konvention vom 20. April 1779.
- 1382 Die in Ansehung des Mobilgemachten und in Campagne befindlichen Chur-Sechßischen Corps d'Armeé ergangenen Anordnungen und was dem anhaengig betr.
- 1383 Nach dem Einmarsch preußischer Truppen in Sachsen ergangene Anordnungen zur Deckung des Bedarfs an Quartieren und Verpflegung.

11338 Generalfeldmarschallamt
- Loc. 11003/07 Journal derer von dem commandirenden Herrn General-Lieutenant Grafen zu Solms an das unter seinem Commando stehende Corps d'Armée ergangen Parolen und täglichen Befehle, nebst denen von den Regimentern hierauf eingereichten Anzeigen 1778.
- Loc. 11004/15 Ausfertigungen das Commando des mobilen Corps betreffend.
- Loc. 11004/16 Befehle des Prinzen von Anhalt-Bernburg an das sächsische Armeekorps während des Bayerischen Erbfolgekrieges.

Printed Primary Sources

Berenhorst, Georg Heinrich von, *Betrachtungen über die Kriegskunst, über ihre Fortschritte, ihre Widersprüche und ihre Zuverläßigkeit, Erste Abtheilung* (Leipzig: Fleischer Verlag 1798).
Prussian Academy of Sciences (eds), *Politische Korrspondenz Friedrichs des Großen* (Berlin: Reimar Hobbing, 1925-1929).
Seidel, Carl von, *Versuch einer militärischen Geschichte des bayerischen Erbfolge-Kriegs, im Jahre 1778: Im Gesichtspunkte der Wahrheit betrachtet* (Königsberg: unknown publisher, 1781).
Seyfarth, Johann, *Unpartheyische Geschichte des Bayerischen Erbfolgekriegs in welcher nicht allein aus allen bey Gelegenheit desselben erschienen Staatsschriften Auszüge geliefert und von allen kriegerischen Vorfällen die beyderseitige Berichte angeführet, sondern auch in den beygefügten Anmerkungen alle vorkommende Städte, Dörfer etc. beschrieben und die Lebensumstände der merkwürdigsten Personen aus zuverlässigen Nachrichten beygebracht worden* (Leipzig: Paul Gotthelf Kummer 1780).
Schöning, Kurd Wolfgang von, *Der Bayerische Erbfolgekrieg … nach der Original-Correspondenz Friedrich des Grossen mit dem Prinzen Heinrich und seinen Generalen aus den Staats-Archiven bearbeitet* (Berlin – Potsdam: Ferdinand Riegel, 1854).
Volz, Gustav Berthold (ed.), *Die Werke Friedrichs des Großen in deutscher Übersetzung* (Berlin: Reimar Hobbing, 1913).
Wraxall, Nathaniel, *Memoirs of the Courts of Berlin, Dresden, Warsaw and Vienna* (Dublin: T. Cadell and W. Davies, 1799).

Secondary Sources

Allmayr-Beck, Johann Christoph, *Das Heer unter dem Doppeladler. Habsburgs Armeen 1718–1848* (Munich: Bertelsmann, 1981).
Baumgart, Peter, Kroener, Bernhard R., and Stübing, Heinz (eds), *Die preußische Armee zwischen Ancien Régime und Reichsgründung* (Paderborn: Ferdinand Schöningh, 2009).
Beck, Lorenz Friedrich, and Göse, Frank (eds), *Brandenburg und seine Landschaften. Zentrum und Region vom Spätmittelalter bis 1800* (Berlin: Lukas Verlag, 2009).
Berkovich, Ilya, *Motivation in War. The Experience of Common Soldiers in Old-Regime Europe* (New York: Cambridge University Press 2017).
Beyrich, Rudolf, 'Der geheime Plan der kursächsischen Räte zur Österreichischen Erbfolge vom Jahre 1738', in *NASG* 37 (1916), pp. 56-67.
Birk, Eberhard, Loch, Thorsten, and Popp, Peter Andreas (eds), *Wie Friedrich 'der Große' wurde. Eine kleine Geschichte des Siebenjährigen Krieges* (Freiburg i. Br. – Berlin – Vienna: Rombach, 2012).
Black, Jeremy, *The Rise of the European Powers 1679-1793* (London: Eward Arnold, 1990).
Black, Jeremy, *A Military Revolution? Military Change and European Society 1550 – 1800* (Basingstoke: Palgrave MacMillan, 1991).
Black, Jeremy, *From Louis XIV to Napoleon. The Fate of a Great Power* (London: Routledge, 2003).
Bleckwenn, Hans (ed.), *Das altpreußische Heer. Erscheinungsbild und Wesen 1713-1807* (Osnabrück: Biblio-Verlag, 1970-2007).
Bleckwenn, Hans, *Unter dem Preußen-Adler. Das brandenburgisch-preußische Heer 1640-1807* (Munich: Bertelsmann, 1978).

Bleckwenn, Hans, 'Altpreußischer Militär- und Landadel. Zur Frage ihrer angeblichen Interessengemeinschaft im Kantonwesen', *Zeitschrift für Heereskunde* 49 (1985), pp.93-95.

Brewer, John, *The Sinews of Power. War, Money and the English State, 1688-1783* (London: Unwin Hyman, 1989).

Bringmann, Wilhelm, *Preußen unter Friedrich Wilhelm II. 1787-1796* (Frankfurt a. M.: Peter Lang. 2001).

Büsch, Otto, *Militärsystem und Sozialleben im alten Preußen 1713 – 1807. Die Anfänge der sozialen Militarisierung der preußisch – deutschen Gesellschaft* (Berlin: De Gruyter, 1962).

Craeybeckx, Jan, 'The Brabant Revolution. A Conservative Revolt In A Backward Country?`, *Acta Historiae Neerlandica* (4/1970), pp.48-83.

Criste, Oskar von, *Kriege unter Kaiser Josef II: nach den Feldakten und anderen authentischen Quellen bearbeitet in der kriegsgeschichtlichen Abteilung des k. und k. Kriegsarchivs* (Wein: Verlag von L. W. Seidel & Sohn, 1904).

Duchhardt, Heinz, *Balance of Power und Pentarchie. Internationale Beziehungen 1700-1785* (Paderborn: Ferdinand Schoeningh, 1997).

Duffy, Christopher, *The Army of Frederick the Great* (second edition) (Warwick: Helion and Company, 2020).

Duffy, Christopher,: *Instrument of War. Volume 1 of the Austrian Army in the Seven Years War* (Warwick: Helion & Company, 2020).

Edelmair, Hans, 'Der Caputrock und seine Aufschläge, Umschläge und Überschläge`, *Pallasch* 31 (2009), pp.31-46.

Fichtenbauer, Peter, and Ortner, M. Christian (eds), *Die Geschichte der österreichischen Armee von Maria Theresia bis zur Gegenwart in Essays und bildlichen Darstellungen* (Vienna: Militaria Verlag, 2015).

Friedrich, Wolfgang, *Die Uniformen der Kurfürstlich/Königlich Sächsischen Armee 1763-1810* (Dresden: self published. 1997).

Glaser, Hubert, *Krone und Verfassung: König Max I. Joseph und der neue Staat* (Munich R. Piper & Co, 1980).

Görler, Carl, 'Studien zur Bedeutung des Siebenjährigen Krieges für Sachsen`, *NASG* 29 (1908), pp.118-149.

Göse, Frank (ed.), *Friedrich der Große und die Mark Brandenburg. Herrschaftspraxis in der Provinz* (Berlin: Lukas Verlag, 2012).

Guddat, Martin, *Grenadiere, Musketiere, Füsiliere. Die Infanterie Friedrichs des Großen* (Hamburg: Nikol Verlag. 1986).

Guddat, Martin, *Kürassiere, Dragoner, Husaren. Die Kavallerie Friedrichs des Großen* (Hamburg: Nikol Verlag, 1989).

Guddat, Martin, *Kanoniere, Bombardiere, Pontoniere. Die Artillerie Friedrichs des Großen* (Hamburg: Nikol Verlag, 1992).

Guddat, Martin, *Handbuch zur preußischen Militärgeschichte 1688-1786* (Hamburg: E. S. Mittler & Sohn, 2011).

Hanke, René, *Brühl und das Renversement des alliances. Die antipreußische Außenpolitik des Dresdner Hofes 1744 – 1756* (Münster: LIT Verlag, 2006).

Hauser, Oswald (ed.), *Friedrich der Große in seiner Zeit* (Cologne, Vienna: Böhlau 1987).

Hebelmann, Georg, *Das preußische 'Offizierskorps' im 18. Jahrhundert. Analyse der Sozialstruktur einer Funktionselite* (Münster: Uni Press, 1998).

Historische Kommission für die Provinz Sachsen und für Anhalt (eds), *Mitteldeutsche Lebensbilder Vol 3 Lebensbilder des 18. und 19. Jahrhunderts* (Magdeburg: Historische Kommission für die Provinz Sachsen und für Anhalt, 1928).

Hochedlinger, Michael, *Krise und Wiederherstellung. Österreichische Großmachtpolitik zwischen Türkenkrieg und "Zweiter Diplomatischer Revolution" 1787–1791* (Berlin: Duncker & Humblot, 2000).

Hochedlinger, Michael, *Austria's Wars of Emergence. War State and Society in the Habsburg Monarchy 1683-1797* (London: Longman, 2003).

Hoffmann, Johannes, *Die kursächsische Armee 1769 bis zum Beginn des Bayerischen Erbfolgekrieges* (Leipzig: S. Hirzel, 1914).

Hohrath, Daniel, *Friedrich der Große und die Uniformierung der preußischen Armee von 1740 bis 1786* (Vienna: Militaria, 2011).

Jany, Curt, *Geschichte der Königlich Preußischen Armee bis zum Jahre 1807. Vol 3 1763-1807* (Berlin: K. Siegismund 1929).

Jany, Curt, 'Die Kantonverfassung Friedrich Wilhelms I.' in *FBPG* 38 (1926), pp.225-272.

Keller, Katrin, 'Der Siebenjährige Krieg und die Wirtschaft Kursachsens`, in: *Sachsen und Dresden im Siebenjährigen Krieg* (=Dresdner Hefte 68), pp. 74-80.

Kling, Carl, *Geschichte der Bekleidung, Bewaffnung und Ausrüstung des Königlich Preußischen Heeres* (Weimar: Königl. Kriegsministerium, 1902-1912).

Knobelsdorff, Wilhelm von, *Zur Geschichte der Familie von Knobelsdorff* (Berlin: Unknown Publisher, 1857).

Kordel, Jacek, *Sachsen, Preußen und der Emperorhof im Streit um die Schönburgischen Herrschaften (1774-1779)* (Leipzig: Leipziger Universitätsverlag, 2021).

Johannes Kunisch, *Der kleine Krieg. Studien zum Heerwesen des Absolutismus* (Wiesbaden: Steiner, 1973).

Kunisch, Johannes (ed.), *Fürst – Gesellschaft – Krieg. Studien zur bellizistischen Disposition des absolutistischen Fürstenstaates* (Cologne – Weimar – Wien: Böhlau 1992).

Kunisch, Johannes, *Friedrich der Große. Der König und seine Zeit* (Munich: C.H. Beck, 2004).

Kroener, Bernhard R., and Pröve, Ralf (eds), *Krieg und Frieden. Militär und Gesellschaft in der Frühen Neuzeit* (Paderborn and Munich: Ferdinand Schöningh, 1996).

Kroener, Bernhard R. (ed.): *Europa im Zeitalter Friedrichs des Großen. Wirtschaft, Gesellschaft, Kriege* (Munich: Oldenbourg Verlag, 1989).

Kroll, Stefan, 'Kursächsische Soldaten in den drei Schlesischen Kriegen`, in Sachsen und Dresden im Siebenjährigen Krieg (=Dresdner Hefte 68), pp.35-41.

Kroll, Stefan, *Soldaten im 18. Jahrhundert zwischen Friedensalltag und Kriegserfahrung. Lebenswelten und Kultur in der kursächsischen Armee 1728 – 1796* (Paderborn: Ferdinand Schöningh, 2006).

Lange, Gerhard, *Die Reduktion und Reorganisation des sächsischen Heeres unter August dem Starken. Inaugural–Dissertation zur Erlangung der Doktorwürde der hohen philosophischen Fakultät der Universität Leipzig* (Leipzig: self published, 1922).

Litschel, Rudolf Walter, *Der bayerische Erbfolgekrieg 1778/79 und der Erwerb des Innviertels* (Linz: Oberösterreichischer Landesverlag, 1978).

Luh Jürgen, 'Sachsens Bedeutung für Preußens Kriegführung`, in *Sachsen und Dresden im Siebenjährigen Krieg* (=Dresdner Hefte 68), pp.28-34.

Luh, Jürgen, *Kriegskunst in Europa* (Cologne, Weimar, Vienna: Böhlau, 2004).

McLennan, Ken, 'Liechtenstein and Gribeuaval. "Artillery Revolution" in Political and Cultural Context', *War and History* 10/3 (2003), pp.249-264.

Merta, Klaus-Peter, *Das Heerwesen in Brandenburg und Preußen von 1640 bis 1806. Die Uniformierung* (Berlin: Brandenburgisches Verlagshaus, 2001).

Meumann, Markus and Pröve, Ralf (eds), *Herrschaft in der Frühen Neuzeit. Umrisse eines dynamisch-kommunikativen Prozesses* (Münster: LIT, 2004).

Mielsch, Rudolf, 'Die kursächsische Armee im Bayerischen Erbfolgekrieg`, *NASG* 53 (1932), pp.73-103 and 54 (1933), pp.46-74.

Möbius, Sascha, *Mehr Angst vor dem Offizier als vor dem Feind?. Eine mentalitätsgeschichtliche Studie zur preußischen Taktik im Siebenjährigen Krieg* (Saarbrücken: VDM Verlag Dr. Müller e. K., 2007).

Müller, Heinrich, *Das Heerwesen in Brandenburg und Preußen von 1640 bis 1806. Die Bewaffnung* (Berlin: Brandenburgisches Verlagshaus, 2001).

Museum für Naturkunde und Vorgeschichte Dessau, *Fürst Leopold I. von Anhalt-Dessau (1676-1747) 'Der Alte Dessauer'. Ausstellung zum 250. Todestag* (Dessau: Museum für Naturkunde und Vorgeschichte Dessau, 1997).

Oestreich, Gerhard, 'Strukturprobleme des europäischen Absolutismus', *Vierteljahreshefte für Sozial- und Wirtschaftsgeschichte* 55 (1969), pp.329- 347.

Franz Persendorfer, *Feldmarschall Loudon. Der Sieg und sein Preis* (Vienna: ÖBV, 1989).

Price, Munro, 'The Dutch Affair and the Fall of the Ancien Régime, 1784–1787`, *The Historical Journal* 38/4 (1995), pp.875–805.

Pröve, Ralf (ed.), *Klio in Uniform? Probleme und Perspektiven einer modernen Militärgeschichte der frühen Neuzeit* (Cologne – Weimar – Vienna: Böhlau 1997.

Pröve, Ralf, 'Zum Verhältnis von Militär und Gesellschaft im Spiegel gewaltsamer Rekrutierungen (1648-1789)', *Zeitschrift für Historische Forschung* 22 (1995), pp.191-223.

Querengässer, Alexander (ed.) *Die Schlacht bei Roßbach* (=Beiträge zur Geschichte des Militärs in Sachsen 2) (Berlin: Zeughaus Verlag, 2017).

Querengässer, Alexander, *Kesselsdorf 1745. Eine Entscheidungsschlacht in der Frühen* (Berlin: Zeughaus Verlag, 2020).

Querengässer, Alexander, *The Saxon Mars and his Force. The Saxon Army during the Reign of John George III 1680-1691* (Warwick: Helion & Company, 2020).

Ranke, Leopold von, *Die deutschen Mächte und der Fürstenbund. Deutsche Geschichte von 1780 bis 1790* (Leipzig: Duncker & Humblot, 1871-1872).

Rehfeld, Paul, 'Die preußische Rüstungsindustrie unter Friederich dem Großen', *FBPG* 55 (1944), pp.1-31.

Reichl-Ham, Claudia, 'Der Türkenkrieg Josephs II.`, *Pallasch. Zeitschrift für Militärgeschichte* 50 (2014), pp.5–31.

Reiman, Emil, 'Friedrich August III. und Carl Theodor`, *NASG* 4 (1883), pp.316-339.

Reimann, Eduard, *Geschichte des Bayerischen Erbfolgekrieges* (Leipzig: Duncker und Humblot, 1869).

Rink, Martin, *Vom 'Parheygänger' zum Partisanen. Die Konzeption des kleinen Krieges in Preußen 1740-1813* (Frankfurt a. M.: Peter Lang, 1999).

Rothenberg, Gunther E., *The Austrian Military Border in Croatia, 1522–1747* (Urbana: University of Illinois Press, 1960).

Rothenberg, Gunther E., *The Austrian Military Border in Croatia, 1740–1881. A Study of an Imperial Institution* (Chicago: University of Chicago Press, 1966).

Rudert, Otto, *Die Reorganisation der Kursächsischen Armee 1763-1769* (Leipzig: Self-published, 1911).

Scharf, Claus (ed.), *Katharina II., Russland und Europa. Beiträge zur internationalen Forschung* (Maynce: Philipp von Zabem, 2001).

Scheffler-Knox, J.L.P. von, 'Die preußische Sparsamkeit im Spiegel der Bekleidungsordnung', *Zeitschrift für Heeres- und Uniformkunde* 7 (1959), pp. 7-12.

Schmid, Alois, and Weigand, Katharina (eds), *Die Herrscher Bayerns. 25 Historische Portraits von Tassilo III. bis Ludwig III.* (Munich: C.H. Beck 2001).

Schuster, Oskar, and Francke, Friedrich August, *Geschichte der Sächsischen Armee von der Errichtung bis in die neueste Zeit* (Leipzig: Duncker & Humblot, 1885).

Schultz, Wilhelm von, *Die preußischen Werbungen unter Friedrich Wilhelm I. und Friedrich dem Großen bis zum Beginn des Siebenjährigen Krieges mit besonderer Berücksichtigung Mecklenburg-Schwerins* (Schwerin: Schulze, 1887).

Sösemann, Bernd, and Voigt-Spira, Gregor (eds), *Friedrich der Große in Europa. Geschichte einer wechselvollen Beziehung* (Stuttgart: Franz Steiner 2012).

Straubel, Rolf, *'Er möchte nur wissen, daß die Armée mir gehöret'. Friedrich II. und seine Offiziere. Ausgewählte Aspekte der königlichen Personalpolitik* (Berlin: Brandenburgische Landeshauptarchiv, 2012).

Stollberg-Rillinger, Barbara, *Maria Theresia. Die Emperorin in ihrer Zeit* (Munich: C.H. Beck, 2019).

Wehrgeschichtliches Museum Rastatt (ed.), *Die Bewaffnung und Ausrüstung der Armee Friedrichs des Großen. Eine Dokumentation aus Anlass seines 200. Todesjahres* (Rastatt: Wehrgeschichtliches Museum Rastatt, 1986).

Winkel, Carmen, *Im Netz des Königs. Netzwerke und Patronage in der preußischen Armee 1713-1786' (Krieg in der Geschichte 79)* (Paderborn: Ferdinand Schönling, 2013).

Wollschläger, Thomas, *Die Military Revolution und der deutsche Territorialstaat. Determinanten der Staatskonsolidierung im europäischen Kontext 1670-1740* (Norderstedt: BOD, 2004).

Zöllner, Erich (ed.), *Österreich im Zeitalter des aufgeklärten Absolutismus* (Vienna: Bundesverlag, 1983).

From Reason to Revolution – Warfare 1721-1815

http://www.helion.co.uk/series/from-reason-to-revolution-1721-1815.php

The 'From Reason to Revolution' series covers the period of military history 1721–1815, an era in which fortress-based strategy and linear battles gave way to the nation-in-arms and the beginnings of total war.

This era saw the evolution and growth of light troops of all arms, and of increasingly flexible command systems to cope with the growing armies fielded by nations able to mobilise far greater proportions of their manpower than ever before. Many of these developments were fired by the great political upheavals of the era, with revolutions in America and France bringing about social change which in turn fed back into the military sphere as whole nations readied themselves for war. Only in the closing years of the period, as the reactionary powers began to regain the upper hand, did a military synthesis of the best of the old and the new become possible.

The series will examine the military and naval history of the period in a greater degree of detail than has hitherto been attempted, and has a very wide brief, with the intention of covering all aspects from the battles, campaigns, logistics, and tactics, to the personalities, armies, uniforms, and equipment.

Submissions

The publishers would be pleased to receive submissions for this series. Please contact series editor Andrew Bamford via email (andrewbamford@helion.co.uk), or in writing to Helion & Company Limited, Unit 8 Amherst Business Centre, Budbrooke Road, Warwick, CV34 5WE

Titles

No 1 *Lobositz to Leuthen: Horace St Paul and the Campaigns of the Austrian Army in the Seven Years War 1756-57* (Neil Cogswell)

No 2 *Glories to Useless Heroism: The Seven Years War in North America from the French journals of Comte Maurés de Malartic, 1755-1760* (William Raffle (ed.))

No 3 *Reminiscences 1808-1815 Under Wellington: The Peninsular and Waterloo Memoirs of William Hay* (Andrew Bamford (ed.))

No 4 *Far Distant Ships: The Royal Navy and the Blockade of Brest 1793-1815* (Quintin Barry)

No 5 *Godoy's Army: Spanish Regiments and Uniforms from the Estado Militar of 1800* (Charles Esdaile and Alan Perry)

No 6 *On Gladsmuir Shall the Battle Be! The Battle of Prestonpans 1745* (Arran Johnston)

No 7 *The French Army of the Orient 1798-1801: Napoleon's Beloved 'Egyptians'* (Yves Martin)

No 8 *The Autobiography, or Narrative of a Soldier: The Peninsular War Memoirs of William Brown of the 45th Foot* (Steve Brown (ed.))

No 9 *Recollections from the Ranks: Three Russian Soldiers' Autobiographies from the Napoleonic Wars* (Darrin Boland)

No 10 *By Fire and Bayonet: Grey's West Indies Campaign of 1794* (Steve Brown)

No 11 *Olmütz to Torgau: Horace St Paul and the Campaigns of the Austrian Army in the Seven Years War 1758-60* (Neil Cogswell)

No 12 *Murat's Army: The Army of the Kingdom of Naples 1806-1815* (Digby Smith)

No 13 *The Veteran or 40 Years' Service in the British Army: The Scurrilous Recollections of Paymaster John Harley 47th Foot – 1798-1838* (Gareth Glover (ed.))

No 14 *Narrative of the Eventful Life of Thomas Jackson: Militiaman and Coldstream Sergeant, 1803-15* (Eamonn O'Keeffe (ed.))

No.15 *For Orange and the States: The Army of the Dutch Republic 1713-1772 Part I: Infantry* (Marc Geerdinck-Schaftenaar)

No 16 *Men Who Are Determined to be Free: The American Assault on Stony Point, 15 July 1779* (David C. Bonk)

No 17 *Next to Wellington: General Sir George Murray: The Story of a Scottish Soldier and Statesman, Wellington's Quartermaster General* (John Harding-Edgar)

No 18 *Between Scylla and Charybdis: The Army of Elector Friedrich August of Saxony 1733-1763 Part I: Staff and Cavalry* (Marco Pagan)

No 19 *The Secret Expedition: The Anglo-Russian Invasion of Holland 1799* (Geert van Uythoven)

No 20 *'We Are Accustomed to do our Duty': German Auxiliaries with the British Army 1793-95* (Paul Demet)

No 21 *With the Guards in Flanders: The Diary of Captain Roger Morris 1793-95* (Peter Harington (ed.))

No 22 *The British Army in Egypt 1801: An Underrated Army Comes of Age* (Carole Divall)

No 23 *Better is the Proud Plaid: The Clothing, Weapons, and Accoutrements of the Jacobites in the '45* (Jenn Scott)

No 24 *The Lilies and the Thistle: French Troops in the Jacobite '45* (Andrew Bamford)

No 25 *A Light Infantryman With Wellington: The Letters of Captain George Ulrich Barlow 52nd and 69th Foot 1808-15* (Gareth Glover (ed.))

No 26 *Swiss Regiments in the Service of France 1798-1815: Uniforms, Organisation, Campaigns* (Stephen Ede-Borrett)

No 27 *For Orange and the States! The Army of the Dutch Republic 1713-1772: Part II: Cavalry and Specialist Troops* (Marc Geerdinck-Schaftenaar)

No 28 *Fashioning Regulation, Regulating Fashion: Uniforms and Dress of the British Army 1800-1815 Volume I* (Ben Townsend)

No 29 *Riflemen: The History of the 5th Battalion 60th (Royal American) Regiment, 1797-1818* (Robert Griffith)

No 30 *The Key to Lisbon: The Third French Invasion of Portugal, 1810-11* (Kenton White)

No 31 *Command and Leadership: Proceedings of the 2018 Helion & Company 'From Reason to Revolution' Conference* (Andrew Bamford (ed.))

No 32 *Waterloo After the Glory: Hospital Sketches and Reports on the Wounded After the Battle* (Michael Crumplin and Gareth Glover)

No 33 *Fluxes, Fevers, and Fighting Men: War and Disease in Ancien Regime Europe 1648-1789* (Pádraig Lenihan)

No 34 *'They Were Good Soldiers': African-Americans Serving in the Continental Army, 1775-1783* (John U. Rees)

No 35 *A Redcoat in America: The Diaries of Lieutenant William Bamford, 1757-1765 and 1776* (John B. Hattendorf (ed.))

No 36 *Between Scylla and Charybdis: The Army of Friedrich August II of Saxony, 1733-1763: Part II: Infantry and Artillery* (Marco Pagan)

No 37 *Québec Under Siege: French Eye-Witness Accounts from the Campaign of 1759* (Charles A. Mayhood (ed.))

No 38 *King George's Hangman: Henry Hawley and the Battle of Falkirk 1746* (Jonathan D. Oates)

No 39 *Zweybrücken in Command: The Reichsarmee in the Campaign of 1758* (Neil Cogswell)

No 40 *So Bloody a Day: The 16th Light Dragoons in the Waterloo Campaign* (David J. Blackmore)

No 41 *Northern Tars in Southern Waters: The Russian Fleet in the Mediterranean 1806-1810* (Vladimir Bogdanovich Bronevskiy / Darrin Boland)

No 42 *Royal Navy Officers of the Seven Years War: A Biographical Dictionary of Commissioned Officers 1748-1763* (Cy Harrison)

No 43 *All at Sea: Naval Support for the British Army During the American Revolutionary War* (John Dillon)

No 44 *Glory is Fleeting: New Scholarship on the Napoleonic Wars* (Andrew Bamford (ed.))

No 45 *Fashioning Regulation, Regulating Fashion: Uniforms and Dress of the British Army 1800-1815 Vol. II* (Ben Townsend)

No 46 *Revenge in the Name of Honour: The Royal Navy's Quest for Vengeance in the Single Ship Actions of the War of 1812* (Nicholas James Kaizer)

No 47 *They Fought With Extraordinary Bravery: The III German (Saxon) Army Corps in the Southern Netherlands 1814* (Geert van Uythoven)

No 48 *The Danish Army of the Napoleonic Wars 1801-1814, Organisation, Uniforms & Equipment: Volume 1: High Command, Line and Light Infantry* (David Wilson)

No 49 *Neither Up Nor Down: The British Army and the Flanders Campaign 1793-1895* (Phillip Ball)

No 50 *Guerra Fantástica: The Portuguese Army and the Seven Years War* (António Barrento)

No 51 *From Across the Sea: North Americans in Nelson's Navy* (Sean M. Heuvel and John A. Rodgaard)

No 52 *Rebellious Scots to Crush: The Military Response to the Jacobite '45* (Andrew Bamford (ed.))

No 53 *The Army of George II 1727-1760: The Soldiers who Forged an Empire* (Peter Brown)

No 54 *Wellington at Bay: The Battle of Villamuriel, 25 October 1812* (Garry David Wills)

No 55 *Life in the Red Coat: The British Soldier 1721-1815* (Andrew Bamford (ed.))

No 56 *Wellington's Favourite Engineer. John Burgoyne: Operations, Engineering, and the Making of a Field Marshal* (Mark S. Thompson)

No 57 *Scharnhorst: The Formative Years, 1755-1801* (Charles Edward White)

No 58 *At the Point of the Bayonet: The Peninsular War Battles of Arroyomolinos and Almaraz 1811-1812* (Robert Griffith)

No 59 *Sieges of the '45: Siege Warfare during the Jacobite Rebellion of 1745-1746* (Jonathan D. Oates)

No 60 *Austrian Cavalry of the Revolutionary and Napoleonic Wars, 1792–1815* (Enrico Acerbi, András K. Molnár)

No 61 *The Danish Army of the Napoleonic Wars 1801-1814, Organisation, Uniforms & Equipment: Volume 2: Cavalry and Artillery* (David Wilson)

No 62 *Napoleon's Stolen Army: How the Royal Navy Rescued a Spanish Army in the Baltic* (John Marsden)

No 63 *Crisis at the Chesapeake: The Royal Navy and the Struggle for America 1775-1783* (Quintin Barry)

No 64 *Bullocks, Grain, and Good Madeira: The Maratha and Jat Campaigns 1803-1806 and the emergence of the Indian Army* (Joshua Provan)

No 65 *Sir James McGrigor: The Adventurous Life of Wellington's Chief Medical Officer* (Tom Scotland)

No 66 *Fashioning Regulation, Regulating Fashion: Uniforms and Dress of the British Army 1800-1815 Volume I* (Ben Townsend) (paperback edition)

No 67 *Fashioning Regulation, Regulating Fashion: Uniforms and Dress of the British Army 1800-1815 Volume II* (Ben Townsend) (paperback edition)

No 68 *The Secret Expedition: The Anglo-Russian Invasion of Holland 1799* (Geert van Uythoven) (paperback edition)

No 69 *The Sea is My Element: The Eventful Life of Admiral Sir Pulteney Malcolm 1768-1838* (Paul Martinovich)

No 70 *The Sword and the Spirit: Proceedings of the first 'War & Peace in the Age of Napoleon' Conference* (Zack White (ed.))

No 71 *Lobositz to Leuthen: Horace St Paul and the Campaigns of the Austrian Army in the Seven Years War 1756-57* (Neil Cogswell) (paperback edition)

No 72 *For God and King. A History of the Damas Legion 1793-1798: A Case Study of the Military Emigration during the French Revolution* (Hughes de Bazouges and Alistair Nichols)

No 73 *'Their Infantry and Guns Will Astonish You': The Army of Hindustan and European Mercenaries in Maratha service 1780-1803* (Andy Copestake)

No 74 *Like A Brazen Wall: The Battle of Minden, 1759, and its Place in the Seven Years War* (Ewan Carmichael)

No 75 *Wellington and the Lines of Torres Vedras: The Defence of Lisbon during the Peninsular War* (Mark Thompson)

No 76 *French Light Infantry 1784-1815: From the Chasseurs of Louis XVI to Napoleon's Grande Armée* (Terry Crowdy)

No 77 *Riflemen: The History of the 5th Battalion 60th (Royal American) Regiment, 1797-1818* (Robert Griffith) (paperback edition)

No 78 *Hastenbeck 1757: The French Army and the Opening Campaign of the Seven Years War* (Olivier Lapray)

No 79 *Napoleonic French Military Uniforms: As Depicted by Horace and Carle Vernet and Eugène Lami* (Guy Dempsey (trans. and ed.))

No 80 *These Distinguished Corps: British Grenadier and Light Infantry Battalions in the American Revolution* (Don N. Hagist)

No 81 *Rebellion, Invasion, and Occupation: The British Army in Ireland, 1793 -1815* (Wayne Stack)

No 82 *You Have to Die in Piedmont! The Battle of Assietta, 19 July 1747. The War of the Austrian Succession in the Alps* (Giovanni Cerino Badone)

No 83 *A Very Fine Regiment: the 47th Foot in the American War of Independence, 1773–1783* (Paul Knight)

No 84 *By Fire and Bayonet: Grey's West Indies Campaign of 1794* (Steve Brown) (paperback edition)

No 85 *No Want of Courage: The British Army in Flanders, 1793-1795* (R.N.W. Thomas)

No 86 *Far Distant Ships: The Royal Navy and the Blockade of Brest 1793-1815* (Quintin Barry) (paperback edition)

No 87 *Armies and Enemies of Napoleon 1789-1815: Proceedings of the 2021 Helion and Company 'From Reason to Revolution' Conference* (Robert Griffith (ed.))

No 88 *The Battle of Rossbach 1757: New Perspectives on the Battle and Campaign* (Alexander Querengässer (ed.))

No 89 *Waterloo After the Glory: Hospital Sketches and Reports on the Wounded After the Battle* (Michael Crumplin and Gareth Glover) (paperback edition)

No 90 *From Ushant to Gibraltar: The Channel Fleet 1778-1783* (Quintin Barry)

No 91 *'The Soldiers are Dressed in Red': The Quiberon Expedition of 1795 and the Counter-Revolution in Brittany* (Alistair Nichols)

No 92 *The Army of the Kingdom of Italy 1805-1814: Uniforms, Organisation, Campaigns* (Stephen Ede-Borrett)

No 93 *The Ottoman Army of the Napoleonic Wars 1798-1815: A Struggle for Survival from Egypt to the Balkans* (Bruno Mugnai)

No 94 *The Changing Face of Old Regime Warfare: Essays in Honour of Christopher Duffy* (Alexander S. Burns (ed.))

No 94 *The Changing Face of Old Regime Warfare: Essays in Honour of Christopher Duffy* (Alexander S. Burns (ed.)

No 95 *The Danish Army of the Napoleonic Wars 1801-1814, Organisation, Uniforms & Equipment: Volume 3: Norwegian Troops and Militia* (David Wilson)

No 96 *1805 – Tsar Alexander's First War with Napoleon* (Alexander Ivanovich Mikhailovsky-Danilevsky, trans. Peter G.A. Phillips)

No 97 *'More Furies then Men': The Irish Brigade in the service of France 1690-1792* (Pierre-Louis Coudray)

No 98 *'We Are Accustomed to do our Duty': German Auxiliaries with the British Army 1793-95* (Paul Demet) (paperback edition)

No 99 *Ladies, Wives and Women: British Army Wives in the Revolutionary and Napoleonic Wars 1793-1815* (David Clammer)

No 100 *The Garde Nationale 1789-1815: France's Forgotten Armed Forces* (Pierre-Baptiste Guillemot)

No 101 *Confronting Napoleon: Levin von Bennigsen's Memoir of the Campaign in Poland, 1806-1807, Volume I Pultusk to Eylau* (Alexander Mikaberidze and Paul Strietelmeier (trans. and ed.))

No 102 *Olmütz to Torgau: Horace St Paul and the Campaigns of the Austrian Army in the Seven Years War 1758-60* (Neil Cogswell) (paperback edition)

No 103 *Fit to Command: British Regimental Leadership in the Revolutionary & Napoleonic Wars* (Steve Brown)

No 104 *Wellington's Unsung Heroes: The Fifth Division in the Peninsular War, 1810-1814* (Carole Divall)

No 105 *1806-1807 – Tsar Alexander's Second War with Napoleon* (Alexander Ivanovich Mikhailovsky-Danilevsky, trans. Peter G.A. Phillips)

No 106 *The Pattern: The 33rd Regiment in the American Revolution, 1770-1783* (Robbie MacNiven)

No 107 *To Conquer and to Keep: Suchet and the War for Eastern Spain, 1809-1814, Volume 1 1809-1811* (Yuhan Kim)

No 108 *To Conquer and to Keep: Suchet and the War for Eastern Spain, 1809-1814, Volume 2 1811-1814* (Yuhan Kim)

No 109 *The Tagus Campaign of 1809: An Alliance in Jeopardy* (John Marsden)

No 110 *The War of the Bavarian Succession, 1778-1779: Prussian Military Power in Decline?* (Alexander Querengässer)

No 111 *Anson: Naval Commander and Statesman* (Anthony Bruce)

No 112 *Atlas of the Battles and Campaigns of the American Revolution, 1775-1783* (David Bonk and George Anderson)

No 113 *A Fine Corps and will Serve Faithfully: The Swiss Regiment de Roll in the British Army 1794-1816* (Alistair Nichols)

No 114 *Next to Wellington: General Sir George Murray: The Story of a Scottish Soldier and Statesman, Wellington's Quartermaster General* (John Harding-Edgar) (paperback edition)

About the author

Alexander Querengässer was born in 1987 in Dresden. He studied history at the University of Leipzig and wrote his PhD about the Saxon Army in the Great Northern War at the University of Potsdam. He currently works as a freelance historian and visiting lecturer at the University in Halle an der Saale. He has written more than 20 books and is the editor of the series "Beiträge zur Geschichte des Militärs in Sachsen" (contributions to Saxon Military History). Recent titles for Helion include *The Saxon Mars and His Force: The Saxon Army During the Reign of John George III 1680–1691* (2019) and an edited collection, *The Battle of Rossbach 1757: New Perspectives on the Battle and Campaign* (2022).

About the artist

Alexandr Chernushkin lives in Poznan, Poland and for more than 20 years has been engaged in military history, specialising in the uniforms of various European armies during the 17th-19th centuries. His particular interest is the history of military and civil uniforms of the Russian Empire and Poland.